ARRESTING DRESS

PERVERSE MODERNITIES

A Series Edited by Jack Halberstam and Lisa Lowe

ARRESTING DRESS

Cross-Dressing, Law, and Fascination

in Nineteenth-Century San Francisco

CLARE SEARS

Duke University Press

Durham and London

2015

Printed in the United States of America on acid-free paper ∞

Typeset in Minion Pro by Westchester Publishing Services

Library of Congress Cataloging-in-Publication Data
Sears, Clare, 1970–
Arresting dress : cross-dressing, law, and fascination in nineteenth-century
San Francisco / Clare Sears.
pages cm—(Perverse modernities)
Includes bibliographical references and index.
ISBN 978-0-8223-5754-4 (hardcover : alk. paper)
ISBN 978-0-8223-5758-2 (pbk. : alk. paper)
ISBN 978-0-8223-7619-4 (e-book)
1. Transvestism—California—San Francisco—History—19th century.
2. Transvestites—Legal status, laws, etc.—California—San Francisco—
History—19th century. 3. San Francisco (Calif.)—Social life and
customs—19th century. I. Title.
II. Series: Perverse modernities.
HQ77.2.U6S43 2015
306.77'8097946109034—dc23
2014023499

Cover art: Police photograph of Geraldine Portica, arrested for violating
cross-dressing law in 1917. Courtesy of The Bancroft Library,
University of California, Berkeley.

CONTENTS

Acknowledgments vii

Introduction: Not Belonging 1

1 Instant and Peculiar 23

2 Against Good Morals 41

3 Problem Bodies, Public Space 61

4 A Sight Well Worth Gazing Upon 78

5 Indecent Exhibitions 97

6 Problem Bodies, Nation-State 121

Conclusion: Against the Law 139

Notes 149

Bibliography 175

Index 191

ACKNOWLEDGMENTS

First and foremost, I am indebted to the staff and volunteers of numerous archives who helped me to locate the sources for this book. The Gay, Lesbian, Bisexual, Transgender Historical Society has been a constant source of inspiration, and I am grateful to Rebekah Kim and Marjorie Bryer for overseeing its rich archival collections, as well as to volunteers past and present for their pioneering work in community-based queer history. The staff at the University of California, Berkeley's Bancroft Library were particularly helpful and patient during the initial months of this study, while I learned how to move back and forth between my research questions and the mass of documents available. Archivists at the California Historical Society, California State Archives, California State Library, Huntington Library, and San Francisco History Center also provided invaluable assistance tracking down materials, and I thank them for their enthusiasm and diligence. I owe special thanks to the staff at the San Francisco Public Library's Magazines and Newspapers Center for creating a wonderfully open research space where local school kids, homeless adults, community college students, and elderly people seeking the obituaries of friends could work side by side. Finally, I give special thanks to Estelle Freedman and Gerard Koskovich for generously sharing their personal collections with me.

I began research for this book as a doctoral student at the University of California, Santa Cruz, and I am indebted to my dissertation committee members for their insights and direction. Nancy Stoller, my committee chair, worked long and hard to create space within academia for community-oriented, politically engaged studies of sexualities. I am thankful for her support and guidance through the long and often confusing process of research and writing. I also thank Melanie DuPuis for her exceptional mentorship. I first conceived of this project during Melanie's historical methods seminar, and her interdisciplinary insights pushed me to engage with a wide range of scholarly debates, broadening the analytic scope of my work. I am enormously grateful to Herman Gray for his critical engagement with my project and for challenging me to deepen my theoretical analyses, particularly of representation and criminalization. Beyond my committee, this project benefited from conversations with numerous UCSC faculty, particularly Gina Dent, who encouraged me to think of "the law" more culturally and critically; Anjali Arondekar, who introduced me to critical thinking about archival practices; and George Lipsitz, who influenced my approach to California historiography. I also thank Craig Reinarman for being an exceptional academic advisor and Julie Bettie for her support and encouragement during my early graduate years.

I first imagined my work reaching a wider audience when I attended UCLA's QGRAD conference in 2003 and 2004. I am very grateful to the conference organizers and for the generous encouragement of Jennifer Terry and James Schultz. Conversations with Nayan Shah, Susan Schweik, Eithne Luibhéid, and Erica Rand were also instrumental as I took up the daunting task of writing this book. I am particularly grateful for the generosity of Jack Halberstam and Susan Stryker. Jack provided many brilliant insights that enriched my analysis, but I am most grateful for his practical support and unswerving advocacy as I navigated the ups and downs of establishing an academic career. Susan has been an exceptional mentor and friend. Her groundbreaking work made this book possible, and her belief in the value of my research sustained me through difficult times. Our conversations were the highlight of my postdoctoral year, and I hope for many more to come.

Many people have read drafts of my work, and I am particularly grateful for the comments and suggestions of Barbara Barnes, Jen Reck, Julie Beck, Don Romesburg, Ian Carter, Rebekah Edwards, and Nan Alamilla Boyd. In addition to diligently reading my manuscript, these friends and colleagues counteracted the isolation of writing and helped me to keep going when publication seemed an elusive goal. I am also grateful to Duke's two anonymous reviewers for terrific suggestions that significantly improved my work. Finally, I am thankful for the patience and encouragement of Duke's magnificent editorial team, particularly Ken Wissoker, Jade Brooks, and Liz Smith.

I am thrilled to complete this book in the Department of Sociology and Sexuality Studies at San Francisco State University, which is now my academic home. sfsu is a teaching university, and I am consistently impressed by the brilliance and tenacity of my students, who teach me something new each semester and always keep me on my toes. I am particularly indebted to my student research assistants Hollis Fleischer, Shideh Teimoori, and Amy Clements. I am very fortunate to have wonderful supportive colleagues, and I am particularly grateful to those who have created campus spaces where I can share my work: Ed McCaughan, Jessica Fields, Andreana Clay, Jen Reck, Amy Sueyoshi, Colleen Hoff, Alexis Martinez, and Chris Bettinger. I am also incredibly thankful for my long-term office mate Hulya Gurtuna's great friendship and humor.

Writing this book took time and money, and I thank the friends and family who helped out in big and small ways over the years. I am grateful for institutional funding from ucsc's Department of Sociology and Graduate Student Association, the uc Humanities Research Institute's Kevin Starr Postdoctoral Fellowship, sfsu's Presidential Award for Probationary Faculty, and sfsu's Vice-President's Assigned Time Award. I am also grateful to Allen LeBlanc for helping me seek funding at sfsu and to the Beatrice M. Bain Research Group at uc Berkeley.

The personal journey from small-town Essex girl to San Francisco scholar was bumpy, and many people helped along the way. Barbara Barnes is the best friend a socially awkward introvert could hope for. As a consummate intellectual, Barb provided the scholarly conversations, sharp insights, and unending encouragement that helped me to complete this book. She also reminded me to drink more beer, watch tv, and never stop listening to music. I also thank Jessie Aguirre, Jen Reck, Christina Cicoletti, Eric Chesmar, and Amy Buzick for excellent talks, occasional vodka, and ongoing reminders that I live in the twenty-first century rather than the nineteenth. Beth Steinberg was pivotal in helping me navigate the relationship between past, present, and future. I am also indebted to Susan Thompson, my sixth-form sociology teacher, for encouraging me to go to university; it would not have happened without her. Many of my ideas about public space, social problems, and embodiment were first developed when I worked in Golden Gate Park's homeless encampments, and I am grateful to Damon Kurth, Aleasha Hover, Aironn Cook, Matt Dodman, and Dave Willis for their conversations and insights. I am also grateful to Khaya Clark for her wonderful friendship during the early years of graduate school and to Jeffery Brown for making much of this possible. In recent years, Elizabeth Chavez and Leah Abiol have become close friends, and it is difficult to imagine my life without them. Finally, I thank my family in England for their love and support: my parents, Brenda and Colin Sears; my sister, Karen Cantwell, and her family Joe, Tom, Amy, Dan, and Joseph; and my brother, Pete Sears, and his family Dawn, Emma, and Katie.

Two incredibly important people died during the course of this project. My academic advisor, Lionel Cantú, died unexpectedly in April 2002. Lionel was central to the early stages of this work, and his mentorship, teaching, and scholarship profoundly influenced its direction. In particular, Lionel encouraged me to think of mid-nineteenth-century San Francisco as a contested site of immigration and to explore the influence of these migratory flows on the organization and policing of sexuality, as well as the influence of sexuality on processes of racialization. My dear friend and sister-in-law Emily Martinez died in September 2005. Emily was witty, brilliant, cynical, and sensitive. She understood me like nobody else. When I am not reflecting on San Francisco's past, I sometimes imagine a different future in which she would read this book, quietly judging, before taking a long nap. I also acknowledge my in-laws/out-laws who are alive and very much kicking: Danny, Serene, and Thor Martinez, Ben and Shelley Martinez, and the wonderful Meg Margolis.

Finally, I thank Tia Martinez for her love, creativity, and inspiration over the past twenty(!) years. Tia encouraged my initial interest in graduate school, convinced me that bookstores were (almost) as cool as record stores, and never complained when I stopped writing love letters and started writing academic papers. Life has changed a lot since she first drew my blood in a health department RV parked outside a lesbian bar in 1993, but her brilliance and kindness continue to amaze me. Tia's influence and enthusiasm run throughout this book, and as I finish the project and wonder what's next, I rest easy knowing that she'll be by my side. In recent years, our kids have brought boundless imagination and energy into my life, inspiring me in ways I never expected. I dedicate this book to Joaquin, who came in the middle; Frankie, who came at the end; and Tia, who was there all along.

Not Belonging

On May 9, 1866, San Francisco's leading daily newspaper published a front-page story describing a "tremendous sensation" that occurred the previous evening in the downtown district, caused by a woman dressed "in black doe-skin pants, men's boots, riding jacket, hat, etc., full masculine apparel." The woman was "leaning on the arm of what appeared to be a man although it might have been a woman," and her appearance drew "a mob of small boys, some hundreds in number," who shouted insults until restrained by police. The police, however, did not arrest the woman, despite her violation of a local cross-dressing law, prompting the newspaper to comment, "As the police arrest every man caught on the street in women's clothing, we see no reason as to why the rule should not be applied to the other sex as well." The next day San Francisco police dutifully arrested the woman, a feminist dress reformer named Eliza DeWolf, launching a court case and newspaper scandal that gripped the city for months.[1]

The following decade, in December 1874, San Francisco police arrested John Roberts for appearing in public in "female attire," or more specifically, in the clothing of a "pretty waiter girl," consisting of "a red striped dress with train *de mud a la Barbary Coast*, a straw hat with a bit of lace and artificial flowers in it, a heavy veil which concealed his face, and a comforter which he wore around his neck." During these years Barbary Coast bars, in the heart of the vice district, employed "pretty waiter girls" and some female impersonators to sell liquor and sex on the premises. We do not know whether Roberts worked in these bars or merely dressed in the style of their employees. Passing over such details, court reporters stated that Roberts was drunk at the time, had a "mania" for wearing women's clothing, and had been recently arrested for the same offense.[2]

Twenty years later, in 1895, San Francisco police staked out a residential neighborhood to investigate complaints about a "strange woman" who walked the streets every evening. After close surveillance, they arrested Ferdinand Haisch, a middle-aged carpenter who lived in the neighborhood, on charges of "masquerading in female attire." At the time of her arrest Haisch was wearing the latest women's fashions: a three-quarter-length melton coat, green silk skirt, red stockings, silver-buckled garters, high-heeled shoes, and stylish hat. Unable or unwilling to provide a reason for this clothing, Haisch simply stated that apart from her carpenter's outfit, it was the only clothing she had. Reporting on the arrest, newspapers stated that Haisch went to considerable lengths to present as a woman, making her own clothing and feminizing her voice. Following a brief stint in the city prison, Haisch was released by a judge on the condition that she never wear women's clothing in public again.[3]

DeWolf, Roberts, and Haisch were just three of the people arrested for cross-dressing in nineteenth-century San Francisco. Specifically they fell afoul of the law that animates this book—a law that made it a crime for a person to appear in public "in a dress not belonging to his or her sex."[4] Passed by the San Francisco Board of Supervisors in 1863, this prohibition occurred in the context of a broader indecency law that also criminalized public nudity, indecent exposure, lewd acts, and immoral performances. In the hands of police and judges, the law became a flexible tool for regulating a wide range of cross-dressing practices, facilitating more than one hundred arrests before the century's end. Those arrested faced public exposure, police harassment, and up to six months in jail; by the turn of the century they also risked psychiatric institutionalization or deportation if not a U.S. citizen.

Arresting Dress examines the emergence, operations, and legacies of San Francisco's cross-dressing law during the second half of the nineteenth century. At first glance this may seem an obscure topic. After all, the law was passed almost 150 years ago, it targeted an arguably marginal cultural practice, and it created only a misdemeanor offense. However, if cross-dressing histories teach us anything, it is that first appearances can be deceiving. Far from a marginal practice, cross-dressing was a central component of nineteenth-century urban life. Indeed cross-dressing emerged as peripheral only in the wake of cross-dressing law; consequently this book scrutinizes marginality as one of the law's effects. Moreover cross-dressing laws were not idiosyncratic or archaic regulations but foundational city codes that were central to the project of modern municipal government. Such laws were passed in over forty U.S. cities between the Civil War and World War I, with remarkably long lives, remaining in force until the 1970s. These laws had wide circulation, reaching beyond the legal realm of courtrooms and codebooks into newspaper scandals, freak-show performances, tourist entertainments, and vaudevillian theater. They also had immense effects, producing new definitions of gender normality and abnormality that haunt us today. Finally, cross-dressing laws extended beyond the policing of normative gender to impact the social meanings of city space, race, and citizenship. In particular they crossed paths with federal immigration laws to limit the terms of national belonging and construct a gender-normative nation. Far more than a local government order that created a misdemeanor offense, cross-dressing law represented a specific strategy of government that constructed normative gender, reinforced inequalities, and generated new modes of exclusion from public life.

A Brief Overview of Cross-Dressing Law

Although cross-dressing laws are rarely, if ever, enforced in U.S. cities today, they were a central component of urban life from the mid-nineteenth century to the mid-twentieth. Between 1848 and 1900 thirty-four cities in twenty-one states passed prohibitions against cross-dressing, as did eleven more cities before World War I.[5] Most of these cities, including San Francisco, passed laws that specifically targeted a person "wearing a dress not belonging to his or her sex" or "wearing the apparel of the other sex" as part of broader prohibitions against public indecency. Other cities, such as Los Angeles and New Orleans, passed laws prohibiting "indecent dress" or wearing "disguises" that did not mention gender or sex but encompassed cross-dressing when they were enforced. Cross-dressing laws were local innovations, passed by municipal governments, and no state or federal legislature passed a law that directly prohibited cross-dressing practices. However, California and New York did pass state laws that criminalized public "disguise" or "masquerade" for the purpose of avoiding identification.[6] As with local disguise laws, the state statutes were not specifically aimed at cross-dressing practices but were nonetheless used to arrest people for wearing gender-inappropriate clothes.

Far from being nineteenth-century anachronisms, cross-dressing laws had remarkable longevity and became a key tool for policing lesbian, gay, and transgender communities in the mid-twentieth century. In particular, numerous oral histories and memoirs document their frequent—and frequently brutal—enforcement in working-class bars and neighborhoods during the 1950s and 1960s. For example, in their study of a working-class lesbian community in mid-twentieth-century Buffalo, New York, Elizabeth Kennedy and Madeline Davis interviewed several women who remembered the police arresting butch lesbians for wearing less than three pieces of women's clothing, in violation of local law. In Nan Alamilla Boyd's book *Wide Open Town* San Francisco residents describe similar harassment on the West Coast, where the police used cross-dressing law to arrest transgender women and gay men in drag, as well as butch lesbians. Several law review articles provide additional support for what these histories suggest: city police departments across the United States used cross-dressing laws to harass queer and transgender communities in the mid-twentieth century, particularly when they raided bars but were unable to catch customers soliciting or having sex. In San Francisco this police harassment helped spark the 1966 Compton's Cafeteria riots that mark the birth of U.S. transgender activism. Even the more widely known Stonewall riots in New York in 1969 appear to have been at least partially fueled by cross-dressing laws; according to the social historian Martin Duberman, the crowd in the Stonewall Inn fought back only after the police attempted to arrest a butch lesbian for wearing men's clothing.[7]

Given the high number of U.S. cities that passed cross-dressing laws and their central role in twentieth-century queer and transgender life, surprisingly little is known about their history, particularly during the nineteenth century, when they were initially passed.[8] Consequently this book breaks new ground by providing the first in-depth study of U.S. cross-dressing laws in one city, San Francisco, during the second half of the nineteenth century. Of course, San Francisco does not represent all of the U.S. cities that passed cross-dressing laws, but it does provide a particularly rich site for analyzing the production and policing of normative gender in relation to broader societal trends.[9]

Between 1848 and 1900 San Francisco experienced unprecedented growth, as a series of economic, political, and social upheavals transformed the region from a small, coastal village in recently Mexican territory into an epicenter of U.S. capitalist investment, urban development, and imperial expansion. This rapid development made questions of governance, social order, and urban space particularly pressing, as the burgeoning city struggled to develop a system of government that benefited its white, male, merchant elite. The same half century also encompassed a crucial period in the reformulation of gender and sexual norms, as well as the redrawing and consolidation of racial and national boundaries against a backdrop of U.S. territorial expansion, manifest destiny ideology, changing patterns of immigration, the end of slavery, and the birth of Jim Crow segregation. Once again emergent questions of morality, difference, racialization, and citizenship assumed particular urgency in San Francisco, where city life was profoundly shaped by the multinational gold rush migrations and the aftermath of the Mexican-American War. San Francisco's cross-dressing law thus emerged in an acutely charged political and cultural climate, where broad societal trends were condensed and accentuated. In this context the interplay of multiple boundary formations comes into view—of normative gender, race, and nation and governable city space. Using cross-dressing law as a window onto these formations, *Arresting Dress* uncovers an important component of lesbian, gay, and transgender history that has consistently appeared in the footnotes of twentieth-century studies but has yet to be brought to the fore.

The significance of cross-dressing laws, however, extends beyond their historical prevalence to encompass their political effects as strategies of government that produced new definitions of normative gender during a period of rapid social change. In using the term *normative gender* I refer, in part, to the multiple taken-for-granted rules and assumptions that dictate how men and women are supposed to be in a given society, including how they should look, act, feel, and think. In this book, however, I primarily use the term to refer to something more fundamental: the modern Western insistence that all bodies and ways of being can be meaningfully divided into discrete, opposing binary categories of male and female, man and woman, masculine and feminine. These binary gender norms are cultural products, not biological absolutes, and they seem to be everywhere and nowhere at the same time; they permeate our assumptions, our interactions, and even our language but can be difficult to isolate and pin down. However, despite their seemingly elusive character, there are moments in history when the boundaries of normative gender are thrown into question, disrupting our classification schemes. During these moments social institutions often intervene to define and regulate normative gender, restricting who can lay claim to femininity or masculinity and who is permitted to be a woman or man. Such institutional impositions create new contested terrain, as normative gender boundaries are formed, deployed, policed, negotiated, and resisted with varying degrees of success.

In the second half of the nineteenth century local governments across the United States took up the project of normative gender in a particularly explicit way, through laws that made it a crime for a person to appear in public in "a dress not belonging to his or her sex." At first glance today these laws seem to focus exclusively on clothing, banning women from wearing pants, for example, and men from wearing dresses. On closer examination, however, cross-dressing laws come into focus as a central mechanism for policing a whole series of "belongings"—not only the items of clothing that "belonged" to a specific sex but also the types of people that "belonged" in public space and the types of bodies that "belonged" in the categories of man and woman.

A Scholarship of "Not Belonging"

Written in opposition to the restrictions on "belonging" that cross-dressing laws incited, this book resists three theoretical or methodological judgments of "not belonging" that can hamper cross-dressing histories. First, it resists the division of cross-dressing phenomena into groups that do and do not "belong" in sexuality and gender studies. It does so through transing analysis, a new interpretive approach that can reinvigorate and open up cross-dressing histories, without embracing every cross-dressing trace as indicative of a lesbian, gay, or transgender past. Second, the book resists the isolation of nonnormative gender as a formation that does not "belong" alongside classifications of race, sex, disability, and citizenship. In doing so it introduces the concept of problem bodies to signal the wide range of bodies that local government targeted for legal regulation in nineteenth-century San Francisco. Finally, it resists the elevation of law as an autonomous domain that does not "belong" in popular culture and the downgrading of popular culture as an apolitical domain that does not "belong" in studies of law. In doing so it highlights the mutual operations of regulation and fascination in the production of gender marginality.

The book's analytic innovations primarily speak to queer and transgender studies, even as they draw from and contribute to additional bodies of scholarship, including gender history, urban studies, critical legal studies, and critical race studies. Specifically the book builds upon several historical studies of cross-dressing in the nineteenth-century United States, which developed out of the lesbian and gay studies movement in the late 1970s and 1980s. Much of this work emphasized the political utility of social history and uncovered a wealth of evidence on cross-gender practices in the nineteenth century, particularly material on females who dressed and lived as men.[10] Many of these studies represented the purposeful efforts of queer scholars to reclaim a shared and recognizable past, and they frequently affirmed cross-dressing females as prototypical lesbians, and later as transgender men. Indeed significant debate occurs within this literature concerning the (homo)sexual versus (trans)gender identities of historical cross-dressers.[11]

The lesbian and gay studies movement carved out critical space in academia for the study of cross-dressing histories. It also provided me with invaluable leads toward some of the archival sources that I use in this book. However, while these studies are based on rich historical evidence and a laudable political desire to reclaim and validate past experiences, they have important analytic limitations.[12] In particular the imposition of contemporary gender and sexual identities onto past cross-dressing practices rests on the assumption that past experiences can be accurately understood in terms of present-day categories and concepts. This, however, is not the case. As numerous historians have documented, the ways that Western societies organize gender and sexuality today are quite different from the ways they did so in the past. In particular the concepts of transvestite, transsexual, and transgender did not exist for most of the nineteenth century, nor did the concepts of lesbian, homosexual, and heterosexual. This, of course, does not mean that people did not dress, live, and identify as the "opposite" sex or have sex with others of the same sex. It does mean, however, that the social and subjective meanings of these practices cannot be assumed but need to be carefully investigated, both to shed light on the past and to gain insight into the ways that contemporary understandings of gender normativity and difference emerged.[13]

In sharp contrast to the cross-dresser as prototype trope found in early lesbian and gay studies, 1990s queer theory presented the cross-dressing figure as a metaphor for the instability and fluidity of gender and sexual identities. Most notably Judith Butler used the cross-dressing, cross-gender figure to deconstruct the binary of authentic versus imitative gender. Butler highlighted butch/femme and drag performances as sites of gender contestation, arguing that the contradiction between sex and gender contained in these performances exposes the construction of all gender performances. Marjorie Garber extended Butler's insights by analyzing the possibilities of transvestite representations to signify the artifice of gender binaries. Garber argued that the persistent popular appeal of transvestism stems from its extraordinary power to indicate "category crises," or moments of turmoil when the naturalness of binary classifications is called into question. Moreover these category crises are not limited to sex, gender, and sexuality but can include race, class, and national classifications, as accompanying cultural anxieties are displaced onto the transvestite as "a figure that already inhabits, indeed incarnates, the margin."[14]

While Butler's and Garber's work is invaluable for troubling the ostensibly natural relationships between binary sex, gender, and sexuality, their theoretical insights can appear disconnected from specific sociohistorical contexts in which "gender trouble" and "category crises" emerge. As a result some scholars argue that Butler's and Garber's metaphoric use of drag erases transgender subjectivities, celebrating the "gender trouble" caused by transgender representation while neglecting the "gender trouble" experienced in transgender lives. While acknowledging that these criticisms are part of a broader, ongoing dialogue between queer theory and transgender studies, this book shows that both forms of "gender trouble" can be usefully brought together through close attention to the specific ways that normative gender boundaries are produced, policed, negotiated, resisted, and deployed.[15]

Trans-ing Analysis

This book presents a new critical approach for studying cross-dressing histories that I term *trans-ing analysis*. This approach incorporates insights from the burgeoning field of transgender studies, as well as from scholarship that seeks to queer history, either by focusing on nonnormative sexual practices (without reducing them to lesbian or gay identities) or by excavating the sexual meanings and dynamics of phenomena that are not transparently sexual (as in scholarship that seeks to queer the state).[16] Trans-ing analysis follows a similar logic but with specific focus on the historical production and subsequent operations of the boundary between normative and nonnormative gender. As such it brings together a range of cross-gender phenomena that are rarely considered alongside one other— not only people and practices that are marked as nonnormative but also cross-gender practices that do not provoke censure and cross-gender discourses that represent men as feminine, women as masculine, and gender difference as impossible to read. Trans-ing analysis thus expands the framework for examining the political significance of attempts to produce and police normative gender boundaries through cross-dressing laws.[17]

In this book I use trans-ing analysis to shift attention—at least provisionally—away from the recognizable cross-dressing *figure* to multiple forms of cross-dressing *practices*. In doing so I carve out analytic space for practices that do not always or easily attach to recognizable cultural figures— the cross-dressing practices of men who donned women's clothing at gold rush dances, for example, or of white women who wore men's clothing to visit Chinese prostitutes. This shift also facilitates expanded analysis of the variety of cultural figures that cross-dressing practices did sometimes coalesce around, incorporating not only the familiar figures of sexuality studies, such as the "passing woman" or the "fairie," but also the feminist dress reformer, the female stowaway who lived as a man aboard ship, the male gender illusionist who performed as a woman on the respectable vaudevillian stage, and the female prostitute who wore men's clothing to advertise her sexual services. By bringing together a wide range of cross-gender practices, trans-ing analysis provides space to highlight their potentially disparate cultural meanings and contradictory effects.

In addition to encompassing multiple cross-gender *practices*, I use transing analysis to bring cross-gender *representations* into the framework of study, focusing on popular and expert discourses that depict hyperfeminine men, hypermasculine women, and illegible gender. Such discourses proliferated in nineteenth-century San Francisco, as newspapers and political tracts published texts and images that were not specifically about cross-dressing but nonetheless used cross-dressing as a rhetorical device to comment on social and political issues of the day. Most notably, popular and political discourses used cross-gender imagery to represent Chinese men as hyperfeminine in an effort to mobilize support for exclusionary immigration laws. Placing cross-dressing imagery alongside practices and prohibitions, trans-ing analysis facilitates a richer exploration of the production and circulation of normative gender.

Problem Bodies

Just at this book proposes trans-ing analysis to assemble a wide range of cross-dressing practices and representations, it introduces the concept of "problem bodies" to collectively refer to the multiple sets of bodies that local government officials defined as social problems and targeted for intervention. In nineteenth-century San Francisco these included bodies that were marked as a social threat because of their performance of cheap labor (the Chinese laborer) or participation in marginal street economies (the disabled beggar, the city prostitute), as well as bodies that were marked as a threat due to their departure from emerging gender norms (the "degenerate" female impersonator, the feminist dress reformer, the "bogus man"). Placing problem bodies alongside one another, this book shows that cross-dressing laws were not an isolated or idiosyncratic act of government but one part of a broader legal matrix that was centrally concerned with the boundaries of sex, race, citizenship, and city space.

Laws that targeted problem bodies appeared in the "Offensive Trades and Nuisances" chapter of the municipal codebook. This body of law defined the atypical human body as an unsightly public nuisance, akin to sewage, trash, and slaughterhouses that operated within city limits. As such it positioned problem bodies on the margins of humanness—not as some *body* whose actions created public disorder but as some *thing* whose existence constituted urban blight. At the same time, nuisance law acknowledged the everyday character of the bodies and objects it regulated; it insisted not on their complete eradication but on their relocation to a different space where they could be concealed or confined. Under the proscriptions of nuisance law, problem bodies existed at the vexing intersection of commonplace and contemptible—an "everyday other" to be socially and spatially contained.

The "problem bodies" concept has clear parallels with Jennifer Terry and Jacqueline Urla's term *deviant bodies*.[18] In their formulation, the term critically interrogates the scientific and popular belief that deviance is locatable within the body—a belief that gained particular currency in the United

States during the nineteenth century as social conflicts were displaced onto the individual aberrant body. The concept of problem bodies performs comparable analytic work but with a specific focus on the practices of local government. In particular it spotlights a distinct process, observable in nineteenth-century cities such as San Francisco, whereby disparate sets of bodies were framed as undermining the municipal project of administering urban life. Certainly some problem bodies, at some times, were subjected to scientific scrutiny and viewed through the lens of embodied abnormality. Many others, however, were marked by a nuisance law framework as an annoying but ordinary presence in city space. The problem bodies concept is particularly useful for cross-dressing history, as it facilitates analysis of the overlapping ways that cross-dressing bodies were constructed and policed—not only as indecent bodies that threatened public morals but also as nuisance bodies that threatened public order and as illegible bodies that threatened the cultural imperative of verifiable identity in an anonymous city. Foregrounding the role of municipal government over science, I use problem bodies to spotlight a distinct terrain in the production of marginality: the local management and policing of city space.

I primarily developed the problem bodies concept to make sense of the persistent coappearance of these bodies in archived texts. Within nineteenth-century municipal codebooks, for example, cross-dressing, prostitute, and disabled bodies appeared alongside one another as (il)legal equivalents in public space, through general orders that banned the public appearance of a person wearing "a dress not belonging to his or her sex," in "a state of nudity," or "deformed so as to be an unsightly or disgusting object." Problem bodies were also brought together in the local police court, as cross-dressing offenders shared the holding cells and court benches with Chinese laborers who violated the city's lodging house laws and city prostitutes who engaged in "indecent" displays. Freak-show amusements similarly brought these bodies together, as cross-dressing performers shared the spotlight with the racialized "Missing Link" and "What-Is-It?" characters and multiple performances of disease and "deformity." In city newspapers reports of cross-dressing arrests appeared alongside stories of Chinese immigrants who "sneaked" into the country in cross-gender disguise. It would take considerable effort to "unsee" such connections, when legal and popular practices persistently grouped these bodies as sharing a common existence on the margins of urban citizenship. The problem bodies concept is thus an archival approach as much as a theoretical framework, which refuses to obscure the clear historical connections among nonnormative gender, sex, race, disability, and citizenship.

By using the concept of problem bodies to construct and interpret cross-dressing history, this book pays particularly close attention to the interplay of gender, racial, and national formations. It draws from scholarship that demonstrates that race has no biological or scientific basis but is a socially constructed category that emerged through historically specific processes of racialization. In the United States the social and political creation of "race" served to justify European American dominance by resolving a fundamental paradox at the heart of the republic: founded on principles of democracy and freedom, the nation's economic and political development was rooted in the enslavement of Africans, the genocide of Native Americans, the exclusion of Asian immigrants, and the conquest of Mexican land. The construction of race helped to explain this contradiction by masking social inequalities as natural.[19]

Claims about gender and sexuality played a key role in processes of racialization, and I am indebted to numerous scholars who have analyzed these complex historical entanglements, especially in the American West.[20] In particular I draw on scholarship that examines the historical linkages among nonnormative gender, racial politics, and national belonging. Karen Leong, for example, argues that American orientalism relies heavily on tropes of feminization that depict Asian nations and peoples in feminine forms. In the late nineteenth century such representations played a key role in national politics, legitimizing federal laws that barred Chinese immigrants from the nation. Nayan Shah further highlights these connections by documenting the ways that officials in nineteenth-century San Francisco viewed economic and domestic arrangements in Chinese communities through a lens of gender "deviance" that justified systematic marginalization and disenfranchisement. *Arresting Dress* builds on this work by sharpening the focus on cross-dressing practices, prohibitions, and representations. Specifically it shows how the cultural circuits of cross-dressing laws sharpened lines between white and Chinese San Franciscans, paralleling and intersecting concurrent attempts to manage racial and national conflicts.[21]

Legal Borders

I argue that San Francisco's cross-dressing law did not operate through prohibitions alone but through a constitutive power that produced new definitions of normative and nonnormative gender. As Barbara Young Welke argues, legal institutions have remarkable power to construct "borders of belonging" that delimit the terms of citizenship along axes of gender, race, and ability. Legal scholars have long recognized the law's productive capacities, and historians have paid particular attention to its role in racialization. In the second half of the nineteenth century multiple laws promoted white supremacy, including federal laws that restricted citizenship to "white persons and persons of African descent," state antimiscegenation laws that outlawed interracial marriages, and state Jim Crow laws that mandated racial segregation in public facilities. As Ariela Gross argues, these laws assumed that racial identity was fixed and transparent, but their enforcement revealed otherwise, requiring courts to explicitly define racial categories and actively sort people among them. I argue that cross-dressing laws performed parallel work on the grounds of gender, shaping the legal categories of man and woman and limiting who could lay claim to each.[22]

San Francisco's cross-dressing law did not simply *police* normative gender by enforcing preexisting standards and beliefs but actively *produced* it by creating new definitions of normality and abnormality and new restrictions on participating in public life. It did so, in part, by sorting out a wide range of cross-dressing practices, classifying some as acceptable, harmless, or entertaining and others as marginal, dangerous, or criminal. In targeting "a dress not belonging to his or her sex," the legal text lent itself easily to this task, focusing on practices that were transparently social (i.e., what clothing does and does not "belong" to whom) and hence subject to contestation and change. This imbued cross-dressing law with the flexibility to police a shifting sartorial boundary and hence to prosecute a range of dress practices judged to not belong.

Cross-dressing laws mobilized two overlapping strategies of containment that circumscribed cross-dressing discursively, within the category of criminality, and spatially, within the private sphere. This had profound effects on the gendered meanings of urban space at a time when city living assumed an increasingly central place in the nation. The rapid growth of the city prompted the development of new modern forms of municipal governance that proactively intervened in local affairs. In particular, modern municipal governments increasingly relied on early forms of zoning to govern urban space, limiting specific industries (such as slaughterhouses and hospitals) to designated areas of the city.[23]

Cross-dressing laws relied on the same logic as early zoning laws, seeking to confine nonnormative genders to designated private spaces and to reduce their public visibility. In the process it not only impacted the lives of those whose gender appearances fell within its reach; it also impacted the sociogeography of the city, marking public city space as exclusively gender normative and limiting gender difference to private or hidden realms. This consolidated definitions of gender normativity by overstating the rarity of "difference" and exaggerating the prevalence of the "norm." Far from an idiosyncratic prohibition on marginal practices, cross-dressing laws were a specific form of governance that played a central role in the production of modern city space.[24]

When foregrounding the productive capacities of cross-dressing laws, this book resists the temptation to view "the law" as a coherent autonomous domain that exists independently of other cultural practices. It draws from scholarship that calls for a critical cultural studies approach to law, focusing on the cultural lives of legal forms.[25] *Arresting Dress* thus traces the operations of cross-dressing laws outside of the juridical realm of courtrooms and codebooks into sites of popular culture where they ostensibly do not belong: the newspaper scandal, vaudevillian theater, the dime museum freak show, and the commercial slumming tour. As a result we see that cross-dressing laws had remarkably wide circulation, as offenders appeared as objects of scandal in newspaper stories and even as star attractions in local freak shows. Rather than point to distinct processes of legal regulation and cultural fascination, these popular sites reveal their overlaps and reinforcements, with regulation inciting interest and a desire to see, and fascination having disciplinary effects that circle back to law.

Archival Belongings

Complementing these analytic innovations, the book rests on a novel and expansive archive that assembles social processes, relations, and subjectivities that allegedly do not belong together. As authoritative and public acts of government, cross-dressing laws left a trail of documentation in their wake, found in codebooks, arrest records, and court reports. As cultural texts that incited public outrage and fascination, cross-dressing laws also left their mark in newspaper scandals, freak-show publicity, theater reviews, and slumming tour guides. I spent many months in California libraries and museums locating these records, bringing together a wide range of documents that are frequently held apart by the disciplinary terms of scholarship and the structure of the archive.[26] For example, I read police records alongside freak-show catalogues, legal texts alongside novels, and government reports on Chinese immigration alongside newspaper scandals about cross-dressing. In doing so I was influenced by scholarship that challenges the concept of the archive as a neutral repository of facts and foregrounds its historical constitution and political effects.[27] This scholarship shows that the logic of the archive—its classifications, adjudications, inclusions, and exclusions—is a "discursive formation" that constrains what can be found, known, and narrated as "history." I interrupt such archival reasoning to foreground social relations and processes that may otherwise have been obscured. As a result I bring together historical characters that seldom share the pages of academic inquiries, despite sharing nineteenth-century city streets: gold rush miners and freak-show performers; slumming tourists and dress reformers; female impersonators and stowaways.

Although this book focuses on cross-dressing laws, it does so expansively, extending in multiple directions to include the concurrent policing of race, sex, citizenship, and city space and the mutual operations of regulation and fascination in processes of marginalization. Despite this expansiveness, it does not—in fact it could not—provide a complete and accurate picture of cross-dressing laws in nineteenth-century San Francisco. In part this is because I rely exclusively on archived documents, which provide only a partial window onto the past. Moreover the documents that were available to me, such as government reports, newspapers, and private papers that somebody deemed worthy of preserving, reflect a particularly narrow and elite set of voices. Certainly different people's voices occasionally appear in these documents, but only within institutional contexts (such as court trials or newspaper interviews) over which they had little control. The picture these documents present, then, reveals virtually nothing about cross-dressing practices that did not result in official investigation or newspaper scandal, nor about the subjective experiences of people who broke the law. However, these documents do reveal plenty about the stories that government officials, judges, and journalists told about cross-dressing, regardless of their "truth." Consequently I use these documents not to provide a complete and accurate account of the past but as windows onto dominant ideologies, anxieties, and classifications of the time.[28]

As a study of nineteenth-century municipal law, this book confronts a problem that is well known to San Francisco historians: the sweeping destruction of local government documents by the 1906 earthquake and fire. Of particular consequence, the earthquake and fire destroyed virtually all records of the local police court, which had jurisdiction over cross-dressing crimes and other misdemeanor offenses.[29] California state court records can mitigate this problem for some researchers, as they document the appeal of cases that began in local courtrooms, including San Francisco's police court. Cross-dressing offenders, however, did not appeal to the state courts or generate the higher level of legal discourse preserved in state records. The earthquake and fire also destroyed records that detailed everyday police work, including the police chief's daily register of arrests and a register of "suspicious activities."[30]

Given the absence of local and state records, I relied on two main sources to reconstruct police and courtroom activity related to cross-dressing laws. First, I used the local government publication *Municipal Reports* to determine when cross-dressing arrests occurred. Published every fiscal year, *Municipal Reports* included annual arrest statistics, disaggregated by type of offense, and sometimes reported by month.[31] Second, I combed the "local items" and "police court" columns of city newspapers to locate cross-dressing cases. These daily columns provided information on offenders' names and alleged crimes, as well as on police court verdicts and sentences. These reports were often incomplete, describing a person's arrest and conviction, for example, but failing to report his or her sentence. Moreover they overwhelmingly focused on white cross-dressing criminals and overlooked Chinese and Mexican offenders. These news reports played a key role in the operations of cross-dressing laws, establishing gender normativity as the property of whites. Consequently, although I use city newspapers to reconstruct cross-dressing cases, I do so critically, reading closely for silence and its effects.[32]

Arresting Dress is not a conventional social history, and it does not primarily aim to recuperate lost histories. Nonetheless the book is grounded in a wealth of archival material, compiled in years of research, and readers who seek the new "stories" that new histories promise should not be disappointed. Alongside Eliza DeWolf, John Roberts, and Ferdinand Haisch, for example, readers will meet Wong Ah Choy, a stowaway who wore men's clothing in violation of local law and attempted to evade immigration inspectors during the years of Chinese exclusion. They will also meet Dick/Mamie Ruble, a person who rejected all gender classifications and invited the police court judge to feel his/her muscles before stating, "I couldn't pass for a woman anywhere, even if I tried."[33] The book also introduces new characters who wore women's clothing that "did not belong to [their] sex," including Bert Larose, a "female impersonator" who sold liquor and picked pockets on the Barbary Coast and engaged in sexual acts with drunken male patrons, and Geraldine Portica, who lived in San Francisco from girlhood until her cross-dressing arrest triggered deportation to Mexico in 1917. Readers will also gain fresh perspective on some of the city's characters that have appeared in earlier cross-dressing histories, learning of Jeanne Bonnet's courtroom defiance after multiple cross-dressing arrests, for example, and Milton Matson's insistence that judges recognize his manhood, even as the police insisted he had a female body. Finally, readers will learn of new venues that provided cross-dressing entertainments in nineteenth-century San Francisco, including Bottle Meyer's bar on Pacific Street, which hired female impersonators in the 1890s, and commercial slumming tours through Chinatown and the Barbary Coast that encouraged female patrons to dress as men. Consequently, although this book focuses on the proscriptions and punishments that impinged on gender difference in nineteenth-century San Francisco, it also details the tenacity and persistence of those outlawed—people who defied the law, spoke out when sentenced, and articulated different gender possibilities.

Organization of the Book

Chapter 1, "Instant and Peculiar," explores the cultural forms, contexts, and meanings of cross-dressing in the years leading up to criminalization. A wide range of cross-dressing practices occurred during these years, shaped by the multinational, predominantly male migrations of the gold rush and the U.S. annexation of California from Mexico after less than three decades of independence from Spanish colonial rule. In the wake of these social upheavals, cross-dressing practices performed contradictory cultural work, with some destabilizing dominant notions of gender and race and others consolidating the power of European-American men. Despite their disparate cultural meanings, these cross-dressing practices were legal equivalents, unhampered by government interference in a heterogeneous public sphere. This virtual legal vacuum was short-lived, however, and as the gold rush years came to a close San Francisco's government passed a local law that made it a crime for a person to appear in public "in a dress not belonging to his or her sex." This marked a new approach to managing gender in the rapidly developing city, positioning cross-dressing as a social problem in need of clear legal response.

Chapter 2, "Against Good Morals," examines the emergence of San Francisco's cross-dressing law in the context of a broader antiprostitution law. In the early 1850s multiple indecencies proliferated in the city, largely ignored by a municipal government that rarely intervened in local affairs. As the gold rush years came to a close, however, the social, political, and economic landscape changed, prompting new formulations of local government responsibility and new concerns about gender, sexuality, and family life. In this context political movements targeted cross-dressing and prostitution as problems of indecency and demanded government intervention through local law. This did not indicate a shift from a "wide-open" frontier town to a "locked-down" police state, but it did signal the debut of a proactive local government that assumed new responsibilities for the social and moral order of the city. In particular the law's emergence tightened the bounds of normative gender, pushing previously tolerated cross-dressing and commercial sex practices to the margins, as acts that no longer belonged in everyday public life.

Chapter 3, "Problem Bodies, Public Space," shifts the focus away from cross-dressing law's emergence to explore its legal operations and effects. Despite its roots in antiprostitution law, cross-dressing law soon became a tool for policing multiple gender offenses, including those of feminist dress reformers, female impersonators, fast young women who dressed as men for nights out on the town, and people whose gender identification did not match their anatomy in legally acceptable ways. The law did not respond to all cross-dressing practices equally, however, but selectively targeted those deemed to pose a social threat. Containing cross-dressing threats discursively (within the category of criminal) and spatially (within the private sphere), the law dictated the terms of urban belonging and marked city streets as gender-normative space. In the process it dovetailed with a host of nuisance laws concerned with the public visibility of multiple problem bodies, particularly those of Chinese immigrants, prostitutes, and those deemed maimed or diseased. Cross-dressing law did not eradicate all cross-dressing practices, but it did ensure that those who continued to engage in them would be classified as criminal, aberrant, not belonging. In the process it set in motion new definitions of gender normality and abnormality and new modes of exclusion from public life.

None of this, however, means that cross-dressing practices completely disappeared from sight. In chapter 4, "A Sight Well Worth Gazing Upon," I show how cross-dressing law increased the visibility of cross-dressing practices under the sign of criminality. After all, cross-dressing law consisted of not only a legal text that formally prohibited public cross-dressing practices but also a set of legal and cultural procedures that brought them into view. Specifically, everyday law enforcement mobilized intimate forms of surveillance and spectatorship as multiple actors *looked for* and *looked at* cross-dressing criminals in police photographs, court sketches, and newspaper crime reports. Visibility was partial, however, as newspaper reports focused on white cross-dressing criminals only and *looked past* similar offenses by Chinese and Mexican men and women. These representations played a crucial role in the operations of cross-dressing law, linking the politics of gender normativity to whiteness and framing cross-dressing offenders as criminal nuisances and queer freaks.

Chapter 5, "Indecent Exhibitions," explores the relationships between cross-dressing law and three entertainment venues that placed cross-dressing performers on display: vaudevillian theater, dime museum freak shows, and commercial slumming tours. These city entertainments commercialized the law's penchant for display and exploited the fascination that enforcement stirred up. At first glance these venues seemed to undermine the law, promoting and celebrating the public visibility of cross-dressing practices. On closer examination, however, they offered their own strategies of containment that dramatized, popularized, and democratized the normative gender boundaries that cross-dressing law produced.

Chapter 6, "Problem Bodies, Nation-State," examines multiple points of convergence between cross-dressing laws and the federal immigration controls that developed in the late nineteenth century and early twentieth. Immigration law did not target cross-dressing as a specific practice, but supporters produced political narratives of nonnormative gender to mobilize restrictions on national belonging. In particular, political campaigns for Chinese exclusion relied heavily upon cross-dressing imagery to vilify Chinese immigrants as hyperfeminine, deceptive men. Federal immigration law also ensnared people who wore clothing that did not "belong" to their sex, including Chinese women stowaways who tried to enter the nation undetected and resident immigrants who were deported following a cross-dressing arrest. By the early twentieth century the federal government was using immigration law to police problem bodies through exclusion from the nation. Together with cross-dressing laws, immigration laws positioned gender normativity as a precondition for full belonging.

In the book's conclusion, "Against the Law," I revisit my main arguments and consider the strategies of resistance employed by people who fell afoul of cross-dressing laws. Collective opposition was difficult, but individual protests arose, as people resisted arrest, argued in court, and insisted upon alternative forms of gender that undermined legal logic. These protests rarely resulted in courtroom victories, but they reached large audiences through the city press. As such they provided a counternarrative to cross-dressing laws and carved out critical space to resist their normalizing effects.

Terminology

A brief note on terminology is necessary. First, as a study of cross-dressing practices and punishments, this book inevitably confronts the challenge of representing—in the gendered English language—people whose gender identifications are unknown. Certainly this challenge is not pervasive, since some of the people who populate this book left at least partial records of their gender identification. Based on these records, for example, it is likely that Ferdinand Haisch identified as a woman, as did Eliza DeWolf. In these cases I follow my historical subjects' lead and use pronouns and names (when known) that correspond to their self-identifications. In other cases, however, the available historical evidence is far less clear, as with John Roberts. In such cases the burden of proof often falls on the gender-variant person; the cross-dressing criminal in pants is assumed to be a woman, and the offender in a dress is assumed to be a man, unless there is compelling evidence to the contrary. In contrast, when there is no evidence of self-identification, I leave the subject's gender identity open, using the terms s/he and his/her. Admittedly this can make for cumbersome reading, but

I choose to burden the reader with occasional awkward prose rather than burden the gender-variant subject with constant misidentification, even across the centuries. This strategy also avoids overstating the prevalence of normative gender identities, simply because they are the "norm," without imposing cross-gender identities on all "uncertain" cases.

This book also navigates the challenges of writing about race during an era when racial categories were in flux. Chapter 1 begins in the mid-nineteenth century as multiple nationalities assembled in San Francisco, prompted by the discovery of gold and the conquest of Mexican territory. As Tómas Almaguer argues, European American migrants, from within and outside the United States, quickly joined together under the category "white," seeking to monopolize the legal, political, and economic privileges it entailed. Chinese migrants, in contrast, were deemed a nonwhite race, with ancestral connections to Native Americans, while upper-class Mexicans were granted an intermediary status and legal classification as white, even as lower-class Mexicans were viewed as an "inferior" nonwhite race. In this book I use the terms *Chinese*, *Mexican*, and *white* to pinpoint the processes and consequences of this racialization, not to reify or essentialize race.[34]

Finally, throughout the book I use the terms *cross-dressing* and *cross-dressing law*. However, these terms are not without their problems. First, cross-dressing does not refer to one specific style of dress but to a wide range of clothing worn by multiple people for many different reasons. The specificities of these different practices are obscured when all are grouped under the concept of cross-dressing. Second, the term *cross-dressing* erroneously assumes that the type of clothing that "belongs" to each sex is easily agreed upon, when in fact such determinations are subject to fierce social debate as well as to change over time. For example, in the nineteenth century the question of whether pants exclusively "belonged" to men or could legally be worn by women was hotly debated in city newspapers and courtrooms, as the limits of cross-dressing laws were tested. Finally, cross-dressing is a problematic concept because it assumes that people can also be easily and consensually classified as "belonging" to one of two discrete, opposite sexes. In nineteenth-century San Francisco this was transparently not the case, and numerous people self-identified as a sex they had not been assigned at birth. These identifications undermine the integrity of cross-dressing as a concept, as clothing and self-identity could be aligned even as self-identity and legal sex were not.[35] These problems with the term *cross-dressing* do not render it unusable for the purposes of this book—it is, after all, what the law targeted in its ban on a person's wearing "a dress not belonging to his or her sex." However, these problems do make clear that *cross-dressing* is not a neutral descriptor but a politically loaded term, laden with assumptions about binary sex and gender and the meanings of their transgression. In this book I use the term only to spotlight, interrogate, and dismantle these assumptions, not to obscure and perpetuate them.

1

Instant and Peculiar

In early 1849 a young man named George Dornin left his home in New York to travel by ship to San Francisco, seeking his fortunes in the newly discovered gold mines of northern California. The journey was long, and Dornin later recalled how the ship's passengers celebrated the Fourth of July: they read the Declaration of Independence, flew the U.S. flag, prayed, held a thirty-gun salute, and enjoyed an evening of cross-dressing and same-sex dance where "the lack of lady dance partners . . . [was] made up by the substitution of the younger, and smoother-faced gentlemen, in calico gowns." As one of the ship's "patriotic Americans," Dornin happily participated in the evening's festivities: "Thanks to Mrs. Longley, I was made presentable as a young lady, and though I could not dance I could manage to walk through the figures and was, in consequence, in active demand." Dornin later served as a Republican member of the California state legislature, and his cross-dressing recollections appear in his published memoirs.[1]

When Dornin slipped into his calico gown and embraced his male partners, he participated in a cultural practice that was common among gold rush migrants, consisting of cross-gender dress and same-sex dance. Indeed multiple cross-dressing practices proliferated in gold rush San Francisco among men who wore women's clothing at predominantly male dances, women who dressed and lived as men when working in the gold mines, female prostitutes who dressed as men to advertise their sexual services, and feminist dress reformers who wore men's pants for increased freedom and mobility on the city streets. These practices took place against the backdrop of two transnational events that structured mid-nineteenth-century San Francisco life: the multinational, predominantly male migrations of the gold rush and the U.S. annexation of California from Mexico after less than three decades of independence from Spanish colonial rule. These events shaped the meanings, pleasures, and anxieties that attached to cross-dressing practices, some triggering considerable gender and racial anxieties and others supporting the growing regional dominance of European American men with remarkable ease. As suggested by Dornin's invocation of "American" patriotism, on Independence Day, on a U.S. vessel bound for newly conquered California, not all cross-dressing practices were as "transgressive" as they may at first appear. To understand the significance of cross-dressing laws—what they targeted, what they overlooked, why they mattered—this chapter turns to the cultural forms, contexts, and meanings of cross-dressing in the fifteen years preceding its criminalization.

A Sweeping Wave of Desire

In early 1848, on the eve of the gold rush, San Francisco was a small, coastal settlement with approximately eight hundred residents, including Californios, Native Americans, and European American settlers and their children. Within two years the town's population had boomed to thirty-five thousand, and within ten years it had surpassed fifty-five thousand as the discovery of gold in the Sierra foothills brought thousands of migrants to the port of San Francisco.[2] Over 95 percent of these migrants were young men, and over half traveled from outside of the United States, arriving first from Mexico, Chile, and Peru and later from Hawaii, France, Australia, China, Britain, Ireland, and Germany. The sudden arrival of these young men from multiple nations, in search of their fortunes, had a tremendous effect on San Francisco, transforming it from a small, sleepy settlement to "an instant city" in a handful of years.[3] The vast preponderance of men among these migrants also transformed gender relations in the region, as thousands of young men struggled to organize their social, sexual, and domestic lives in the virtual absence of women.

When these migrants arrived in San Francisco, they stepped into a social world that was not only adjusting to the chaos of the gold rush but also reeling from the recent Mexican-American War and the U.S. annexation of California. The war resulted in major territorial changes, and the United States seized more than one million square miles of land that became the states of California, Nevada, Utah, New Mexico, and Arizona, as well as portions of Colorado, Wyoming, Oklahoma, and Kansas. This massive transfer of land was formalized by the 1848 Treaty of Guadalupe-Hidalgo, signed just weeks after the discovery of gold. In the following months, as thousands of migrants crossed national borders to reach gold rush San Francisco, national borders crossed resident Californios, who ceased to be nationals of Mexico and became "foreigners" in U.S. territory without traveling an inch. U.S. rule produced dire consequences for Californios, despite treaty reassurances to the contrary, as legal maneuvering robbed them of land rights and accompanying status, lifestyle, and political power.[4] The U.S. conquest of Mexican California also shaped the ideological form of the gold rush, particularly for migrants from the eastern states, fueling beliefs in manifest destiny and infusing travel to California with nation-making, as well as wealth-making, meanings. Indeed some of the first European American men to arrive in San Francisco were soldiers from East Coast regiments who had crossed the continent for battle, not gold, but arrived too late to fight in the Mexican-American War. The territory that these and other migrants arrived in was not only a new U.S. possession but also a new home to thousands of other migrants, from multiple nations, who were staking claims to the land and the riches it promised. Undoubtedly the sudden national diversity of the region was a variation of its earlier cultural diversity rather than a completely new phenomenon.[5] Nonetheless this national diversity combined with the region's gender demographics to produce a social world in which complex and intersecting claims about identity, difference, and morality were made. In particular the postconquest gold rush context created spaces of possibility for male femininities and female masculinities that most visibly manifested in cross-dressing practices.[6]

Although the California gold rush quickly swelled San Francisco's population beyond recognition, the discovery of gold initially promised to be the town's death knell, as established residents flocked to the mines, causing the local newspaper, school, and even the military fort to cease all operations. However, the small settlement housed the region's only developed port, and as word of gold spread around the world hundreds of ships steamed into the Yerba Buena cove and thousands of gold-hungry men poured into town. These would-be miners needed a place to buy supplies, and San Francisco quickly became "an emporium for its hinterland," offering food, lodging, entertainment, mining tools, and clothing at exorbitant prices.[7] Additionally, because mining was a seasonal enterprise, thousands of miners returned to San Francisco every year to ride out the winter and spend whatever gold they had gained. The sleepy hamlet was soon overwhelmed. As one newspaper editor explained in mid-1849, "We were prepared for a large emigration, but we were not prepared for such a sweeping wave of *desire*."[8]

During these early gold-hunting years San Francisco was a chaotic and crowded place, lacking the physical spaces and social relationships that many associated with home. For example, there were few buildings to accommodate the new arrivals, so people bedded down in hastily erected tents, on large wooden boards nailed to the walls of overcrowded lodging houses, or simply on the ground where they fell. Multiple men shared the few beds available, and while some men presumably enjoyed such arrangements, others wryly complained that "however anxious a man may be to cultivate an extensive acquaintance he is not always exactly anxious to be imbedded in friendship."[9] Empty ships crowded the harbor, abandoned by crews and passengers rushing to the mines. Conditions were unsanitary, disease was rampant, and by the end of 1849 many gold rush migrants had died.

Within two years, however, the chaos of the late 1840s had been replaced with more ordered—though equally rapid—growth. As early as mid-1850 streets had been planked, multilevel brick houses had been built, and a banking and financial district developed. Saloons, gambling dens, and brothels similarly sprang up, providing some of the social and sexual companionship that could stand in for home. The town expanded spatially, too, westward toward the Presidio and eastward into Yerba Buena cove, as merchants converted abandoned ships into saloons and hotels—and even a city jail. San Francisco became the key hub for imported merchandise, serving as a transfer point between arriving clipper ships and departing steamers that transported supplies upriver to Sacramento and the surrounding mines. Certainly San Francisco's development remained unstable, and major fires destroyed the fledgling canvas-and-wood city six times between 1849 and 1852. Nonetheless, by 1851 San Francisco was one of the nation's leading ports, its foreign commerce topped only by the long-established cities of New York, Boston, and New Orleans.[10]

If twentieth-century historians have been struck by San Francisco's emergence as an "instant city," nineteenth-century chroniclers were equally impressed—or perhaps disturbed—by its "peculiar" population. During the gold rush years San Francisco was an overwhelmingly male town; women constituted only 2 percent of the population in 1849 and 15 percent in 1852. This gender imbalance featured prominently in gold rush participants' diaries, letters, and memoirs, frequently as a "peculiarity" to be remarked upon. One chronicler, for example, observed, "The most striking peculiarity observable in this city is the plentiful lack of women," while others claimed that the preponderance of young men "naturally tended to give a peculiar character to the aspects of the place and habits of the people."[11] Perhaps unsurprisingly some migrants viewed this "peculiarity" with dismay, with one stating, "One great cause of a loose state of morals in San Francisco is the absence of female society and female influence."[12] Others were even more grim, claiming that San Francisco had a uniquely high rate of "corruption, villainy, outlawry, intemperance, licentiousness, and every variety of crime" as a direct result of women's absence.[13] Indeed the imagined link between unrestrained bachelor men and rampant immorality led some religious leaders to develop schemes for importing "respectable" women to San Francisco to become dutiful wives—or, as one newspaper editor described it, to "bring a few spare-ribs to this market."[14]

Assessments of San Francisco's gender imbalance provide a window onto some of the ways that women were perceived during this period, most frequently as a "humanizing influence" or "civilizing force." However, the gender ratio "problem" in gold rush San Francisco also provides a window onto colonial relations, particularly between European American men, indigenous women, and Mexican women. Perceptions of a gender imbalance had existed in California long before the gold rush, since the Spanish conquest in 1769 instituted colonial ideologies that literally did not count indigenous women as women when calculating gender ratios.[15] Moreover the political and economic "value" of indigenous and Mexican women had fallen since the early days of conquest, as European colonizers no longer relied upon marriage to gain access to land, military alliances, and political and economic resources.[16] The problem of there being too few women in gold rush California, then, was more accurately a problem of there being too few women acceptable for marriage to European American men, and it had several causes that predated midcentury mass migrations. These included an ideological sphere that now condemned sexual relations between European American men and indigenous or Mexican women, except for rape and prostitution, and long-standing practices of land appropriation, violence, and Indian Removal policies that had forced indigenous people from the area. Moreover some miners were acutely aware (if not critically so) of the impact of these changes on gender relations. In his study of sex and gender in gold rush California, for example, Albert Hurtado quotes a Yuba County miner writing to his cousin of his plan "to go back to Michigan to get a Wife." This was not because there were no women in Yuba County but because—in his derogatory and dehumanizing words—"Squaw time is over in California."[17] Consequently when gold rush migrations brought thousands of men, and far fewer women, into midcentury San Francisco, they produced a gender imbalance that extended and modified a preexisting phenomenon, shaped by colonial practices, rather than creating something new. Far from being distant history, these colonial legacies continued to inform social relations in the region, manifesting in the ways this gender imbalance was perceived, as well as in the gender and sexual order created in response.

Mid-nineteenth-century San Francisco was thus located at the crossroads of two transnational events: the multinational, predominantly male mass migrations of the gold rush and the conquest of Mexican California by a U.S. government hungry for land and continental domination. At this crossroads national and racial identities were in flux, as were sexual and gender identities and the social relations they informed. This state of flux was temporary and was gradually replaced with a social and legal order that protectively consolidated the interests of a European American propertied elite and criminalized a wide range of public indecencies, including cross-dressing practices. These changes, however, occurred slowly and unevenly, and throughout the first half of the 1850s the gold rush migrations prompted a reorganization of gender and sexual relations under conditions of national heterogeneity and gender homogeneity, characterized by male predominance. This reorganization did not equalize gender relations between men and women, but it did allow some reconfiguration of the connections between sex, gender, and sexuality. Specifically, European American cultural demands for a strict coherence between anatomy and gender loosened their grip, providing spaces of possibility for some men to experiment with femininity in dress and labor, some women to perform masculinity in predominantly male social worlds, and some people to live as a gender they were not assigned at birth. However, these spaces of possibility were intimately shaped by the region's colonial experiences—with Spain in the past and the United States in the present.

The Place of the Women Would Be Taken by Men

In the fifteen years preceding San Francisco's passage of cross-dressing law, a wide range of cross-gender practices flourished, emerging in multiple and sometimes unexpected sites. The predominantly male, racially segregated gold mining camps, for example, were home not only to hard labor, heavy drinking, disease, and violence but also to cross-dressing recreations, as European American miners used items of clothing to gender the homosocial spaces of their men-only dances. Although these dances received only a footnote mention in Hubert Howe Bancroft's multivolume history of midcentury San Francisco ("The place of women at dances would be taken by men"), other observers provided more generous details of the dress and dance practices of European American men. After attending such a dance at Angel's Camp in the southern mines of Calaveras County, for example, a Scottish artist named J. D. Borthwick explained how several men became women for the night, wearing a sackcloth patch to indicate their new gender: "The absence of ladies was a difficulty which was very easily overcome, by a simple arrangement whereby it was understood that every gentleman who had a patch on a certain part of his inexpressibles should be considered a lady for the time being. These patches were rather fashionable, and were usually large squares of canvass, showing brightly on a dark ground, so that the 'ladies' of the party were as conspicuous as if they had been surrounded by the usual quantity of white muslin." Music at such dances was usually provided by an amateur fiddler, who encouraged cross-gender dancing by directing the miners to "lady's chain" and "set to your partner." According to Borthwick, when the fiddler instructed the dancers to "promenade to the bar, and treat your partners," cross-gender practices would continue, as "the 'ladies' . . . tossed off their cocktails and lighted their pipes just as in more polished circles they eat ice-creams and sip lemonade."[18]

At similar dances in the northern mines handkerchiefs were used to temporarily transform men into women, as at a Nevada City dance in 1850, where numerous men compensated for the gender imbalance of twelve women to three hundred men by tying a handkerchief around their arm and assuming the woman's part. Luzena Stanley Wilson attended the dance and reported that the men "airily assumed the character of ball-room belles. Every lady was overwhelmed with attentions, and there was probably more enjoyment that night, on the rough pine floor . . . than one finds in our society drawing-rooms."[19] Women's clothing was also sometimes worn to indicate a man's temporary new gender. Just as George Dornin donned a calico dress to compensate for the "lack of lady dance partners," several women who attended a ball at Marysville in Yuba County persuaded a minister's son from Boston to supplement their number by wearing a woman's gown, shawl, and fan.[20]

San Francisco also had its own predominantly male dance halls—in the words of a French journalist named Etienne Derbec, "What dance halls, good heavens!"[21] The city's popular masquerade balls, held in large gambling saloons on Saturday nights, attracted men in "female attire" as well as women in "male attire" and a host of other masqueraders and onlookers. Unlike the men-only dances in the mining camps, city masquerade balls frequently brought together cross-gender and commercial sex practices, as sex workers mingled with masqueraders on the dance floor and at the bar. These masquerades were often described as venues of wanton indecency, encouraged by the anonymity of masking. For example, one San Francisco journalist, Frank Soulé, and his colleagues claimed that "the most extraordinary scenes were exhibited" at the city's masked balls, led by "hot-headed young men, flush of money and half frantic with excitement, and lewd girls free from the necessity of all moral restraints."[22] Soulé does not mention whether any of these "lewd girls" were men in women's clothing. However, Borthwick, who provided the lavish account of the Angel's Camp dance, did not mention the presence of women at San Francisco's masquerade balls but did write of "half-a-dozen masks in female attire."[23]

The frequent description of these dances in gold rush diaries and memoirs highlights the entertainment value of men's cross-dressing practices and the symbolic power of clothing to transform men into women dance partners. Some of these practices challenged normative gender boundaries and provided spaces of possibility for people to experiment with cross-gender dress and presentation. Many dancers and masqueraders took advantage of these opportunities, some perhaps enjoying the thrill of temporary costuming and others taking more specific pleasures from the gender transformations triggered by women's dress. However, these transformations had multiple meanings and performed different, even contradictory types of cultural work. Consequently not all of these practices were as transgressive as they may at first appear.

For example, cross-dressing practices at gold rush dances provided the temporary fantasy of binary gender, which facilitated—if somewhat ironically—the appearance of heteronormative relations. Moreover these cross-gender dress and dance practices provided some European American men not only with a way to negotiate the region's gender imbalance but also with the means to actively produce and police new racial boundaries in the postwar context. After all, the gender imbalance these men negotiated was a racialized phenomenon, as acknowledged by a derisive "California Correspondent" to an East Coast newspaper, who explained that gold rush dances were "pretty much of the stag order": "We are short of pettycots—except the squaws, which indeed wear no pettycots, but only a light wrapper."[24] At these gold rush dances European American men chose to dance with each other, wearing dresses, while refusing to acknowledge, and humanize, indigenous women.

Cross-dressing dance practices were also joined by racial mockery at some gold rush dances, particularly at San Francisco's masquerade balls. In July 1851, for example, a Mexican-American War veteran and leading city merchant attended a masked ball at the city's Cairo Coffee House, wearing "blackface, petticoats and a woman's dress."[25] Such dress practices drew from the racial parodies and cross-dressing mimicry popularized by minstrel shows, which spread across the United States in the 1840s and 1850s. As the historian Eric Lott has argued, minstrel performances expressed a complex set of anxieties and longings but ultimately worked to consolidate white working-class masculinity and to reinforce prevailing ideologies of separate male and female spheres. Minstrel shows dominated San Francisco's nascent entertainment industry, with over sixty-six troupes performing in the 1850s alone. Their cultural logic also infused masquerade balls, shaping the racial mockery and disavowal that some cross-dressing costumes performed.[26]

City masquerade balls also sometimes placed "exotic" peoples on display, foreshadowing the racialized exhibition practices of freak shows and world's fairs, which grew in popularity as the century progressed. In 1850, for example, a group of shipwrecked Japanese sailors attended a San Francisco masquerade ball following their rescue by a U.S. ship off the California coast. One young crew member, Hikozō Hamada, later recalled that the U.S. ship's captain brought them on shore to "see the grand dances," stipulating that they first change into "native dress." The captain took the group to a masquerade ball on Kearney Street, leading them backstage, where they saw masqueraders "paint their faces and put on masks. We saw some females put on men's clothes, while some men arrayed themselves in women's garments." Unlike other people attending the ball, however, the Japanese crew had little time to enjoy these cross-gender performances. Instead they were forced on stage in front of a large crowd that eagerly awaited their display. City newspapers had advertised the sailors' exhibition, encouraging "everyone who is desirous of seeing them" to attend. Such episodes clearly complicate the meanings of cross-dressing practices at masquerade balls, underscoring the racialized context and exploitative form of at least some gold rush entertainments.[27]

Certainly as California grew in wealth and power, the homosocial, cross-gendered spaces of these dances did not become an embarrassing secret from the region's past but a celebrated symbol of its early years under U.S. rule. For example, in 1887, when the artist W. P. Bennett produced an illustrated version of James Hutchings's best-selling letter-sheet *The Miners' Ten Commandments*, originally published in 1853, the image of a presumably male miner dancing in a skirt appeared alongside scenes of mining, gambling, and crossing the plains as illustrations of gold rush life.[28] Even more striking, when the state capital hosted a lavish inaugural ball for Governor James Budd in 1895, the commemorative edition of the *San Francisco Examiner* ran a full-page cartoon of the state's white male elite dancing together, half of them in women's clothing (see figure 1.1).[29] As this cartoon demonstrates, cross-dressing practices and same-sex dancing retained a central place in high-society entertainment long after the gold rush passed, as cultural symbols of the state's economic and political development. In the late nineteenth century, then, at least some cross-dressing practices were fondly remembered as part of "official" history, as their potential threat to normative gender relations was counterbalanced, at least partially, by their support of racialized, heteronormative "American" masculinity.[30]

The mutual operation of cross-gender practices and racialization also found expression in the organization of domestic labor. After all, in post-conquest gold rush California, European American men crossed gender boundaries not only by dancing and dressing as "ladies" but also by per-

HUMORS OF THE BALL.

FIGURE 1.1. Newspaper cartoon commemorating the California State Inaugural Ball in 1895. *San Francisco Examiner*, Inaugural Ball Supplement, January 29, 1895.

forming domestic labor, for themselves and others, which they had previously viewed as beneath them. For example, Eliza Farnham, one of the region's few female migrants, wrote that in California "it is no more extraordinary for a woman to plough, dig and hoe with her hands . . . than for men to do all their household labor for months, never seeing the face nor hearing the voice of [a] woman during that time."[31] Similarly in her work on the social world of the gold rush, the historian Susan Johnson cites a letter by Lucius Fairchild, a future governor of Wisconsin, who wrote to his family about his seemingly unusual job waiting tables in a hotel: "Now in the states you would think that a person . . . was broke if you saw him acting the part of hired Girl . . . but here it is nothing, for all kinds of men do all kinds of work. . . . I can bob around the table, saying 'tea or coffee Sir' about as fast as most hombres."[32] As Johnson notes of this letter, Fairchild attempted to distinguish between "acting" in a woman's role and being an authentic man, although his attempt was betrayed by his reliance on the Spanish *hombres* rather than the English *men* to shore up his masculine identity. In a world where gender divisions of labor were thus disrupted, even the supposedly masculine labor of mining could be feminized, as San Francisco newspapers occasionally pointed out to their readers. Some men, for example, used women's sidesaddles when riding their horses through the mines, to help them work longer hours when digging from side canyons. Using a woman's saddle, the *Alta* claimed, was easier than "sitting woman-like on a man's saddle."[33] Even the miners' stock-in-trade equipment, a heavy-duty frying pan, was a household item from a woman's domain. One newspaper editor compared dispirited, pan-clutching miners to "good housewives . . . hurrying to some grand *clam bake*, to which all the world *except* his wife had been invited."[34]

These cross-gender labors were embedded in an economy that European Americans strove to organize for their sole benefit.[35] Geographic proximity had ensured that Californios, Mexicans, and Chileans began working the mines long before most European Americans arrived, but the latter group nonetheless believed that the recent war gave them exclusive rights to the land and the riches it produced. Consequently in an era before immigration controls the recently formed California state government passed a law in 1850 that imposed a special tax on "foreign" miners. Two years later, as the population grew, European Americans pressured the legislature to pass a second foreign miners tax, this time aimed at Chinese migrants. Combined with intensifying racial violence, the tax prompted many Chinese men to leave the mines and seek other forms of employment in San Francisco. Given the city's "peculiar" gender demographics, one segment of the labor market was particularly eager for new workers: the domestic and service occupations deemed "women's work."

Chinese gold rush migrants primarily hailed from Guangdong Province, on the south coast of China, where domestic labor was viewed as the responsibility of women.[36] However, when economic pressures pushed Chinese men into these occupations in California, many European American observers deemed them to have a natural, feminine propensity for women's work. Albert Richardson described San Francisco's Chinese residents as excellent house servants: "Perfect in imitation, where female labor is scarce he proves unrivaled at nursing, cooking, washing and ironing. Babies intrusted to him he dandles with so much caution and tenderness, that all the maternal instinct must lurk somewhere: under his long pig-tail, in his yellow face, or moony eyes. My friend had a masculine domestic named Afoy, who scrubbed floors, washed dishes and cooked dinners with grave and deliberate fidelity."[37] In Richardson's account, Chinese men's domestic skills did not derive from an ability "to bob around the table . . . as fast as most hombres" but from a maternal instinct located in a racially distinct body. Richardson focused in particular on the distinctive hairstyle of Chinese men as the site of femininity, issuing a potent claim about racial and gender difference that came to shape anti-Chinese politics far beyond the gold rush period. Such accounts positioned Chinese men as natural stand-ins for white women, obscuring the effects of discriminatory laws and containing gender trouble in the body of a racialized, feminized Other. Chinese men bore the brunt of feminizing critiques, but the anti-Chinese writer Hinton Helper made similar claims about Jewish men, stating they did not "engage in any sort of manual labor, except, perhaps, that which is of the most trivial and unmanly nature."[38] Similar to the dance practices described earlier, cross-gender labor provided not only a way for European American men to negotiate the region's gender imbalance but also a way to construct and consolidate ideas of naturalized racial difference.

Metamorphose Extraordinary

At the same time that European American migrant men were negotiating the gender imbalance of the gold rush era by experimenting with cross-gender practices in dress and labor, another set of cross-gender practices flourished among men with bodies that could be classified as female. Of course, these men came to public attention only when their anatomy was somehow discovered. In early 1850, for example, a San Francisco newspaper reported the arrival of "an individual whose sex would certainly never have been satisfactorily ascertained from outward appearances." The passenger, named Charley, had lived as a man during the voyage from Panama, but the newspaper editor claimed that he was actually a "lady" who had accomplished a "Metamorphose Extraordinary."[39] Another person, also named Charley, lived as a man for a much longer period of time. Charley Parkhurst drove the Wells Fargo stagecoach across central California during the 1850s and lived as a man for thirty years, until he died of cancer at age sixty-seven and the coroner reported that he had a female body.[40] Indeed, according to one gold rush migrant, Albert Richardson, men such as Parkhurst were so common in gold rush California that when a newspaper photographer advertised for a "lad" to help him, he was compelled to specify that "no young women in disguise need apply."[41]

In the predominantly male world of gold rush California, men who risked classification as "women in disguise" navigated a complex sexual terrain and their gender crossings inevitably raised questions of intimacy and desire. How did female masculinity inform and enliven their sexual relationships with other men, for example? How did it animate and complicate their relationships with women? Some observers sidestepped such questions by denying these men any sexual interests. One San Francisco newspaper acknowledged that Charley Parkhurst was "one of the boys" but insisted that he was "not a love-maker, and petticoats, even when surmounted by a trim bodice and a pretty face, were without special attractions." Other observers imposed a narrative of opposite-sex attraction, transforming these men into women the moment a man caught their eye. Ironically such narratives exposed the anxieties they sought to assuage, highlighting the sexual possibilities mobilized by gender crossings, as well as the instability of opposite-sex desire.[42]

The degree of gender confusion caused by cross-dressing practices in the years preceding cross-dressing law is indicated by the complex career of a popular daguerreotype image that circulated widely during the gold rush era (see figure 1.2). The picture was allegedly of a "girl miner" and featured a full-length image of a young miner dressed in men's pants, shirt, and tie, with a large hat pulled down over shoulder-length hair. According to the artist who took the picture, the young woman had adopted men's clothing to work in the mines, after her parents died crossing the plains in 1849. Having made her fortune, she left the mines and had her picture taken as she passed through San Francisco in 1850. The artist sold hundreds of copies of this picture to men in the area, until one of his customers, a young man named John Colton, recognized the image as a picture of himself. Confronting the artist, Colton allegedly demanded his share of the profits: "Why, that's my picture you are selling to these miners, and I want you to divide the profits, as you have evidently made a pretty good clean up from the enterprise."[43] Whether the artist yielded to Colton's demand and whether he continued to sell the picture following this confrontation is unknown. However, for the following 150 years historians continued to interpret the picture as evidence of cross-dressing women's presence in the mines, until Jennifer Watts, the curator of photographs at Huntington Library, uncovered the story of John Colton.[44]

FIGURE 1.2. Daguerreotype of John Colton that was widely sold in gold rush San Francisco as a "girl miner." Lorenzo Dow Stephens, *Life Sketches of a Jayhawker of '49* (San Jose: Nolta Brothers, 1916).

While Colton's claim that he was purposefully misidentified and marketed as a woman suggests that the "girl miner" picture lacks historical value as evidence of women's cross-dressing, the photograph's career more than confirms the cultural currency of such indeterminate gender images. First, in featuring the likeness of a man who is identified as a woman who is then identified as a man, the photograph highlights the slipperiness of gender identifications and the possibilities of dress to make gender difficult to read. Moreover even before John Colton claimed to be the "girl miner," the picture's popularity among gold rush men points to the complexity of gender relations in a predominantly male migrant world. On the one hand, the picture's popularity highlights the commodification of women that occurred in gold rush San Francisco, with men flocking to purchase even a picture of a "genuine" woman. On the other hand, the picture's popularity reveals that, under these conditions, men would cherish a picture that resembled their workmates, perhaps with the hope that one of them would also turn out to be a "girl." Female masculinity and male femininity thus converge in this image to highlight the spaces of possibility, as well as the difficulties of interpretation, that characterized the operations of gold rush gender.

Certainly not all females who wore men's clothing during the gold rush identified or lived as men. Some women donned men's clothing for temporary practical reasons en route to California, such as riding a mule during the Isthmian crossing—a treacherous short-cut through Panama, which allowed migrants to greatly reduce their travel time. One such woman, Mrs. D. B. Bates, expressly disliked wearing men's clothing and was eager to return to women's attire as soon as possible: "Rest assured, O ye of the opposite sex, that I, for one, will never attempt to appropriate to myself the indispensables, or the love of lordly power which usually accompanies them."[45] Others, however, had more permanent attachments to men's clothing and the female masculinity it signified, even as they continued to live as women. For example, in a Sierra Nevada mining camp, a European American woman described a Mexican woman who "has always worn male attire," and when violence broke out between Anglos and Mexicans in the camp, she drew "a pair of pistols" and "fought like a very fury."[46] Similarly when Mary Seacole, a Jamaican-born woman of color, was traveling to San Francisco via the Isthmus, she encountered many female migrants who resembled men not only in their choice of clothing but also in their riding skills, recklessness, and vulgar language. According to Seacole, these women were "in no hurry to resume the dress or obligations of their sex," which made it "somewhat difficult to distinguish the majority from their male companions."[47]

Women in men's clothing were also a relatively common sight in San Francisco, leading one newspaper editor to note, "Ladies are very fond of . . . a certain article of apparel which has, from the time Adam donned the first fig leaf, been appropriated by the sterner sex."[48] Some of these women wore clothing that had been made for men, while others wore the new "bloomer costume" designed to help women escape the confines of conventionally feminine dress.[49] Perhaps the most striking instance of female cross-dressing in gold rush San Francisco involved prostitutes who wore men's clothing to indicate their availability for commercial sex.[50] Similar to the "girl miner" picture, men's clothing did not render these women inaccessible as objects as men's desire but confirmed their potential sexual availability, perhaps by indicating a transgressive sexuality that distinguished them from "respectable" ladies, but also perhaps by likening them to "one of the boys."

Given the gold rush gender imbalance, women were generally welcomed in San Francisco, even if they were clad in items of men's clothing. Nonetheless gender anxieties bubbled beneath the surface, centering on the challenges this clothing posed to male privilege and gender legibility. The cross-dressing practices of European American women also stirred up racial anxieties, as some European American men drew parallels with Chinese women's dress. Not all observers cast these parallels in a negative light. One newspaper editor hoped that European American women would adopt bloomer style from "our neighbors of the Sun and Moon, or Celestial birth," who "can furnish us the fashions . . . and show us how they are worn."[51] Others, however, decried bloomer fashion, citing Chinese women as evidence of its desexualizing and masculinizing effects. The editor of one weekly broadsheet lamented the popularity of bloomers and rhetorically asked his readers, "Who that sees our 'Celestial maidens' from day to day in the streets, will deny that a woman *nately* rigged out in nice corduroys, with broad hat, and tight jacket, is one of the 'B'hoys.'" To this editor, bloomers brought European American women closer to Chinese women *and* European American men; consequently they needed to be opposed, otherwise "what man, married or single, will *dare* to call his *breeches* his own"?[52] Merging women's independence, Chinese migration, and cross-gender dress into a combined assault on European American men's dominance, such arguments highlighted the complex political context in which cross-dressing practices occurred.

The cross-gender landscape of gold rush San Francisco was dense and contradictory, consisting of multiple cross-dressing practices that rubbed up against each other in public space. These practices did not indicate a "wide-open" permissive frontier town—at least not in a straightforward sense. Instead they were the product of a complex web of power shaped by the city's rapid growth, "peculiar" gender demographics, and concurrent processes of migration, racialization, and nation formation. At the same time, these cross-dressing practices did exist with little government interference, unhampered by the dense net of public order, morality, and nuisance laws that would soon govern city life.

This virtual legal vacuum was relatively short-lived, and as the gold rush era drew to a close a series of economic, political, and social changes prompted a new era of regulation through municipal law. This marked a significant shift in official responses to gender transgressions and transformed public cross-dressing into a newly criminal offense. Not all cross-dressing practices would fall afoul of this law; the calico-clad same-sex dancing enjoyed by Dornin, for example, would remain legal entertainment and become a celebrated symbol of gold rush life, as newspaper coverage of Governor Budd's inauguration illustrates. Instead cross-dressing law would impose legal categories and consequences onto selected practices, bringing new specificity to the previous muddle of meanings and promising a clearly delineated response to cross-dressing threats. This promise would not be completely fulfilled, and multiple cross-dressing practices would persist, some in clear defiance of the law. The terms of these practices, however, would be radically and enduringly transformed, as cross-dressing law produced new definitions of gender normativity that shaped the city's landscape for decades to come.

Against Good Morals

In November 1857 an "infamous young woman" named Sophia Sherwood was arrested in San Francisco for wearing men's clothing. The legal grounds for the arrest were tenuous at best. On the one hand, some city officials claimed that cross-dressing was a misdemeanor offense under common law since it disturbed the peace and outraged public morals. On the other, the scope of common law in California was debatable, and no specific legislative act banned cross-dressing at the city or state level. Sherwood challenged her arrest and brought this legal ambiguity before Judge Henry Coon in the local police court. Although unsympathetic to Sherwood's position, Coon dropped the charges and conceded that cross-dressing practices were permitted in San Francisco, as long as they did not prompt a public outcry.[1] This tentative legality, however, was relatively short-lived; six years later, with Coon now mayor, the Board of Supervisors passed a new general order that explicitly banned cross-dressing in public spaces. This law marked a new approach to managing gender in the rapidly developing city, positioning cross-dressing as a social problem in need of a clear legal response.

The criminalization of cross-dressing in San Francisco emerged at the crossroads of three specific forces that I examine in this chapter: the joining of cross-dressing and prostitution as indecency, the framing of indecency as a societal problem in need of intervention, and the identification of local law as the solution. The classification of indecency as a problem to be addressed by law would have been unforeseeable at the beginning of the 1850s, when multiple indecencies were widely tolerated and local government rarely intervened in city life. However, as the decade unfolded, San Francisco underwent a series of changes that redefined the boundaries of normative gender and reworked local government into a proactive regulatory force. As such the city's cross-dressing law reflected not only changing conceptions of gender but also changing notions of governance.[2]

Giving Orders

San Francisco's Board of Supervisors criminalized cross-dressing in 1863 in a general order that prohibited a person from appearing in public in "a dress not belonging to his or her sex." The law did not target cross-dressing as a distinct offense but as one manifestation of the broader offense of indecency. The full text stated, "If any person shall appear in a public place in a state of nudity, or in a dress not belonging to his or her sex, or in an indecent or lewd dress, or shall make any indecent exposure of his or her person, or be guilty of any lewd or indecent act or behavior, or shall exhibit or perform any indecent, immoral or lewd play, or other representation, he should be guilty of a misdemeanor, and on conviction, shall pay a fine not exceeding five hundred dollars."[3] Such wide-reaching indecency laws were common in U.S. cities in the second half of the nineteenth century and were primarily concerned with reducing the public visibility of prostitution. Although later editions of the municipal codebook obscured this legal relationship, the emergence of cross-dressing law was intimately bound up with the regulation of prostitution.

The legal coupling of cross-dressing and prostitution would not have surprised San Francisco residents in the 1850s and 1860s. Both sets of practices were linked under English common law as "acts of an evil character" that were "contrary to decency and good morals."[4] Moreover both sets of practices were connected in daily public life, as female sex workers regularly advertised their sexual services by wearing men's clothes on the street. Describing San Francisco in 1849, for example, Frank Soulé and colleagues wrote, "Occasionally . . . the crowd would make way for the passage of a richly dressed woman, sweeping along, apparently proud of being recognized as one of frail character, or several together of the same class, mounted on spirited horses, and dashing furiously by, dressed in long riding skirts, or what was quite as common, in male attire." Similarly Eliza Farnham, a gold rush migrant, described "bold-faced unfortunates" who appeared "hatless and habitless [skirtless] on horseback in the streets," and three decades later Hubert Howe Bancroft recalled gold rush San Francisco as a place where "loose characters flaunted costly attire in elegant equipages, or appeared walking or riding in male attire."[5] Cross-dressing and prostitution, then, were connected not only conceptually, as two sides of the same gender-transgressive coin, but also materially, in the public presentations of midcentury sex workers.

Although these linkages explain why local government would view cross-dressing and prostitution as related phenomena, they do not explain how they came to be viewed as the social problem of indecency, nor how municipal law became the solution. After all, during the early gold rush years local authorities had permitted a wide range of public practices that would later be targeted by "good morals" laws, most strikingly public prostitution, particularly when practiced by European American women. Certainly some residents disapproved of the inverted moral order that this represented, but their protests were isolated and failed to mobilize social or legal change.[6] During the second half of the 1850s, however, the tide began to turn, as antivice crusades gathered supporters and momentum, and a merchant-led campaign to "purify" local government seized political power. By the early 1860s antivice forces held sway in the city and the Board of Supervisors passed its first set of "good morals" laws.

Becoming Indecent

The enactment of cross-dressing law inaugurated a new direction in San Francisco governance, as one of the city's very first "good morals and decency" laws. In the same way that cross-dressing law was not a distinct prohibition but one component of a wide-reaching indecency law, the ban on indecency was not an isolated act of government but one part of a new chapter, "Offenses against Good Morals and Decency," in the municipal codebook.[7] This chapter detailed a set of previously tolerated behaviors that were now criminal offenses: public indecency (including cross-dressing), public intoxication, profane language, and bathing in the bay without appropriate clothing. Taken together these laws signaled a significant shift in San Francisco's approach to governing moral life.

For the previous fifteen years San Francisco governments had paid surprisingly scant attention to morals offenses, making little concerted effort to regulate gambling, drinking, prostitution, or cross-dressing. A handful of early antivice laws were generally understood to be ineffective, and despite occasional protests multiple "indecencies" flourished in the city, including public cross-dressing.[8] However, from 1863 through at least the end of the century, every new edition of the municipal codebook presented additional antivice laws that extended the ban on gambling and prostitution and created new morals offenses, such as selling obscene material, visiting an opium room, permitting women in bars after nightfall, and engaging in acts that injured public morals.[9] The 1863 "good morals and decency" laws, then, not only marked the transformation of cross-dressing into a newly criminal offense but also signaled a turning point in local government affairs and initiated a new trend of municipal intervention into moral life.

The relative absence of morality laws in 1850s San Francisco reflected, in part, the toleration of vice in a predominantly male town; after all, if indecency was not viewed as a problem, there was no need for legal solutions. Perhaps most strikingly, commercial sex work was openly accepted in gold rush San Francisco, particularly when practiced by European American women, including those who wore men's clothing. Newspaper editors and city leaders frequently welcomed the arrival of European women who migrated to the city to sell sex. In 1850 the *Alta* newspaper happily reported that "flotillas of young men" had paddled out into San Francisco Bay to meet an "extraordinary importation" of women by ship. "One Frenchman brings twenty," the *Alta* proclaimed, "all, they say, beautiful!" Several months later the *Pacific News* announced that "nine hundred women of the French demimonde [were] expected" to take residence on Stockton and Filbert streets. Although it was widely acknowledged that many of these women migrated to work as prostitutes, newspapers described them as "fair but frail" ladies and "ladies in full bloom."[10] This terminology indicated more than a polite use of euphemism; it also represented a space of possibility between the act of selling sex and the identity of prostitute. This space of possibility allowed some European American women who sold sex to engage in other forms of labor—and other sexual relationships—without being circumscribed by the stigma of prostitution. It also allowed men who purchased sexual services to construct themselves as gender-normative masculine men—both sexual and respectable—in relation to these "ladies."

The social organization of sexual labor in San Francisco, however, was shaped not only by the city's gender imbalance but by concurrent processes of racial formation. As Tomás Almaguer argues, postwar gold rush San Francisco brought together multiple nationalities against the backdrop of conquest, mass migration, and the ideology of manifest destiny. Seeking to dominate the new social and economic structure, European Americans deployed racializing discourses that subordinated migrants from Mexico, Chile, Peru, and China as "inferior races" and subsumed the wide range of European nationalities and European Americans into the elevated category "white." Sexuality played a central role in these processes, fracturing the sex work economy along racialized lines.[11]

While European American men lauded their female compatriots (including sex workers) as respectable ladies, they criticized Mexican, Chilean, Peruvian, and Chinese women (including those who were not sex workers) as indecent "whores." The city journalists Soulé, Gihon, and Nisbet described the women who lived in a district dubbed "Little Chile" as follows: "This class of the foreign population was generally of the lowest, most debased character. . . . The men seemed deceivers by nature, while the women . . . were immodest and impure to a shocking degree. These were washer-women by day; by night—and, if a dollar could be earned, also by day—they were only prostitutes."[12] Women from Mexico, Chile, Peru, and China also faced harsher working conditions when selling sex, and they bore the brunt of episodic violence. In large part the disparate meanings, conditions, and consequences of selling sex in gold rush San Francisco reflected historically rooted national conflicts, which impacted sexual labor in the city as much as nonsexual labor in the mines. Equally important, these disparities reflected the ways that conflicts were being rearticulated—and national and racial boundaries were being redrawn—on the potent ground of sexuality.[13]

In this context it is no surprise that early attempts to police prostitution targeted Chinese and Mexican women, overlooking similar acts by European Americans. In April 1854, for example, the Board of Supervisors passed a local law to "suppress houses of ill-fame," which granted police the power to close any "place of prostitution" or any "ball, dance, fandango or assembly" where "people of ill-fame" gathered.[14] On paper the law applied to all sites of prostitution, but in practice the district attorney singled out Mexican and Chinese houses of ill fame, starting with Charles Walden's Golden Rule House on Pacific Street and moving on to establishments run by Ah-Choo, C. Lossen, and Ah Yow. The ordinance was poorly worded, as it required witness testimony to secure a conviction and rested on the undefined concept of ill fame. Nevertheless judges convicted the defendants, ruling that "bad reputation" constituted legal proof of prostitution.[15]

Even this racially selective policing strategy was short-lived. Only one month after the law's passage, the police arrested a European American woman named Mary Blane for keeping a house of ill fame. Blane hired a prominent defense attorney who skewered the prosecution for lack of evidence and secured witness testimony that she ran a respectable boardinghouse. Although Charles Walden and Ah Yow had presented similar arguments several weeks earlier, the jury acquitted Blane. The ruling had twofold significance. First, it highlighted the racial stratification of San Francisco's sex work economy and the racial underpinnings of the antiprostitution law. An 1855 cartoon satirized these inequalities, depicting two policemen forcefully arresting fully clothed Chinese women while ignoring the blatant sexual display of a seminaked European American woman who beckoned a man into a brothel (see figure 2.1). Second, the ruling neutralized the city's attempts to regulate prostitution. Following Blane's acquittal, the local judge announced that he would not enforce the ordinance, and the police marshal instructed the Board of Supervisors that their efforts had failed. Throughout the 1850s subsequent efforts to "suppress houses of ill-fame" followed a similar pattern: a brief period of racially specific enforcement, the unsuccessful prosecution of a European American woman, and a return to the laissez-faire status quo.[16]

During the 1850s, however, a series of societal changes occurred that led to increased legal controls on sex work and cross-dressing through "good morals" law. First, the end of the gold rush triggered a reorganization of gender relations and urban space that led to an antivice campaign against sexual and gender "indecencies." Specifically, by 1853 the excitement and haste of the gold rush was over, large company-driven mining had replaced small placer claims, and the promise of individuals striking it rich (greatly exaggerated to begin with) had passed. This marked a major transformation in the region's economy, which in turn prompted a reorganization of gender relations and city space.

FIGURE 2.1. Satirical cartoon depicting unequal law enforcement in 1850s San Francisco. "Actualities, San Francisco, California in 1855," Bancroft Library, University of California, Berkeley, BANC PIC 1963.002:0459—B.

Men who had flocked to San Francisco to make their fortunes now faced a decision: to return to the place they came from or to stay and make San Francisco home. Many chose the former, and the city experienced an unusually high population turnover during these years. However, those who chose to stay—and who could afford to do so—sent for their wives and children to join them in the developing city by the bay. As a result San Francisco underwent a profound gender change during the 1850s as the percentage of women increased from 2 percent in 1849 to 39 percent in 1860. Although women were still a statistical minority, the rate of change was astonishing: between 1852 and 1860 the number of women in the city increased 262 percent, from 5,529 to 20,026, while the number of men increased just 14 percent, from 30,625 to 34,776. These new arrivals differed from women who had migrated before 1852; they were more likely to be middle class, European American, and from the northeastern United States, migrating to San Francisco to join their husbands in already established homes and businesses. Consequently "respectable" wives and mothers soon outnumbered "disreputable" women, and the middle-class European American family became an established feature of San Francisco life for the first time under U.S. rule.[17]

Just as many gold rush migrants had previously bemoaned the city's "peculiar" gender demographics as the source of society's downfall, they now celebrated the arrival of middle-class, European American women as its salvation. For such observers, the presence of these women directly impacted moral life because they exerted a "civilizing" influence that curtailed the excesses of masculinity and because their vulnerabilities drew out men's protective instincts. One newspaper editor welcomed women and children as "beautiful aids and corrections to man," while another praised women's "proverbially humanizing influence in society."[18] These interpretations expressed a particular set of ideas about gender, sexuality, and social stability that became increasingly viable as the 1850s progressed, privileging one family formation—white, intraracial, middle class, and heterosexual—as the necessary foundation of social, economic, and political order.

This family unit represented one specific way of organizing sexual, gender, and racial relations, and it had numerous social and political effects as it gained dominance in the city. For example, it undercut the social necessity and public acceptability of gambling saloons, brothels, and bars, since respectable men could now receive social and sexual companionship at home, within the family, without visible external costs. Additionally it meant that men could now assert their masculinity through claims of "protecting the ladies" and "defending the family," options that did not exist before wives, mothers, and daughters arrived. Certainly during the early gold rush years some men had defined European American sex workers as ladies (frail and fair ladies, to be precise). However, the emergence of the respectable middle-class family required the category "lady" to be purged of its association with prostitution so as to leave it "pure" for middle-class wives and mothers to occupy. Consequently shifting gender demographics demanded the policing of new gender boundaries among women, between "ladies" and "non-ladies," particularly those who sold sex and wore men's clothing.

The end of the gold rush had other effects on the city too, signaling the end of seasonal labor patterns that left the city deserted for six months of the year. San Francisco now achieved greater residential stability and could embark on a journey of urban development and land specialization that resembled other cities. During the early gold rush years San Francisco had been a small city, without mass transportation, and its territorial expansion had been limited to distances that could be easily walked. As a result, like other early U.S. cities, it had been compact and congested, with a specific sociospatial structure: land use was mixed, with residential and commercial spaces grouped together; workers lived close to their city center workplaces; and residents of different classes, races, and nationalities lived in close proximity. However, with rapid population growth and the development of mass transportation the city expanded its territorial boundaries and residents dispersed to the periphery and suburbs. This dispersal was class-specific, as the upper and middle classes established new residential areas to the west, leaving the downtown area to working-class and poor city residents. Combined with the population boom, this population dispersal resulted in "a new urban spatial order" that was increasingly fragmented by class, nationality, and race.[19]

Increasing residential segregation was accompanied by increasing specialization of land use for industry. By 1854 wholesaling businesses had moved eastward toward the bay, large-scale manufacturing industries had located south of market, slaughterhouses and stockyards were forced to move outside of the city under local nuisance laws, and the downtown area increasingly focused on commerce, retail, and entertainment. The commercial sex industry, however, was not confined to a discrete vice district and thrived along the city's main streets, particularly Dupont and Stockton, interspersed with "respectable" residences and businesses. These streets were home to middle-class residents who had not relocated to the suburbs, as well as central transportation routes between the suburbs and downtown. Consequently middle-class families were forced to pass through large, highly visible vice areas when they traveled from their suburban homes to the city center, whether to attend work or to visit their church, the opera, or the city's main shopping district.[20]

Shifting gender relations combined with the reorganization of city space to shape San Francisco's early antivice movement. Specifically, antivice crusaders framed prostitution as a problem of public visibility that shocked middle-class European American "ladies" and impeded their movements through the city. According to an 1855 government report, "A virtuous woman cannot walk our streets without meeting the obscene stare, and being jostled against by harlots." The problem was not that ladies insisted upon traveling through the city's seedy back streets late at night, authors insisted, but that prostitutes insisted on working along the populous main thoroughfares "in the most public places, in the full light of day." Antivice crusaders echoed these claims in the city press. One newspaper editor stated that the public visibility of prostitution forced "the wives and daughters of our citizens . . . to avoid certain thoroughfares entirely or have their feelings outraged by . . . indecent exposures." Similarly a letter writer protested the "dens of shame and pollution on the main thoroughfares," asking, "Must our wives and daughters be forever exposed to these revolting and corrupting spectacles whenever they step into the street?" According to the crusaders, respectable middle-class women would be able to move freely through the city only if the use of urban space by other women— emphatically not "ladies"—was curtailed. Summing up this sentiment, one antivice crusader demanded that prostitutes be "*driven* into the dark lanes of our city, where none but the vile and most depraved do congregate."[21]

When proposing spatial solutions to urban prostitution, San Francisco's antivice reformers framed white, Chinese, and Mexican sex work in significantly different terms. On the one hand, they frequently viewed European American prostitution through the lens of temptation and seduction. They worried about the moral example set by European American parlor house prostitutes who "dwell in splendid houses in the principal streets of the city, and endeavor to attract attention by sitting before their open windows and doors, and by flaunting parade on foot and on horseback through the streets." These women, crusaders argued, "should be forced to seclude themselves from public places," lest their dazzling displays of wealth and sex seduce innocent youth. On the other hand, the crusaders framed prostitution practiced by "the other class of low Spanish and Chinese" in terms of disgust. Here concerns about the dynamics of sexual desire and restraint gave way to images of subhuman "vile characters" who "infested" the city and deserved to be "treated with little mercy."[22] In the rhetoric of reformers, claims about prostitution drew racial boundaries among women as well as legal boundaries between virtue and vice.

The Purified City

The popular reframing of prostitution as a racialized social problem played an important role in the criminalization of cross-dressing as indecency. Public outrage alone, however, was insufficient to lead to legal changes; it needed to be transformed into action by a local government willing to intervene into the city's moral life. In the first half of the 1850s this was virtually unthinkable. Besides cross-dressing and prostitution, local officials wished to avoid a wide range of issues occurring within city limits, including repairing and grading streets, managing sewage disposal, providing street lamps, and preventing city fires. Such municipal reluctance was common in U.S. cities at this time, but the rapid expansion of San Francisco's population in recently conquered and still contested territory made the absence of proactive government particularly apparent.

As newspaper correspondents often bemoaned, the U.S. annexation of Mexican California had created a temporary void of political and legal authority, with the territory existing as a U.S. possession—but not a U.S. state—for over eighteen months.[23] Undoubtedly the absence of political authority was most intense in newly settled mining camps, where lynch laws and everyday violence policed public life, particularly targeting Chinese and Mexican miners as well as indigenous people. Unlike these camps, gold rush San Francisco already had a system of government in place, consisting of a legislative body, the Ayuntamiento, which had been established by the 1836 Mexican Constitution. European Americans had controlled the Ayuntamiento since July 1846, and five of these men had already served as *alcaldes* (mayors), before John Geary became the first alcalde under U.S. rule in 1849.

Despite the continued presence of a governing body, San Francisco's legal infrastructure was unable to meet the demands of a rapidly growing city, driven by the mass migrations of the gold rush. Probably the clearest indicator of this was the condition of the police force and jail—or lack thereof. In Geary's inaugural address of 1849 he told San Franciscans, "You are without a single police officer or watchman, and have not the means of confining a prisoner for an hour. . . . In short, you are without a single requisite necessary for the promotion of prosperity, for the protection of property, or for the maintenance of order."[24] The Common Council subsequently appointed a captain of police, who then appointed thirty-four supporting officers. However, during the first half of the 1850s neither government officials nor city residents were particularly invested in developing a permanent and effective police force, even as the population boomed. Consequently in 1856, with over fifty thousand residents, San Francisco still employed only thirty-four police officers—and these had not been paid in eight months. The city also lacked a secure jail; from October 1849 to May 1851 prisoners were detained on a ship in the harbor. This makeshift, floating prison was surrounded by hundreds of other abandoned vessels, and prisoners easily and frequently escaped. Such conditions prompted the *Alta* to proclaim San Francisco "perhaps the worst governed community in existence. . . . She is without law, without proper executive officers, and without the means of confining and punishing offenders, and were it not that gold is so abundant, no man could calculate how long before the assassin's knife would be at his throat."[25]

Significant changes in local governance needed to occur before San Francisco would criminalize cross-dressing as indecency. These changes took place in the mid-1850s and had long-lasting effects on the structure of local politics and policing. While other U.S. cities underwent similar transformations during this decade, San Francisco's path toward "good government" was particularly dramatic, forged by a merchant-led group of armed vigilantes that seized political power for ninety-nine days after a semimilitary coup. The 1856 Vigilance Committee (predominantly Protestant) framed their actions as a citizens' revolt against political corruption, accusing the local Democratic Party (predominantly Catholic) of running a crooked political "machine" of electoral fraud, favors, and bribes. Unlike an earlier merchant-led Committee of Vigilance, formed in 1851, the 1856 Vigilantes had lofty goals that extended beyond the policing of crime to encompass "a thorough and fundamental reform and purification of the social and political body."[26] In pursuing these goals the 1856 Vigilantes "purged" San Francisco of allegedly fraudulent politicians, driving virtually all Democrats from the city, including those in elected office. They also brought together political and moral reform agendas, linking the campaign for good government to gender normativity, sexual propriety, and family life.[27]

Gender normativity and sexual morality took center stage in the Vigilance project from the very start, structuring events that triggered their formation. The first of these began with a confrontation between William Richardson and Arabella Ryan (also known as Belle Cora) and Charles Cora at the American Theater in November 1855. Richardson, a U.S. marshal, was at the theater to see a pantomime with his wife and their female friend. Sitting in an expensive first balcony seat, Richardson was outraged when he realized that Ryan and Cora, a well-known parlor-house madam and a gambler, were seated directly behind him rather than in the general admission seats, cheap pit seats, or velvet-curtained stalls reserved for prostitutes and their companions. Richardson attempted to get the couple removed from the theater, but when the manager refused to evict the couple—who were regular customers of the first balcony—Richardson left, swearing vengeance. Two days later a confrontation between the men left Richardson dead and Cora in jail for murder. Cora was tried two months later, but jurors failed to reach a verdict, as some accepted his claim of self-defense and preferred a manslaughter conviction. Although Cora was returned to jail to await a second trial, the city's leading merchants saw the case as emblematic of San Francisco's woes: gamblers and prostitutes got away with murder, while respectable ladies and gentlemen were consistently affronted in the morally corrupt public sphere.

The second formative event also consisted of a highly publicized fatal shooting against the backdrop of antivice concerns: the shooting of James King, editor of the *Bulletin* newspaper, by James Casey, a member of the Board of Supervisors. One month before the Cora-Richardson confrontation, King had unveiled the *Bulletin* as a new daily newspaper that distinguished itself in a crowded market with sensationalist, crusading reporting against government corruption and vice. For King, political and moral corruption were intimately connected, as gamblers and prostitutes used their "ill-gotten" wealth to bribe city officials, while corrupt politicians turned their back on honest merchants and families to cozy up to the practitioners of vice. Insisting that political and moral reforms must go hand in hand, King emerged as the popular leader of the city's antivice movement, embracing the Cora case as his cause célèbre.

In King's hands, Cora's trial provided unquestionable proof that gamblers and prostitutes ran the city: they dominated public space, destroyed respectable families, and used the "gold of prostitutes" to escape justice. Moreover with Richardson dead and the U.S. marshal position vacant, King saw their power extending to the highest echelons of federal government, claiming that Cora and his allies had persuaded the U.S. president to install a former gambler into the federal law enforcement position. King's incendiary editorials did not focus solely on Cora; in the first half of 1856 he published a series of attacks against James Casey, a member of the Board of Supervisors, alleging that the local Democrat won his seat on the Board through electoral fraud. On May 14, 1856, King published a particularly provocative attack that revealed Casey's prison history and called for his execution by hanging. That evening Casey shot King outside of the *Bulletin*'s office; six days later King died.

In many ways the fatal confrontations between Cora and Richardson and Casey and King were unremarkable. As the San Francisco historian Philip Ethington explains, dueling was a regular feature of the mid-nineteenth-century political landscape, as republican notions of masculinity and virtue required men to respond to slurs on their character with deadly violence. In 1850s San Francisco at least one major political duel took place each year, alongside countless other gunfights between men defending their honor. In this context it is not surprising that the morally charged confrontations between Richardson and Cora and Casey and King would end with fatal gunshots; indeed King had long predicted that one of his enemies would shoot him in the street. Unlike typical gunfights, however, these confrontations dramatically staged the growing social unease about vice and corruption: a notorious gambler shot a respected federal officer following a dispute over a prostitute, and a corrupt politician shot the city's most vocal and popular proponent of reform.[28]

Galvanized by the symbolic power of the combatants, a merchant-led group of men gathered outside the jail as news of King's shooting spread through the city. Four days later, certain that Casey and Cora would escape conviction through a corrupt judicial system, close to three thousand men stormed the jail, armed with rifles and a cannon. Identifying themselves as the 1856 Vigilance Committee, they seized both men, escorted them to Vigilante headquarters, and hurriedly convicted both of murder. Two days later, as King's funeral parade wound its way through the city, the Vigilantes executed Casey and Cora by public hanging, stringing their bodies from the windows of a warehouse in front of a roaring crowd.

The execution of Casey and Cora was merely the start of the 1856 Vigilance Committee's actions. Soon claiming over six thousand members, the Vigilantes formed armed military units that scoured the city to "purge" San Francisco of fraudulent politicians and their henchmen. Organized into infantry and artillery regiments, the Vigilantes launched predawn raids and rounded up the Democratic Party's political operatives, convicted them of ballot box stuffing and "shoulder-striking" (electoral bullying), and banished them from San Francisco. After one prisoner died in Vigilante custody, the California state governor intervened and demanded that the Vigilantes turn over their prisoners. When the Vigilantes refused, the governor declared the city to be in a state of insurrection, but his attempts to raise an army to regain control miserably failed. Now in complete control of the city, the Vigilantes intensified their push for "pure" government by demanding the removal of virtually all elected officials, including supervisors, judges, and the district attorney. When their demands were refused, the Vigilantes selected a Committee of Twenty-One to submit a slate of candidates for the upcoming November election. Presented as the People's Party, the slate scored a major victory and dominated local politics for the next twenty years.

San Francisco merchants played a leading role in the Vigilance Committee, and their economic concerns helped shape its trajectory. As the historian Richard Senkewicz explains, many merchants came to San Francisco during the early gold rush years seeking to exploit the town's position as "an emporium for its hinterland."[29] By the mid-1850s, however, the economic landscape had shifted, as overstocked markets and commercial insecurity replaced the earlier promise of easy riches. According to Senkewicz, merchants scapegoated local politicians and strove to assuage their economic anxieties through vigilante-induced political reforms. In particular they pursued a vision of political and social stability, rooted in fiscal conservatism and family life, which would attract outside investors and enable their commercial success.

As the Vigilantes enacted their plans to "purify" the city, concerns about gender normativity and sexual propriety remained at the forefront of public debate. The Cora and Richardson confrontation, for example, prompted a series of questions concerning respectable womanhood, sexuality, and public space, specifically the presence of an alleged prostitute in a respectable public venue. These questions were hotly debated in the pages of the press. The *Bulletin* attributed Richardson's death to the fact that a "notorious prostitute forces herself . . . *into such close proximity*, that the breath of the harlot *fans the cheek* of virtuous innocence." Once the 1856 Vigilance Committee had seized control of the city, middle-class women entered the political fray, writing letters to the press that urged the Vigilantes to banish prostitutes from the city, along with corrupt politicians. One writer praised the Vigilantes for their work so far but insisted that "one thing more must be done: Belle Cora must be requested to leave this city. . . . The truly virtuous of her sex will not feel the Vigilance Committee have done their *whole* duty till they comply with the request of MANY WOMEN OF SAN FRANCISCO." Another letter writer expanded these demands beyond Belle Cora, urging the Vigilantes to drive all "infamous harlots from our city," else "we, the women of San Francisco, will . . . endeavor to create a moral sentiment in this community which shall render it impossible for these prostitutes and their paramours to remain in our midst." Some letter writers insisted that the Vigilantes target not only prostitution but also other manifestations of sexual impropriety in the public sphere: "I hope the Vigilance Committee, while doing their best to clear the city of scoundrels, will not forget the Ladies, and that they will devise some way to punish those persons who loaf around the corners on Montgomery street and stare us out of countenance when we pass."[30]

As these letters suggest, Vigilante-era newspaper editors permitted "the ladies" to publicly participate in political debate, even as their participation was limited to criticizing another public woman: the city prostitute. However, the ladies were also present in Vigilante discourse in another crucial way: not as its author or its participant but as its underlying, legitimizing ground. In particular the Vigilantes frequently deployed the weighty category of "the ladies" as a powerful rhetorical device that could mobilize support for "pure" government and legitimize the use of extralegal violence. At one mass meeting, for example, a leading Vigilante roused the crowd: "The ladies are always right, and their endorsement of any cause would insure success. . . . It is enough to me to know that the ladies are with the Committee." In their rhetorical use of "the ladies" the Vigilantes forged a new local politics that presented a particular vision of normative gender as the foundation of social order.[31]

The category of "the ladies" was loaded with sexual, class, and racial symbolism; it also signified respectable femininity, untainted by sexual commerce or a range of soon-to-be-criminalized indecencies, such as public intoxication, using vulgar language, or "wearing a dress not belonging to [one's] sex." Reworking the boundaries of acceptable womanhood, the ladies of Vigilante discourse denounced "unsexed" prostitutes who were unworthy of the "name of woman" and also "repugnant" women's rights activists, who were "ambitious of being pigmy men." Called to serve a different set of ambitions, the ladies promised a "pure" domestic sphere where husbands could find respite from the harsh demands of commercial and political life. Here, as the historian Mary Ryan explains, the respectable middle-class family could take root once "the dangerous female was banished from the pantheon of true womanhood."[32]

The increasing presence of "the ladies" facilitated the debut of another figure on San Francisco's political stage: the upstanding family man. Vigilantes were called to action as property owners and citizens of a republic but also as husbands and fathers who epitomized "the manly and the good." One man urged the Vigilantes onward "as a law-abiding man . . . a husband and father of a wife and children," while another equated Vigilante support with patriarchal heroics: "Do not be deaf to the appeal of your wives—do not be blind to the supplicating looks of your children—do not waver when your best interests are at stake!" Dramatically framing San Francisco as a present-day "Sodom and Gomorrah," Vigilantes challenged the debauched masculinity of gamblers, "fancy" men, and theater owners who catered to prostitutes and ladies. "Make your choice gentleman," one supporter demanded. "You can't have *both*. . . . The time has come for you to decide."[33]

Vigilantes positioned the family man as the bedrock of good government and explicitly considered marital status when investigating men for political and moral transgressions. As Philip Ethington points out, the Vigilantes' Investigative Committee did not execute or banish any married men from the city and appeared untroubled about letting bachelors go. When investigating John McCann for political corruption, for example, one Committee member, Alfred Clarke, reported, "He is (I believe) a single man. The City would lose nothing by his absence."[34] Vigilante discourse thus marked a significant shift in the boundaries of normative manhood, as the carousing masculinity of the gold rush era was pushed to the margins and the respectable family man took center stage.

Vigilantes did not directly condemn cross-dressing practices in their battle to purify San Francisco, but they did use cross-dressing imagery to ridicule their opponents, predominantly Catholic Democrats who organized under the name Law and Order. The historian Michelle Jolly reports that a pro-Vigilante artist published a letter-sheet entitled "Dame Partington in California," in June 1856 (see figure 2.2). In political discourse, "Dame Partington" functioned as an insult against those who stood in the way of progress, based on the popular folktale of an English woman who attempted to use a mop to keep the Atlantic Ocean from flooding her coastal cottage during a heavy storm. The Vigilante letter-sheet featured a caricature of Law and Order dressed as Dame Partington—a bearded man, in a bonnet and smock, attempting to hold back the tide of "vigilance" and "reform." The cross-dressing imagery is startling and the political message is clear: Vigilante opponents are weak, laughable, unmanly men.[35]

Vigilante discourse thus put a series of gendered social divisions into play: between respectable women and disreputable harlots; between defenseless ladies and heroic gentlemen; between respectable family men and debauched bachelors; and between manly reformers and the effete opposition. These divisions lay at the heart of the Vigilantes' popular appeal, connecting the crusade for pure government to gender normativity, sexual propriety, and respectable family life.

The Vigilantes not only boosted the fortunes of the city's antivice crusade by linking their social purity agenda to campaigns for pure government but also secured a central place for these concerns within local politics by forcefully installing a municipal government amenable to moral reforms. At the close of their three-month reign the Vigilantes morphed into a new political entity, the People's Party, which operated within a legal framework and smoothed the transition from military coup to municipal rule. The People's Party ran for election in the fall of 1856, and as Jolly demonstrates, gender normativity retained a central role in the campaign. In particular People's Party supporters emphasized their status as respectable family men, while framing their Democratic opponents as rowdy young bachelors who patronized bars, brothels, and gambling saloons, clinging to the now-discredited masculinity of the gold rush era. The campaign was successful, with the People's Party winning all local

DAME PARTINGTON IN CALIFORNIA.

FIGURE 2.2. Pro-Vigilante letter-sheet depicting the cross-dressing opposition. "Dame Partington in California," Bancroft Library, University of California, Berkeley, BANC PIC 1963.002: 24.

offices except the seat for District 1, a working-class, transient area by the waterfront.

The Vigilante-sponsored People's Party ruled San Francisco politics for the next twenty years, pursuing fiscal and moral policies that served merchant interests by seeking a "decent" urban environment that was conducive to outside investment and family life.[36] During these decades it rejected primary elections and selected its candidates behind closed doors, consistently filling key political offices with ex-Vigilantes, including those of chief of police and police court judge. Between 1856 and 1867 all San Francisco mayors were Vigilantes or their close associates, as were most city supervisors.[37] This included Henry Coon, a founder of the People's Party and its first police judge—the same Judge Coon who conceded the legality of cross-dressing in 1857. Perhaps Coon remembered the case when he became mayor in 1863 and oversaw the enactment of "good morals and decency" laws, including cross-dressing law. Whatever his recollections, his actions had monumental effects, setting in motion a new regulatory approach toward gender transgressions in the city.

....

With the passage of cross-dressing law, San Francisco's Board of Supervisors expressed an unprecedented interest in defining and policing normative gender as part of the work of governance. This did not indicate a shift from a "wide-open" frontier town to a "locked-down" police state, but it did signal the debut of a proactive local government that assumed new responsibilities for the social and moral order of the city. In particular the law's emergence denoted a tightening of the bounds of normative gender, pushing previously tolerated cross-dressing and commercial sex practices to the margins, as acts that no longer belonged in everyday public life.

The changing legal status of indecency was a symbolic victory for the city's antivice crusaders, facilitated by the 1856 Vigilance Committee's political coup. Moreover by banning cross-dressing as one manifestation of indecency, the law had material effects that far outlasted the political turmoil of the 1850s. In the hands of police and judges cross-dressing law became a flexible tool for policing multiple gender transgressions, and it remained in force for more than a hundred years. In the process it produced new definitions of normative gender and new understandings of city space.

Problem Bodies, Public Space

In his classic, salacious history of San Francisco's "underground," Herbert Asbury describes one of the many mysterious characters that populated the Barbary Coast in the 1890s, a "middle-aged man" who regularly visited the Parisian Mansion brothel on Commercial Street: "[He] appeared each morning at the Parisian Mansion, carrying a bundle which contained a complete outfit of women's clothing. These garments he donned, and then he swept and dusted the brothel from cellar to garret. His work completed, he resumed his proper attire and departed, leaving a silver dollar on the parlor table. No one but Madame Marcelle knew his name, and she kept the secret."[1] According to Asbury, there was "considerable mystery" about this person—the mystery of why a middle-aged man would repeatedly visit a brothel to trade "his proper attire" for women's clothing and domestic labor. Although we could certainly speculate about these reasons, such dress practices also suggest another "mystery" that is worthy of exploration—not the psychosexual intrigue of why this person wore women's clothing in the brothel but the sociolegal puzzle of why s/he did not wear this clothing when returning to the street.

Certainly Asbury's Commercial Street character would have committed a crime under cross-dressing law if s/he had left the Parisian Mansion wearing women's clothing. However, many questions remain. Was cross-dressing law ever enforced? What happened to those apprehended? How were they punished? Was it really safer to cross-dress behind the doors of a brothel than on the city streets? If so, why? And what were the implications of this—for individual offenders and the gendered meanings of public space?

The answer to the first of these questions is straightforward: although San Francisco police did not enforce all of the city's "good morals and decency" laws, they did enforce cross-dressing law, making over one hundred arrests before the century's end. This amounted to one or two arrests each year, with occasional periods of intensified enforcement. Certainly the number of cross-dressing arrests did not reach the levels reported for some indecency offenses, such as using vulgar language, but it did surpass the number booked for lewd acts, indecent exhibitions, and the felony offense of sodomy.[2]

The answers to the remaining questions are far more complex. The complexity stems from highly selective law enforcement, as police and judges targeted only cross-dressing practices that were perceived to threaten city life and that occurred in public space. As a result the law did not operate with a blanket ban on all cross-dressing practices but through two overlapping modes of containment: discursive containment within the category of criminality and spatial containment within the private realm. In the process cross-dressing law set in motion new definitions of gender normality and new modes of exclusion from public life.

All Dressed Up

San Francisco police used cross-dressing law to regulate multiple gender offenses, including those of feminist dress reformers, "fast young women" who dressed as men for a night on the town, female impersonators, and people whose gender identifications did not match their anatomy in legally acceptable ways. In selectively targeting these offenses, cross-dressing law attempted to draw and fix two interrelated sets of gender boundaries, one between men and women and another between people with typical gender identities (i.e., male masculinities and female femininities) and atypical gender identities (i.e., male femininities and female masculinities). In the process it played a key role in creating new definitions of normative gender, shaping whose gender presentations would be permitted and who could make legal claims to being a man or a woman.

In monitoring the boundary between men and women, San Francisco police enforced cross-dressing law against women who sought a variety of male privileges rhetorically associated with "wearing the breeches": economic independence, political voice, sexual autonomy, and free movement through public space. For example, in 1866 the police arrested Eliza Hurd DeWolf for appearing on the city's fashionable Montgomery Street wearing a dress reform costume consisting of "black doeskin pants, men's boots, riding jacket, hat etc."[3] DeWolf was visiting San Francisco to deliver a series of public lectures on spiritualism, a popular religious movement that centered on communicating with the dead through female mediums. Spiritualism had ties to many radical social movements of the day, including abolition, free love, and women's rights, and DeWolf was a vocal advocate of the need to reform women's dress. Ironically her clothing was not significantly different from that worn by many women during the city's gold rush era fifteen years earlier, but by 1866 its alleged mismatch with her body was now a criminal offense, and police arrested her for wearing "a dress not belonging to her sex."[4]

Two years later, in 1869, police arrested a Chinese woman for similarly violating cross-dressing law after she appeared in public "dressed in Chinese male attire of the finest materials." Unlike the deluge of newspaper articles that accompanied DeWolf's cross-dressing crime, the city press provided scant information about this woman's arrest, even omitting her name from reports. They did, however, relay a story of cross-class romance and danger, alleging that the woman had fled her position in a Mission Street washhouse to elope with a Chinese merchant from Sacramento Street. According to city newspapers, the woman had donned her lover's clothing to avoid recognition as she moved through the city streets, only to fall afoul of cross-dressing law.[5]

The following decade, in 1876, police arrested two more women, Nellie and Lizzie Brown, for the same offense. Similar to DeWolf, these women explained their dress in terms of feminist politics and unsuccessfully attempted to talk their way out of prison by asserting their connection with the Women's Suffrage Association. Their feminism was connected to concerns with a different type of "spirits" than DeWolf's—the ones found in local saloons; they were part of a burgeoning cultural movement of young women who dressed as men to patronize the dive bars and music halls that denied women access after nightfall under "dive law" prohibitions.[6] Indeed the phenomenon of young women wearing men's clothing to "do the town" was so common in the 1860s and 1870s that the weekly *California Police Gazette* described it as an "epidemic" and warned women to resist. Apparently ignoring such warnings, Nellie and Lizzie Brown were arrested while having a "rollicking time" in the heart of the Barbary Coast, decked out with "cocked hat," "gleaming cigar," and roguish swagger.[7]

As these cases suggest, many San Francisco women used men's clothing to transgress gender boundaries, move through city space, and challenge the limited social roles assigned to them; for the most part these women did not seek to become men. Other people in the city, however, did live as a gender they were not assigned at birth. These people were also arrested under cross-dressing law, as the police attempted to purge public space of those whose gender identifications did not match their anatomy in legally permissible ways. For example, in 1895 the police arrested a forty-seven-year-old carpenter named Ferdinand Haisch for "masquerading in female attire" after Hayes Valley residents called the cops on the "strange woman" who walked through their neighborhood every evening. Haisch also lived in Hayes Valley and always wore women's clothing when the workday ended. The police staked out the neighborhood for several weeks, finally identifying and arresting Haisch wearing the latest women's fashions. Unable or unwilling to provide a reason for her dress, Haisch simply stated that apart from her carpenter's outfit, it was the only clothing she had.[8]

San Francisco police also used cross-dressing law to arrest people whose clothing styles signaled involvement in the city's sexual demimonde, centered in the Barbary Coast. In the mid-1870s the police regularly arrested a person called Jeanne Bonnet who always wore "male attire." In contrast with DeWolf's dress reform clothing, Bonnet preferred the stylish "hoodlum" suits worn by the city's young and rowdy working-class men; with her short hair, narrow build, and a penchant for hard liquor, she regularly moved through city space as a man.[9] Bonnet hung out in the bars and brothels along Dupont Street, befriending Barbary Coast women and persuading at least one local sex worker, Blanche Buneau, to leave prostitution and her exploitative lover. The police arrested Bonnet more than twenty times for cross-dressing and occasionally brought additional charges. For example, when the police realized that the masculine figure drinking at the bar was a woman in men's clothing, they arrested Bonnet for violating not only cross-dressing law but also the local dive laws that banned women from entering bars. This harassment ended only in 1876, when an unidentified gunman shot and killed Bonnet in Blanche Buneau's bed. The murder was never solved, and Buneau disappeared from the historical record.[10]

As these cases suggest, San Francisco police used cross-dressing law to arrest a wide range of people for multiple gender offenses, including men who wore "female attire," women who wore "male attire," and men and women who wore clothing that matched their self-identity but diverged from their legal sex. However, the police did not treat everybody who wore "a dress not belonging to his or her sex" in the same way. For example, in May 1903 the police apprehended two wealthy female tourists, one from Chicago and one from New York, who wore male attire while participating in a "slumming tour" of San Francisco's Chinatown. Slumming tours were a standard commercial enterprise in turn-of-the-century San Francisco, led by official guides licensed by the city. These tours, however, were not intended to give tourists license to violate cross-dressing law, and when a police officer spotted Mrs. Dubia and Mrs. Dessar dressed in male attire, he placed them under arrest. When the party arrived at the city prison, however, the arresting officer did not deliver the tourists to the prison cell, as was the usual procedure, but to the chief of police. As respectable, wealthy wives and mothers, they begged to be released, claiming that they had worn men's clothing only at the urging of their tour guide, so as to take in the seedier neighborhood sights that would have otherwise been off-limits. The chief of police initially doubted their story, but after confirming their address at an upscale hotel, he released the two without charges.[11]

Compared to other cross-dressing offenders, the fate of Dubia and Dessar reveals that cross-dressing law was not concerned with clothing per se but with the ability of clothing to mobilize and symbolize specific social threats. These included threats to male dominance posed by dress reform feminists who defied women's confinement in the private sphere, threats to sexual morality posed by cross-dressing "degenerates" who caroused in bars along the Barbary Coast, and threats to the cultural imperative of gender legibility posed by people with a gender identity that diverged from their legal sex. These dangers were more than figments of lawmakers' imaginations; they were real disruptions to an unequal power structure that positioned the respectable family as the basis of social order and systematically reserved economic, political, and social resources for white normatively gendered men.

Occasionally police court judges acknowledged as much when they parsed dangerous cross-dressing crimes from "harmless" cases that could be dismissed. In December 1890, for example, police arrested a person on Kearney Street in the early hours of Sunday morning for wearing women's clothing on a body they judged to be male. According to city newspapers, the offender wore a "complete woman's outfit" and was "effeminate in appearance and voice"; most newspapers identified her as Oscar Johnson, but some reported that she gave the name of Bettie Portel when first arrested. Judge Rix sentenced Portel to six months in jail—the maximum penalty permitted by law—on the grounds that she "was impersonating a female for no good purpose." It is unclear what Rix imagined Portel's "purpose" to be, but his ruling vividly demonstrates the courts' broader interests when judging cross-dressing crimes.[12]

In sharp contrast with Portel's sentence, arrestees who authored a credible claim of legal womanhood and respectable femininity were sometimes able to get charges dismissed. In 1910 a "fatherly" Judge Shortall dismissed cross-dressing charges against May Sullivan and Margaret McCarthy on the grounds that "they were good girls" who "simply made a mistake"; the women had appeared tearful and penitent in court, Sullivan explained that she was soon to be married, and both women claimed ignorance of the law. Three years later Judge Deasy similarly dismissed charges against Lottie Salas following her arrest for wearing men's clothing while accompanying her husband to a boxing match. As the "young society" wife of a millionaire, Salas had money, marriage, and conventional femininity on her side; she appeared in court "stunningly attired" and blushed as the charges were read. In these cases city judges drew a sharp line between the clothing practices of "good girls," which could be absorbed within the respectable family, and the clothing practices of persons with "no good purpose," which posed a serious threat. Policing such threats through cross-dressing law was not an irrational quirk of government but reflected a concerted effort to protect and consolidate gender divisions of power. In the service of these hierarchies, some cross-dressing practices were corralled into the category of criminality, while others were left unmarked.[13]

No Place to Go

Although it signaled a literal attempt to set the boundaries of normative gender through constructions of criminality, San Francisco's cross-dressing law was not an isolated or idiosyncratic act of government but one part of a broader legal matrix that also regulated the boundaries of sexuality, disability, race, and city space. From its inception, cross-dressing law was specifically concerned with public gender displays; any clothing practices that occurred in private were beyond its scope. In targeting the visibility of cross-dressing bodies in public space, the law dovetailed with numerous other local laws concerned with the public visibility of multiple "problem bodies," particularly those of Chinese immigrants, prostitutes, and those deemed maimed or diseased.

As Mary Ryan, Susan Schweik, and others have argued, nineteenth-century cities were dense, unruly spaces packed with heterogeneous crowds; men and women of multiple nationalities shared the same spaces, as did virtuous ladies and their lewd compatriots, "unsightly beggars and mad vagrants," and people who shunned the clothing that "belonged to their sex." San Francisco's social landscape was particularly confusing. Rapid population growth produced large-scale anonymity that robbed people of their ability to order public life through personal ties. At the same time, the zoning practices that would ultimately govern city life were still in a fledgling state. Seeking order in a city of strangers, municipal officials turned to one of the few tools at their disposal, passing general orders and ordinances under the powers granted by nuisance law.[14]

In 1863 the California state legislature granted San Francisco expanded powers to "authorize and direct the summary abatement of nuisances" and "provide by regulation, for the prevention and summary removal of all nuisances and obstructions in the streets, alleys, highways and public grounds." Exercising these powers, San Francisco's Board of Supervisors passed multiple laws that sought to reduce urban blight, targeting sewage disposal, slaughterhouses, and the keeping of hogs within city limits. Alongside these laws the supervisors passed additional general orders that targeted human bodies as a public nuisance. These "problem bodies" laws differed significantly from other nuisance laws in terms of their object of concern, but their mechanisms of control were very similar, seeking to manage public nuisances—animal, object, or human body—by regulating city space.[15]

In San Francisco nuisance law targeted four sets of problem bodies: cross-dressers, prostitutes, disabled beggars, and Chinese immigrants. As I discussed in chapter 2, antivice campaigners identified cross-dressing and prostitution as social problems in the mid-1850s against a backdrop of changing gender relations, shifting geography, anti-Chinese sentiment, and a merchant-led movement for good government. Rewarded with the "good morals and decency" laws of 1863, antivice movements arose periodically throughout the remainder of the century to protest lax law enforcement, highlight new concerns, and demand further legal controls.

Just as reformers persistently worried about the visibility of sexual and gender transgressions on San Francisco's streets, they also agitated about "unsightly" displays of the "maimed or diseased." After the city passed its "good morals and decency laws," journalists called for a police crackdown on disabled beggars, pinpointing a blind man and a young girl whose hands had been amputated as "nuisances which should be speedily abated."[16] According to Schweik, such calls were animated by multiple factors, including anxieties about the status of begging in a free labor economy, a growing commitment to "disappear" the disabled within segregated state institutions, and post–Civil War fears that "sham cripples" falsified war injuries to exploit public sympathy and pocketbooks. As Schweik argues, concerns about "fake" beggars paralleled concerns about cross-dressing; both sets of practices disturbed the cultural desire for legible bodies in an increasingly anonymous city. Certainly both sets of practices unnerved San Francisco's supervisors, who issued similar responses through local law.[17]

San Francisco supervisors also passed multiple local laws that targeted Chinese men and women as public nuisances; indeed the city's Chinese residents were subject to more local regulations than any other group. Legal discrimination began at the state level during the early days of the gold rush as European Americans, both foreign and native born, sought to establish political and economic dominance over the newly conquered territory. In 1852 the California state legislature targeted Chinese residents for a "foreign miners" tax, and in 1854 the California Supreme Court ruled that Chinese people were "not of white blood" and hence were ineligible to testify against whites in court.[18] During the 1850s and 1860s anti-Chinese agitators occasionally called for Chinese migrants to be barred from the country, but their demands were countered by the economic needs of a nascent capitalist class that funneled Chinese laborers into specific segments of the emerging racialized economy, particularly railroad construction and domestic service.[19]

Anti-Chinese politics reached new heights in the 1870s, when a statewide economic crisis led to unprecedented levels of unemployment and destitution among San Francisco's white working class. Triggered in part by the completion of the transcontinental railroad, the economic downturn brought Chinese and white laborers into competition for scarce re-sources. Rather than form a multiracial working-class alliance to protest the instability and exploitation at the heart of the emerging capitalist economy, white workers turned to the Workingmen's Party of California (WPC), based in San Francisco. Formed out of frustration with the two main political parties, the WPC identified two sources of white workers' suffering: unscrupulous capitalist bosses and "degraded" Chinese laborers, who accepted low wages and hence posed unfair competition in the labor market. Occasionally presenting an insightful critique of capitalist exploi-tation, WPC arguments typically morphed into racist attacks on Chinese workers, summed up in the party's slogan "The Chinese must go!" During the 1870s the WPC wielded significant political power in San Francisco. Its anti-Chinese agenda found expression in weekly outdoor public meetings, regular acts of violence, and a series of blatantly discriminatory local laws that attempted to drive Chinese residents from the city.[20]

In the second half of the nineteenth century, then, San Francisco's gov-ernment designated multiple sets of bodies as social problems in need of legal intervention. Adopting a nuisance law strategy, this intervention clas-sified problem bodies as urban blight—an offensive presence on city streets. Nuisance law's significance, however, stemmed not only from its framing of "the problem" but also from its proposed solution: managing problem bodies (and industries and animals) by manipulating city space. According to Sally Engle Merry, these strategies of "spatial governmentality" showed little interest in individual reform, preferring to create safe urban zones by removing or concealing offensive persons. In San Francisco local officials pursued these goals through four strategies of spatial control: exclusion, confinement, concealment, and removal.[21]

First, some laws sought to directly exclude problem bodies from public space. This was the case for cross-dressing law, which specifically made it a crime for a person to "appear in a *public place* . . . in a dress not belonging to his or her sex." It was also the case for an 1867 law that prohibited per-sons "diseased, maimed, mutilated" or an otherwise "unsightly or disgust-ing object" from appearing in public. One part of a broader law "to prohibit street begging, and to restrain certain persons from appearing in streets and public places," this law focused on the intersection of disability and poverty, seeking to exclude the potentially sympathetic figure of the disabled beggar from San Francisco streets. Two years later, in 1869, the supervisors passed a law that prohibited persons from carrying baskets or bags on poles on the city streets—a common way of moving through public space among some Chinese immigrant workers. Similar to cross-dressing law, these laws focused on public appearances and movements and simultaneously policed problem bodies while producing governable city space.[22]

Alongside local laws that sought to exclude problem bodies from public space, a second set of laws sought to reduce their visibility to middle-class white women and children through *confinement* in carefully designated and conveniently racialized vice districts. In the 1890s the Board of Supervisors passed a series of orders that targeted "houses of ill-fame" on middle-class residential streets. Some of these orders focused on those who ran or worked in these houses, while others targeted property owners who rented their buildings for "disreputable purposes." According to the historians Neil Shumsky and Larry Springer, local business owners supported these laws, seeking to remove prostitution from a newly located shopping district. City residents also presented them as necessary for the protection of property values and the active creation of "respectable" city neighborhoods.[23]

In 1898 a group of property owners from Mason Street petitioned the chief of police to "enforce the Penal Code against the people who occupy disreputable houses on the west side of the street between Eddy and Ellis." The *Call* newspaper reported, "The petition alleges that the houses in question depreciate the value of property and prevent respectable people from leasing houses in that block." Similarly a group of residents who lived near Berry Street petitioned the mayor to "vigorously" enforce vice laws against houses of ill fame because respectable people had to pass the street on their way to church, hotel, theater, and high school. In this case the mayor ordered the chief of police into immediate action, stating that it was "scandalous" for such a nuisance to exist "in the midst of such an important section of the city." Subsequent laws and policies went even further in their attempt to confine vice to less "important" areas. For example, when the owner of a Barbary Coast "den" attempted to buy property in the upscale Pacific Heights neighborhood following the 1906 earthquake and fire, the police captain promised to block the sale: "This section of the city must be kept free of such places. They have no business outside of the burned district and I propose to drive them back to where they belong." Two years later, and even more dramatically, the chief of police drew territorial boundaries around the Barbary Coast, ordering the district's female residents to remain east of Powell and north of Bush Street or face arrest and jailing under vagrancy laws. As Shumsky and Springer note, these policing strategies not only constricted the geographic spaces in which prostitution could occur but also compelled women who engaged in sex work to live within designated zones.[24]

A related type of legal intervention did not explicitly exclude problem bodies from general public space or designated neighborhoods but required their concealment from the "respectable" public's view. In 1863 Chief of Police Martin Burke attempted to reduce the visibility of prostitution in Chinatown by requiring the owners of cribs (small, street-level rooms from which women solicited sex) to buy and erect large screens at the entrance of the streets that housed them. These screens marked not only the geographic spaces of concern (i.e., Chinatown) but also the characteristics of "the public" who needed to be shielded from these sights. Chief Burke made this explicit in a subsequent annual report, stating that his purpose was to "hide the degradation and vice . . . from the view of women and children who ride the streetcar" through the newly developing downtown area.[25]

A fourth set of laws bypassed intracity boundaries entirely and sought to completely remove problem bodies from city space. This strategy was used exclusively against Chinese immigrants and encompassed the removal of Chinese prostitutes under a racially specific prostitution law and the removal of all Chinese residents under a nuisance law. In 1865 the Board of Supervisors passed an "order to remove Chinese women of ill-fame from certain limits of the city." As Judy Yung and Sucheng Chan have documented, earlier prostitution laws had been selectively enforced against Chinese women, but this was the first local law to explicitly target a single nationality. Under the advice of the city attorney, the Board of Supervisors removed the word *Chinese* from the legal text prior to publication, but the intent of the law remained unchanged. The following year 137 women—virtually all Chinese— were arrested as "common prostitutes," compared to one arrest the previous year. Frank Pixley, the lawyer who represented the arrested women in police court, claimed that when he objected to Mayor Coon that the law was unequally enforced, Coon "laughed and jeered at him, and told him that they would drive the Chinese women into the interior, where they might pursue their prostitution." These women were subsequently removed from the city, and Chief Burke boasted that he had used the law to expel three hundred Chinese women, with fewer than two hundred remaining.[26]

Alongside their efforts to use indecency laws to remove Chinese women from San Francisco, the Board of Supervisors attempted numerous times to harness the power granted by nuisance laws to remove all Chinese bodies from city space. As Nayan Shah has demonstrated, this possibility circulated in anti-Chinese political discourse since at least the mid-1850s. In 1854, for example, the Common Council (precursor to the Board of Supervisors) declared the Chinese an "unmitigated and wholesome nuisance" and sought the "immediate expulsion of the whole Chinese race from the city, or at least their removal outside the more inhabited line of streets." Similarly in 1876 a state report on Chinese immigration asserted, "The whole Chinese quarter is miserably filthy, and I think that the passage of an ordinance removing them from the city, as a nuisance, would be justifiable." These attempts to remove Chinese residents through the application of nuisance laws reached their peak in 1880, when an investigative committee of the San Francisco Board of Health, led by Mayor Kalloch of the anti-Chinese Workingmen's Party of California, published a report declaring Chinatown a nuisance. Under the power of nuisance law, the committee then called for the condemnation of Chinatown and the removal of all Chinese residents from the city limits: "With all the vacant and healthy territory around this city it is a shame that the very centre be surrendered and abandoned to this health-defying and law-defying population." Judicial restraints ultimately rendered these efforts ineffective, but not before the Board of Health unanimously accepted the committee's recommendations, signaling local government's investments in using nuisance law for racialized removal.[27]

Undoubtedly there are important differences between these laws, as well as between the processes by which cross-dressed, indecent, unsightly, and racialized immigrant bodies were defined as problems and targeted for legal intervention. Nonetheless I bring these laws together here—as they were brought together in nineteenth-century municipal codebooks—for two specific reasons. First, when these laws are considered together it becomes clear that cross-dressing law was not alone in its attempt to minimize the public visibility of problem bodies. Instead it was one part of a broader legal matrix that was concerned not only with gender transgressions but also with race, citizenship, and disease. Moreover these were not independent concerns. As numerous scholars have argued, accusations of sexual deviance have frequently been deployed in processes of racialization, while racialized anxieties have informed the policing of gender and sex. In turn race, gender, and sex have all been linked to disease, and in nineteenth-century San Francisco the management of public health was key to policing Chinese immigrants and prostitutes. In short, there were numerous intersecting cultural anxieties during this period that become more apparent when cross-dressing law is situated in its broader legal context.[28]

Second, analyzing cross-dressing law within this context also makes clearer the ways that the law was concerned not only with managing gender but also with managing city space. As the legal historian Lawrence Friedman has stated about nineteenth-century morality laws in general, "What was illegal . . . was not sin itself—and certainly not secret sin—but sin that offended public morality. This was what we might call the Victorian compromise: a certain toleration for vice, or at least a resigned acceptance, so long as it remained in an underground state." However, before vice could "remain in an underground state," such spaces had to be created. In San Francisco nuisance laws were instrumental to this process, constituting a dense legal matrix that dictated the types of bodies that could move freely through city space and the types of bodies that could not. Additionally these laws created urban zones where problem bodies could be contained, primarily the racialized vice districts of Chinatown and the Barbary Coast. Consequently they affected not only the movements of problem bodies but also the sociospatial order of the city, operating as early technologies of zoning that drew a series of boundaries between public and private, visible and concealed, and respectable and vice districts.[29]

In the case of cross-dressing law, the boundary between public and private was put into play. Specifically the law did not criminalize cross-dressing in private spaces but produced a public/private divide through which cross-dressing practices could be managed by dictating the terms of public visibility and policing access to public space. As a result some people confined their cross-dressing practices to private spaces and modified their appearance when in public for fear of arrest.

When San Francisco police arrested Ferdinand Haisch in 1895, for example, the police court judge released her from prison on the condition that she cease wearing women's clothes in public. Haisch apparently complied, but her ever-vigilant neighbors were still not satisfied and demanded her rearrest for wearing women's clothing at home. While predictably sympathetic to the neighbors' complaints, the police admitted they were powerless to intervene because the law permitted cross-dressing in private. Similarly, and also in the 1890s, a San Franciscan who identified as a woman named Jenny O. reported that although she preferred to wear women's clothing that did not "belong" to her legal sex, she dared do so only in private, for fear of arrest on the city streets. In a letter to the German sexologist Magnus Hirschfeld, Jenny wrote, "Only because of the arbitrary actions of the police do I wear men's clothing outside of the house. Skirts are a sanctuary to me, and I would rather keep on women's clothing forever if it were allowed on the street." As these cases suggest, the threat of arrest when in public was sufficient to pressure at least some women to restrict their gender expressions to private spaces. Consequently cross-dressing law did much more than police the types of clothing that "belonged" to each sex; it also used the visible marker of clothing to police the types of people that "belonged" in public space.[30]

Haisch and Jenny O. could hardly be blamed for bowing to the pressures of cross-dressing law. Those arrested faced police harassment, public exposure, and up to six months in jail—the maximum penalty permitted under state law. Judges were rarely this punitive, but they sometimes administered stiff fines and imprisoned those unable to pay. Jail sentences could vary considerably: five days for John Wilson in 1878, but forty days for Jeanne Bonnet in 1876, fifty days for Edward Livernash in 1891, sixty days for Milton Matson in 1903, and the maximum six-month sentence for Bettie Portel in 1890.[31] Conditions in the jail were abysmal for all inmates but could be particularly harsh for those with cross-gender identifications. Guards in the men's jail forced one inmate who was wearing a red dress and a straw hat to strip in front of the other prisoners, a scene that one reporter claimed was "highly enjoyed by the inmates of the cells and the crowd of persons in the corridor." The jail was also segregated by sex, and judges approvingly noted that placing cross-dressing offenders in the men's or women's cells, according to their legal sex, could add to the severity of their sentence.[32]

By the late nineteenth century some cross-dressing offenders also risked psychiatric institutionalization, as the state insane asylum assumed increasing responsibility for warehousing people whose behaviors signaled a "disordered mind."[33] In October 1890 a judge sent Dick/Mamie Ruble to the state insane asylum because of "a hallucination that she should wear men's clothing and wants legal authority for doing so." Ruble was arrested for violating cross-dressing law, but the case took a dramatic twist in court, when Ruble refused to identify with available gender categories and explained to the judge, "I'm neither a man nor a woman and I've got no sex at all." While many cross-dressing offenders pled for mercy and claimed their crimes were innocent "pranks," Ruble challenged the judge to locate femininity on his/her muscular body: "Did you ever see a woman with a hand like that Judge . . . ? Look at that muscle. Oh I tell you I couldn't pass for a woman anywhere, even if I tried." Unimpressed by Ruble's declarations, the judge called in the police surgeon, who referred the case to the Insanity Commission, located in a small basement room in city hall. The two-member commission reviewed the case, declared Ruble insane, and ordered his/her indefinite commitment to the Stockton Asylum, where the admitting doctor noted that Ruble "imagines she is a hermaphrodite. Wears male clothing. Wishes to have legal authority to wear men's clothing." Such "evidence of insanity" doomed Ruble to life in the asylum; s/he remained there for eighteen years, until dying from tuberculosis in 1908.[34]

Judges and doctors did not interpret all cross-dressing practices as evidence of insanity, however. One year after Ruble's trial the Insanity Commission heard the case of Maria Rogers, whose husband sought to have her institutionalized on the grounds that she "dressed in male attire and watched his movements." The commission rejected the husband's arguments and declared Rogers to be sane—a rare outcome in a system that returned an insanity verdict in 93 percent of cases. In contrast, in 1894 the Insanity Commission ruled that Henry Pohlmann was insane on the grounds that "he . . . labors under the delusion that he is a woman," wearing makeup and women's clothing. Similarly in 1899 the commission found Sophie Lederer to be insane, noting that the twenty-three-year-old domestic worker "talks irrationally—acts silly and claims to be a boy." Pohlmann spent two months in the Stockton Asylum before being deported to Germany, while Lederer effectively received a life sentence, dying in the asylum of heart disease in 1908. By the late nineteenth century, then, people with cross-gender identifications navigated an increasingly treacherous landscape, as a cross-dressing arrest could trigger an insanity hearing with devastating results. Under these circumstances it is not surprising that some people confined their cross-dressing practices to private spaces, nor that Asbury's "Commercial Street character" wore women's clothing only in the Parisian Mansion brothel.[35]

The legal attempt to exclude cross-dressing practices from public space— and to confine them to private spaces—was a form of segregation that had significant political consequences, both for individuals whose public appearance constituted a crime and for the "general" public. Of course, individuals could sidestep this segregation by changing their clothing when in public, as Jenny O. described. However, while this strategy may have been tenable for people who cross-dressed on occasion, it was far less tolerable for those who wore gendered clothing to present an enduring gender identity that did not match their legal sex. For such gender-variant people, cross-dressing law did more than ban a set of clothing; it effectively outlawed their existence. This fundamental slippage—from criminalizing acts to criminalizing personhood—was central to the law's segregationist effects.[36]

For people criminalized in public space, participation in day-to-day city life was curtailed. Everyday activities, such as going to the shops, enjoying a night on the town, or even walking through one's own neighborhood, brought surveillance and arrest. The ability to participate in these mundane activities was fundamental to urban citizenship, as city planners recognized when they strove to make the city inhabitable for middle-class women by creating "safe" public spaces, including parks, retail districts, and ladies' parlors and drawing rooms in big city hotels. However, the creation of these venues often occurred simultaneously with the purposeful exclusion of a range of people from public spaces, including those whose clothing did not "belong" to their sex.

By criminalizing gender-variant people in public space, cross-dressing law also severely restricted access to the public sphere, which the critical theorist Jürgen Habermas identified as a fundamental precondition of democracy. In Habermas's influential formulation, the public sphere consists of multiple public venues where individuals come together to discuss common public and political affairs, including coffeehouses, saloons, bars, and meeting halls, as well as the mediated venues of newspapers and journals. By restricting access to these public venues, cross-dressing law effectively excluded gender-variant people from civic participation and the democratic life of the city. Of course, many additional barriers to participation existed, and, as Nancy Fraser has argued, Habermas's formulation overlooks the multiple gender, race, and class exclusions that actively constitute the bourgeois public sphere. According to Fraser, however, members of excluded groups were historically able to establish alternative public spheres in which to debate and formulate competing political narratives. By outlawing the use of public space, cross-dressing law restricted access to even alternative public spheres, introducing considerable obstacles to community formation and collective politics.[37]

Finally, the impact of cross-dressing law on gender variance and public space was consequential not only for those marked as criminal in everyday public and political life but also for the "general," gender-normative public, which faced an artificially narrow range of gender identities in city space. After all, when in public there were only two ways that gender-variant people could avoid arrest: either changing their clothing to comply with the law or evading police detection by fully "passing." Involving different risks and benefits, these strategies nonetheless had a similar effect on city space, removing different gender appearances and identities from the public view. Indeed by policing gender hierarchies through public exclusion, cross-dressing law reinforced the very notion of "difference" as anomalous by exaggerating the prevalence of the "norm."

....

Of course, none of this means that the law removed all cross-dressing practices from San Francisco's streets. Arrest records document the persistence of cross-dressing offenses throughout and beyond the nineteenth century, and many more people must have violated the law without being caught. It does mean, however, that people who continued to cross-dress in public did so under threat of sanction, marked as problem bodies that constituted an offensive nuisance on city streets. This had profound effects on the social organization of gender and urban space. Containing cross-dressing practices discursively (within the category of criminal) and spatially (within the private sphere), the law dictated the terms of urban citizenship: public cross-dressing became a criminal offense, private cross-dressing became a shameful secret, and the city became a gender-normative spatial formation. Thus although cross-dressing law did not eradicate all cross-dressing practices, it did ensure that those who continued to engage in them would be classified as criminal, aberrant, not belonging.

A Sight Well Worth Gazing Upon

As a woman whose gender identity diverged from her legal sex, Jenny O. made a careful effort to avoid arrest under San Francisco's cross-dressing law by changing into men's clothing when she appeared in public. Ironically, however, she attained a much higher and more durable level of visibility than would have been likely on San Francisco streets when she was photographed for Magnus Hirschfeld's book *Transvestites: The Erotic Drive to Cross-Dress*. As a sexologist and advocate of homosexual emancipation, Hirschfeld championed the rights of people he termed "transvestites" in both the United States and Europe, and he published a collection of their stories, including Jenny O.'s, in 1910. One edition of the book included an illustrated supplement, which featured photographs of Hirschfeld's subjects. Jenny O. appeared in four photographs: in the first, she wore men's clothing; in the second, she was naked with her genitals exposed; in the third she was naked again, with her penis and testicles tucked between her legs; and in the fourth, she wore the women's clothing she preferred (see figure 4.1). These images provide rare visual documentation of cross-gender identifications in 1890s San Francisco and offer a striking portrait of a woman who navigated the city's cross-dressing law. Moreover they indicate that the politics of visibility surrounding late nineteenth-century

Der amerikanische auf Seite 100 der „Transvestiten" beschriebene Transvestit.

Fig. 1. Als junger Zeitungsverkäufer.   Fig. 2. In nudo.

Fig. 3. Als nackter Transvestit.   Fig. 4. In seinem Frauenkostüm.

FIGURE 4.1. Photographs of Jenny O. in Magnus Hirschfeld's *The Transvestites*. The caption translates as "The American transvestite who appears on page 100 of *The Transvestites*." Magnus Hirschfeld and Max Tilke, *Der erotische Verkleidungstrieb (Die Transvestiten), illustrierter Teil* (Leipzig: Verlag "Wahrheit" Ferdinand Spohr, 1912), plate 22. Courtesy of the Collection of Gerard Koskovich, San Francisco.

cross-dressing were far more complex than an initial review of cross-dressing law suggests.[1]

At first glance Hirschfeld's photographs seem to stand in stark contrast with cross-dressing law, spotlighting the problem bodies that the law sought to conceal. On closer examination, however, sexology's displays and the law's proscriptions come together as related techniques of marginalization that identified, catalogued, and exposed the cross-dressing criminal. In part this is because Hirschfeld's photographs had their own normalizing dynamic, graphically illustrating the objectification that cross-dressing subjects endured, even from their sworn supporters. It is also because cross-dressing law operated through comparable strategies of looking and display, amplifying the visibility of cross-dressing bodies as troubling nuisances and fascinating freaks.

As a local government order, cross-dressing law prohibited public appearance by a person in "a dress not belonging to his or her sex." However, while the legal text sought to reduce the public visibility of cross-dressing practices, everyday law enforcement relied on two strategies of looking that brought them into public view. First, cross-dressing law enforcement required the police to *look for* cross-dressing criminals, which demanded a particularly intimate surveillance of suspects' bodies. As defined by law, cross-dressing was a peculiarly visual crime that rested on the ostensible disjuncture of gendered clothing and sexed body. To detect a cross-dressing offense, then, the police had to look for and uncover the body underneath, just as Hirschfeld's photographs exposed the naked form beneath Jenny O.'s dress. This intimate surveillance promised to reveal the truth of cross-dressing crimes and restore legible, knowable, binary gender.

Second, cross-dressing law provided legal and popular platforms on which to display and *look at* the guilty body. In police photographs, courtrooms, and newspaper crime reports, state officials and reporters exposed and displayed cross-dressing as a criminal offense, imbuing these practices with remarkable visibility and raising public awareness of cross-dressing crimes. Unlike Hirschfeld's photographs, these legal displays did not feature naked bodies, but they similarly transformed the terms of visibility, subjecting the cross-dressing criminal to the harsh light of expert judgment and a normalizing gaze. The terms of this visibility, however, were partial. City newspapers in particular overwhelmingly focused on white cross-dressing crimes, *looking past* similar offenses by Chinese and Mexican men and women. These representations limited the terms of public discourse by persistently framing white cross-dressing subjects as criminal nuisances and queer freaks. They also established the production of normative gender as the prerogative of whites and drained gender variance from Chinese and Mexican communities.

Looking For

Before the police could make a cross-dressing arrest, they had to detect a potential offense, and this demanded a particularly intimate surveillance of suspects' bodies. After all, there was nothing inherently criminal in wearing a pair of pants, a silk skirt, or even a feather boa—it was only the mismatch of this clothing with the legal sex of the wearer that constituted an offense. Consequently to uncover a cross-dressing crime the police had to envision the sex beneath the clothing, and they utilized multiple markers to guide their imaginings: the size of a suspect's hands and feet, the presence or absence of facial hair, and the "swaggering" or "tripping" way he or she walked.[2]

One Sunday evening in December 1874, a San Francisco police officer spotted a woman walking through the city streets wearing a pair of snow shoes. Working from the belief that "snow shoes were not generally worn in the city by ladies," the suspicious officer approached the woman and ripped off her veil, revealing the masculine facial features of a person identified as John Roberts. The officer arrested Roberts for appearing in public in "female attire," or, as the next day's newspapers described it, in the clothing of a "pretty waiter girl," consisting of "a red striped dress with train *de mud a la Barbary Coast*, a straw hat with a bit of lace and artificial flowers in it, a heavy veil which concealed his face, and a comforter which he wore around his neck." Reporters did not relay Roberts's explanations for this clothing. Perhaps *she* simply liked it, dressing as a woman because she identified as a woman; perhaps *he* was returning from a masquerade ball in female costume; perhaps *s/he* wore women's clothing to solicit male sex customers along the waterfront; perhaps *he* was a comic performer in the local theater who hadn't changed back into street clothes; or perhaps *s/he* was part of a nascent queer underground, wearing women's clothing to indicate sexual interest in male "rough trade." Omitting such details, they mocked the appearance of "the female-man" before reporting that Roberts was brought before the municipal police court judge, quickly convicted, and fined $20.[3]

The circumstances surrounding Roberts's arrest were typical, as officers scrutinized suspects for a variety of gender signs that indicated cross-dressing criminality. For example, before the police arrested Dick/Mamie Ruble in October 1890, an officer assessed "her small feet, delicate hands and air of effeminacy" to ensure that "his suspicions were correct." Similarly when two officers spotted a "peculiar" person wearing men's clothes in July 1896, they evaluated the person's bust size, foot size, and lack of facial hair before identifying Mamie Baldwin as a woman in violation of cross-dressing law.[4] Reporting on these arrests, city newspapers praised the police as wise and worldly judges of gender—"too astute to be deceived"—who skillfully detected the "feminine symmetry of limb" beneath a man's suit or the masculine features beneath a woman's veil.[5]

Not all arrests were straightforward, however, and although police officers boasted of their ability to uncover cross-dressing crimes, detection could be difficult. Before arresting Ferdinand Haisch in 1895, for example, police staked out the streets for several weeks, scrutinizing the passers-by and trying to detect "the strange woman . . . who walked like a man." Clearly Haisch did not look significantly "stranger" than many other women in the neighborhood, and according to the *Chronicle*, the police "were not certain that they would catch him. . . . They had a difficult task in hand, for it would have been very unpleasant for them if by mistake they arrested some woman instead of the masquerader." To prevent such mistakes, the police resorted to physical means, such as tearing off a suspect's veil or wig, to identify its wearer's sex and detect a crime. These actions served to confirm an officer's suspicions and to restore gender legibility to the cross-dressing offender. Successful detection of cross-dressing offenses, then, did more than bring a culprit before the court; it also reinforced the fantasy of clear and knowable binary gender boundaries.[6]

In some cases the removal of a wig or a veil was insufficient to determine the wearer's sex, and the police supplemented their "cursory examinations" with a jailhouse medical examination. This medicalized surveillance intensified the law's invasive gaze and served as a juridical equivalent to Hirschfeld's camera in its quest to reveal the bodily "truth" of the cross-dressing criminal. When Ruble appeared in court to insist that s/he was neither a man nor a woman, the judge called in the police surgeon to determine Ruble's sex. Following an examination the police surgeon concluded that s/he was indeed female. This medical judgment set in motion a series of institutional proceedings, triggering both a legal verdict (s/he had violateu cross-dressing law) and a psychiatric one (s/he was deemed insane) that resulted in Ruble's lifelong commitment to the Stockton insane asylum.

Not everyone subjected to these medical examinations was as unfortunate as Ruble. In July 1909 a police officer apprehended a woman named Helena Castle, whose appearance "bordered the masculine," on suspicion of being a man in woman's clothing. At the police station Castle insisted that she was a female, and a skeptical police captain called in the prison matron to determine her sex. Following a "mysterious" exam, the matron concluded that Castle was indeed female and the police issued her with a certificate that documented her sex to prevent future arrests. Saved from Ruble's fate, Castle nonetheless passed through an institutional web of arrest, examination, and certification that accompanied the enforcement of cross-dressing law. As these cases illustrate, the law incited a particularly intimate kind of surveillance that granted the police new, invasive powers to scrutinize gender ambiguity and discover the "truth" of bodily sex beneath the clothes.[7]

Although formal responsibility for cross-dressing law enforcement rested with the police, concerned city residents joined the pursuit, developing their own forms of surveillance and reporting "suspiciously" gendered characters to the police. When Dick/Mamie Ruble took a walk on Market Street one Monday morning, s/he would probably have avoided arrest and its catastrophic aftermath if a vigilant passerby had not called the police, alleging that the person in men's clothing was a "pretty maid." Five years later, in 1895, May Smith might also have avoided arrest if a waiter had not reported his suspicions that the young man eating oysters and drinking gin at his café was actually a woman. Facilitating cross-dressing law enforcement, these San Francisco residents did more than aid in the detection of crimes; they also performed the role of good citizen, enacting a script that linked gender suspicion and legal compliance as prerequisites for urban belonging.[8]

By responding to the law's call for public vigilance, some city residents were able to access the role of good citizen, even as they were denied formal citizenship under local, state, and federal law. In 1869, for example, a group of Chinese men called the police to investigate a fellow countryman whom they suspected of being a woman. The officer complied and found their suspicions to be correct: the woman was arrested and subsequently fined $10 for violating cross-dressing law. In 1908 the police arrested an Oakland youth named So Git, after Sam Kee, "a wealthy merchant who belongs to the peace element," reported that the feminine person who walked Oakland streets in makeup, jade jewelry, silk dress, and tinseled shoes was male. Through such actions Kee subverted dominant narratives that linked Chinese difference to gender deviance, participating in the intimate surveillance and reporting that cross-dressing law required.[9]

City newspapers encouraged public vigilance, broadcasting alleged violations and demanding police action. These news reports performed important cultural work, publicizing the law's existence to large, general audiences and transporting it from the dry, dusty pages of the municipal codebook to the spot-lit, public forum of the newspaper's front page. In 1866 the city's leading newspaper published a front-page letter by the aptly named "Propriety," who expressed outrage that a woman had walked through city streets wearing men's clothing the previous night without arrest. "Is there not such a thing in existence as a statute or ordinance prohibiting women from appearing on the public streets arrayed in men's apparel?" Propriety demanded. "If there is, why is it not enforced?" In 1873 the *Call* published this short but stern call for action: "There is a law on the books which declares that it is a misdemeanor for any person to appear upon the streets in a dress not belonging to his or her sex and many persons are anxiously inquiring why it is that the police do not enforce it in the case of a certain actress who makes it a practice to appear on the streets in male attire." Given such incitements to see, it is unsurprising that embarrassing mistakes occurred, as when a local newspaper ran a front-page story on the outrageous behavior of a woman cyclist in male attire, only to concede the following day that "the girl who shocked the good people . . . proves to be a boy after all." Rather than lead to restraint, however, such events further inflamed the press, heightening people's fascination with gender illegibility and amplifying calls for greater gender scrutiny.[10]

Framing gender suspicion as the responsibility of competent urbanites, city newspapers resoundingly mocked people who failed to spot the cross-dressing offenders in their midst. For example, in 1894 the press reported on the arrest of Bert Larose, a "young female impersonator," who had stolen money from a patron in the Bottle Meyer's bar on the Barbary Coast. The bar employed Larose to boost liquor sales by flirting with customers and encouraging their alcohol consumption. According to the *Chronicle*, Larose had "induced Carl E. Berwick to purchase liquor at the bar and then while sitting on Berwick's lap and fondling him in an affectionate manner picked his pocket of $250." The court punished Larose harshly for these actions, with a six-year prison sentence for the crime of grand larceny. City newspapers, however, were oddly matter-of-fact when describing Larose's transgressions. Although Larose wore women's clothing while "fondling" Berwick, newspapers described the "curious . . . young man" in strikingly mundane terms, as a "beardless youth . . . nicely painted and wearing his skirts," who "made a precarious living by performing as a woman in Barbary Coast theaters and dives." In contrast, they lampooned "old man" Berwick for his gender ineptness, portraying him as a drunken, doddery fool who "confessed that one night two months ago he fell in love with a female impersonator, who drank beer with him, kissed him and robbed him." Extending the emphasis on confession, one newspaper even reproduced Berwick's courtroom testimony, as if he were on trial for failing to tell men and women apart:

> "Now, Mr Bernick [sic], do you mean to tell me that you thought this boy was a woman?"
>> "I did so," faltered the aged one, whose cheeks were slowly reddening.
>> "And you took him into a box at Bottle Meier's [sic] Theater?"
>> "I did."
>> "And you caressed him there?"
>> "I suppose so."
>> "Kissed him?"
>> "Maybe I did."
>> "And hugged him?"
>> "I guess so."
>> "And he hugged you, did he?"
>> "Well, I should say he did. That's how he got my money."
>> "Mr. Bernick, are you a married man?" asked the lawyer in low thrilling tones.
> Bernick confessed that he has a wife who is sick in the East.

Clearly crafted to titillate readers, such reports also raised the specter of cross-gender presentation and same-sex intimacy, framing gender suspicion and scrutiny as a precondition for competent urban citizenship.[11]

Looking At

Cross-dressing law provided the police and press not only with an impetus to *look for* cross-dressing bodies but also with the means to *look at* them, as the drama moved from suspicion and scrutiny to public display. In holding cells, police photographs, courtrooms, and newspaper crime reports, cross-dressing practices were imbued with remarkable levels of visibility. This visibility promised to restore gender legibility and hence counter the threat of cross-dressing crimes. It also fundamentally altered the terms of public presentation, erasing the multiple gender identifications of cross-dressing offenders by displaying them as criminal nuisances and "queer freaks."

Following an arrest under cross-dressing law, offenders were locked up in the city prison or jail to await trial, where they were sometimes forced to strip in front of guards and other inmates. Unlike the medical examination that accompanied some arrests, these forced disrobings had no official function but served to titillate the guards and humiliate the cross-dressing inmate, who was brought to jail or prison wearing clothing that violated the law. When John Roberts spent the night in the city prison in 1874, guards required their new inmate, clad in a red dress and a straw hat, to strip in front of the other inmates and a crowd of onlookers that gathered in the corridor. Similarly when Elsie Stallcup was locked up at the central police station for wearing men's clothes in 1909, a "group of grinning policemen" ripped off her short-haired wig for their own amusement; her gender (and criminality) had already been established. Incarceration thus removed cross-dressing offenders from the general public's view but did not preempt judgmental observation; instead it facilitated a humiliating display before the gaze of guards and inmates. These jailhouse disrobings also framed cross-dressing as a futile offense, restoring gender legibility and serving as a violent reminder to offenders of the always exposable, never escapable bodily "truth" beneath their clothes.[12]

For some cross-dressing offenders, the policeman's gaze continued to linger on their body after arrest, as they were forced to stand in front of a camera to be captured on film for a rogues' gallery of crime photographs. As early as 1855 one San Francisco police officer, Isaiah Lees, began photographing people arrested in the city; several other police photographers joined him as the century moved on.[13] These photographs captured the likeness of people convicted of felony offenses, as well as those convicted of violent misdemeanors and petty thefts. The police department compiled the photographs, six to a page, in mug-shot albums that allegedly helped to identify repeat offenders. People convicted of felony offenses underwent another round of photographing when they were sentenced to San Quentin or Folsom Prison. When Bert Larose was sentenced to San Quentin for grand larceny s/he was photographed three times: first, wearing a stylish hat, scarf, and suit jacket; second, with the hat removed; and third, with head shaved, wearing the standard striped uniform of state prisoners (see figure 4.2). The third photograph took place against a backdrop that appeared in all California state prison photographs: a chalkboard that listed the inmate's age (eighteen), place of birth (Ohio), sentence (six years), identification number (16065), name (Bert Larose), offense (grand larceny), and place of arrest (San Francisco). Taken together, these images strip Larose of clothing, hair, and personal identity, depicting his/her visual transformation from a stylish youth who attracted older men to a generic state prisoner. Once taken, Larose's photographs were filed in the state prison albums, which vividly communicated the racial segregation and dehumanization that characterized police photography during this period: photographs of Chinese offenders were kept in separate books, and some photographs bore the word DEAD scrawled across them in red pen.[14]

As low-level nuisance offenders, most people convicted under cross-dressing law were spared the humiliation of the mug-shot picture; convicted of misdemeanor offenses, they also avoided state prison and the accompanying photographs. Nonetheless several remarkable police photographs depict people arrested under San Francisco's cross-dressing law in the early twentieth century. One of these photographs features Geraldine Portica, a young Mexican American woman arrested in 1917 for wearing women's clothing on a body the police classed as male (see figure 4.3). Unlike the city's official mug shots, which center on the face, this photograph focuses on Portica's whole body, capturing her as a beautifully dressed woman, posing for the camera, with one hand on her hip and the other lifting her skirts away from her body. Portica looks directly at the camera, but with a slightly defeated look on her face; presumably, this staged pose was not her idea. Moving beyond the ostensible goal of identifying repeat offenders, the photograph conveys a fascination with the crime itself, as the full-body shot of Portica's feminine image is contrasted with a police officer's handwritten caption: "This is not a girl, but a boy." At the same time, the caption strives

FIGURE 4.2. California state prison photographs of Bert Larose, convicted of grand larceny while working as a female impersonator in 1894. Department of Corrections, San Quentin Prison, Inmate Photographs, 15950-16201, California State Archives.

FIGURE 4.3. Police photograph of Geraldine Portica, arrested for violating cross-dressing law in 1917. Jesse Brown Cook Scrapbooks Documenting San Francisco History and Law Enforcement, vol. 4, Bancroft Library, University of California, Berkeley, BANC PIC 1996.003—Falb.

to correct the gender trouble that Portica incites by restoring gender legibility and reinscribing maleness on her body.[15]

While jailhouse disrobings and police photography strove to counter the threat of cross-dressing crimes by restoring gender legibility, courtroom displays effectively changed the terms of public presentation by transforming the cross-dressing subject into a criminal nuisance. These displays took place in an unassuming venue, the municipal police court, which processed all cross-dressing cases as misdemeanors under local law. The court was a small basement room in city hall, which the writer Mark Twain described as "the infernalest smelling den on earth." "If I were police judge here," he jeered, "I would hold my court in the city prison and sentence my convicts to imprisonment in the present police court room."[16] The cramped atmosphere of the police court was partly due to its small size but also due to the large number of cases processed; the court had jurisdiction over all local, minor offenses, including public cross-dressing, and it routinely processed over one thousand cases each month. Police court cases were usually cleared quickly and with little procedural protections. The police court judge, an elected official, was the sole arbiter of guilt; those who wanted a jury trial had to request a transfer to the city criminal court. Most defendants waived this right and were quickly convicted or acquitted. As a result the police court did not produce high-profile trials that captured public attention; instead it processed hundreds of cases out of the spotlight in routine and unremarkable ways.[17]

Lacking the spectacle that accompanied some higher court trials, police court proceedings are easy to overlook, yet they played a critical role in displaying cross-dressing under the sign of public nuisance. The police court primarily dealt with the city's low-level nuisance offenders, those accused of vagrancy, petty theft, prostitution, and drunkenness. When John Roberts went to court, for example, s/he shared the defendant's box with two women arrested for begging, two women arrested for using vulgar language, five men arrested for assault and battery, one woman arrested for fast driving, twelve people arrested for assault with a deadly weapon, and forty "common drunkards." On rare occasions a judge would acknowledge the court's lowly status, as when Judge Deasy agreed to hear Elsie Stallcup's case in his chambers so that the "pretty high school girl" would be "spared the ordeal . . . of facing the morbid crowd in . . . court." In most cases, however, cross-dressing offenders appeared in court alongside the vagrants, drunks, and prostitutes who constituted public disorder in city space. Massing these problem bodies together under the sign of public nuisance, the police court thus established cross-dressing's criminality as indisputable, obscuring the social conflicts that surrounded cross-dressing law and transforming the contested limits of normative gender into "common sense."[18]

Although police court proceedings rarely attracted crowds of onlookers to the courtroom, they did reach wide audiences through the police court columns of local newspapers that reported on court activity each day. The quotidian reporting of these offenses dovetailed with police court practices to represent cross-dressing as an unremarkable public nuisance. Similar to Roberts's case, for example, John Wilson's cross-dressing arrest in 1878 received only one mention in the city press, low on a list of processed offenses: "Catherine Krun, drunk, three months; Ah Duck, petty larceny, six months; Ah Ping, same, six months; Frank Seaman, drunk, one month, battery, three months, vulgar language, ten days; John Wilson, drunk, one hundred days, wearing female apparel, five days; Casper Ramer, battery, $30 or 15 days; James Wallace, battery, six months; Thomas Gallagher, cruelty to animals, $10 or 5 days."[19] Listing individual charges and punishments but excluding further details on the offender or offense, such reports effectively collapsed all police court cases into a generalized nuisance that undermined decent orderly city life. Such routine limited attention communicated to offenders and audiences that cross-dressing arrests were not "news"; they did not require public debate in the courtroom, through jury deliberations, or in sustained or serious coverage in the city press. Instead these were mundane public order offenses, akin to vagrancy and drunkenness, to be contained as part of regular city government work.

Although many cross-dressing arrests received scant attention in police court columns, others dramatically captured the headlines, as city newspapers framed some cross-dressing criminals as one-of-a-kind "queer freaks" rather than mundane public nuisances. These sensationalized reports typically focused on aberrant individuals, questioning their sanity and raising the horrifying but intoxicating specter of cross-gender deception and same-sex intimacy. Similar to mundane police court columns, these reports did not discuss cross-dressing crimes as significant news events or situate them within serious political discourse. They did, however, imbue cross-dressing crimes with remarkable levels of visibility, offering up the cross-dressing criminal for their readers' consumption and pleasure.

Most notably, sensationalized newspaper reports invited readers to visualize cross-dressing criminals through vivid descriptions of their attire, even as they expressed outrage that such clothing was permitted in public view. Portrayals of offenders in women's clothing were particularly enticing, as one newspaper's depiction of Edward Livernash, arrested for "masquerading" as a woman in 1891, illustrates: "The prisoner was a sight well worth gazing upon. Not a stitch of masculine clothing was there about him. A blue sateen dress was almost concealed under a fashionable traveling ulster of gray goods with a small check. A splendid sample of the milliner's art—a symphony in gray—surmounted the prisoner's head. On his hands were a pair of new black gloves. Not the least notable feature of the outfit was a brand new russet leather satchel. Everything about the prisoner, in fact, was of an inviting newness." By the 1890s newspapers also began to publish artists' sketches of cross-dressing offenders, visually depicting the crimes they ostensibly wanted hidden from view. As a result readers did not have to take the reporter's word that Livernash was "a sight well worth gazing upon"; an accompanying sketch of the dramatic arrest scene allowed them to see for themselves.[20]

Lavish depictions of cross-dressing criminals were embedded not in sympathetic news narratives but in sensationalist reports that mocked arrestees and emphasized the freakishness and danger of cross-gender "disguise." This visibility could function as punishment, linking the voyeuristic compulsion to see with the regulatory desire to control. One police court judge acknowledged as much during Mamie Baldwin's prosecution in 1896. Arrested while drunkenly celebrating the Fourth of July, Baldwin appeared in court in men's clothing before a large crowd, who "craned their necks to get a look at the woman." Newspapers amplified this visibility with a full-page courtroom sketch that visually depicted Baldwin's "natty suit of blue clothes," "brown Fedora hat," and stylish "scarf, collar, cuffs and shirt" (see figure 4.4). Finding Baldwin guilty, the judge denounced cross-dressing as "dangerous and decidedly improper" but nonetheless issued a nominal fine of $5 since Baldwin had "already been punished thoroughly": "You have had your picture in the paper and all that sort of thing."[21] In these moments newspaper representations played a key role in the operations of cross-

FIGURE 4.4. Courtroom sketch of Mamie Baldwin, arrested for violating cross-dressing law in 1896. "Carried the New Woman Fad Too Far," *San Francisco Chronicle*, July 7, 1896.

dressing law, supplementing its modes of punishment and dramatizing the gender boundaries it policed.

Looking Past

As San Francisco newspapers invited readers to *look for* and *look at* cross-dressing criminals, they paid strikingly little attention to Chinese and Mexican offenders, *looking past* their transgressions to focus overwhelmingly on white crimes. According to arrest records, city police made ninety-nine cross-dressing arrests between 1863 and 1900, and local newspapers reported on forty-seven of these; all but one involved a person presumed to be white.[22] This is striking given the racial dynamics of law enforcement during the period, particularly the zealous prosecution of Chinese people through indecency and nuisance laws. Newspapers' preoccupation with white cross-dressing crimes may reflect law enforcement practices, with local police arresting only white people under cross-dressing law; the absence of racial categories in local arrest statistics makes it difficult to assess this claim. Alternatively it may reflect selective news reporting, with city newspapers documenting white offenses while neglecting all other cross-dressing arrests. Certainly newspapers failed to document some nonwhite arrests in the early twentieth century, overlooking the 1907 cross-dressing arrest of So Git, as well as the 1917 arrest of Geraldine Portica.[23] In their partial reporting on cross-dressing crimes, white journalists wrote of white criminals for a predominantly white readership to communicate the boundaries of permissible white gender. In the process they positioned the forms, benefits, and limits of normative gender as the exclusive property of whites.

When reporting on cross-dressing crimes, newspapers relied on a framework of individual pathology that represented white offenders as isolated deviants. These reports obscured the potential political significance of cross-dressing practices and transformed alternative identities, intimacies, and ideologies into private eccentricities and moral flaws. Dress reform politics, for example, became "much ado about nothing"; same-sex relationships became "gender fraud"; and cross-gender identification became evidence of a "deluded brain." In these reports the figure of the white cross-dressing criminal functioned as a political sponge that absorbed cultural anxieties about shifting gender norms and kept white gender formations stable and "pure." By using the white cross-dressing criminal to mark the margins of permissible gender, newspapers created not only aberrant "outsiders" but also normative "insiders," and their selective reporting ensured that these insiders were exclusively white.

On one occasion only newspapers reported that a Chinese person had been arrested for cross-dressing, after police apprehended a woman in 1869 for wearing men's clothing. The city press provided scant information about the woman's arrest, even excluding her name from reports and referring to her simply as "Jane Doe."[24] Anonymity was unheard of in cross-dressing crime reports, but according to the California historian Daphne Lei, "not naming the Chinese" occurred frequently in popular writing of the time, working to expunge individual identities and construct "the Chinese" as an undifferentiated mass.[25] In this context newspaper silence on Chinese cross-dressing arrests became a form of discourse that erased gender variation within Chinese communities and imposed a uniform gender identity on the city's whole Chinese population.

This does not mean that newspapers imposed a normative gender identity on Chinese San Franciscans, however. Instead city newspapers persistently represented Chinese gender as a foreign and pathological formation, with men and women failing to perform the masculinity and femininity that editors deemed "normal." Cross-dressing featured prominently in these representations, but as confirmation of Chinese difference and danger, not as evidence of individual criminal acts. Most of this discussion focused on immigration cases, as I explore in chapter 6. However, San Francisco newspaper reports on an arrest in the neighboring city of Oakland are also instructive.

In July 1908 Oakland police arrested a Chinese youth named So Git for wearing women's clothing in public. San Francisco newspapers published lavish descriptions of So Git's appearance, with reporters virtually fawning over the youth's "gorgeous oriental costume": "His cheeks were painted and his coiffure was complete in its oily smoothness and wealth of bejeweled hair pins; his dress was of the finest texture and vied with the rainbow in its iridescent hues; his features were small and even in the natural state might easily have been mistaken for a woman's."[26] These descriptions paralleled newspaper accounts of Edward Livernash's cross-dressing arrest the previous decade, albeit in orientalist form. Unlike reports on Livernash, however, newspapers represented So Git's clothing not as evidence of a disturbed individual but as proof of a broader Chinese "plot" that centered on sexual slavery and "tong wars." Some San Francisco newspapers claimed that So Git had adopted the disguise of "a bewitching slave girl" with the aid of an accomplice to swindle money from a gullible Chinese man who planned to "buy a pretty wife." Others connected the slave girl plot to a "recent tong war," depicting So Git as a leading gangland figure who used feminine masquerade to lure enemies into a violent trap. Even law-abiding Chinese families were drawn into violence in these newspaper accounts. In one report the usually peaceful Ching Ling family was now contemplating "gun play" after So Git besmirched their reputation by using their name when first arrested. Throughout these reports newspapers discussed So Git's cross-dressing arrest in relation to organized violence, forced prostitution, and criminal deception. In contrast to the white cross-dresser, who was viewed as an aberrant individual, newspapers constructed the Chinese cross-dressing criminal as indicative of an undifferentiated, all-consuming threat.[27]

....

Despite its stated concern with public gender displays, cross-dressing law did not bury cross-dressing practices under a stack of prohibitions and punishments but amplified their visibility under the sign of criminality. Vacillating between mundane and sensational representations, legal and popular discourse increased public awareness of cross-dressing practices and brought them into general view. Newspapers played a central role in this process, but their displays were partial, focusing on white offenders and overlooking Chinese and Mexican cross-dressing criminals. Far from undermining the logic of the law, visibility was fundamental to its operations, depicting gender normativity as whiteness, framing cross-dressing as criminality, and establishing the marginality of gender difference as common sense.

By dragging people into courtrooms and newspaper columns, however, legal and journalistic practice risked turning offenders into local celebrities, as they splashed gender transgressions across the front page and inadvertently advertised the practices the law sought to proscribe. Admittedly newspapers rarely portrayed cross-dressing crimes in a flattering light or invited readers to identify with the perpetrators. Nonetheless these stories were never monolithic, and alternative readings could arise. In particular, newspaper stories on cross-dressing offenses advertised the possibilities of doing gender differently, and some readers may have been inspired rather than repelled. Moreover police courtrooms and reports occasionally provided glimpses of communities that were supportive of gender difference. Reporting on a cross-dressing trial in 1866, for example, city newspapers noted that Eliza DeWolf's courtroom appearances drew crowds of supporters, even as they dismissed those supporters as "long-haired men" resembling inmates of "Insane Asylums" and "ill-favored women, who had through natural defect failed to otherwise attract the attention of the opposite sex."[28] Similarly newspaper reports on Bert Larose's 1894 prosecution named Bottle Meyer's as a bar that hired female impersonators to provide sexual services to male customers, effectively advertising the venue and its location to interested readers. Certainly these glimpses of community were marginal to the dominant narratives of cross-dressing criminality, nuisance, and insanity. Nonetheless they carved out critical space within these narratives to counter the prohibitory logic of cross-dressing law.

Indecent Exhibitions

As local law drove cross-dressing practices into private spaces while increasing their visibility under the sign of criminality, a remarkable development occurred in city amusements, as entertainment venues began to feature cross-dressing performers, center stage, for audience viewing and appreciation. Mainstream vaudevillian theater, for example, billed female and male impersonators as star attractions; dime museums included cross-dressing characters as one-of-a-kind "freaks"; and commercial slumming tours guided visitors through the Barbary Coast and Chinatown to see multiple cross-gender phenomena in the city's "underworld." These entertainment sites shone a spotlight on cross-dressing bodies and exploited the fascination that law enforcement inadvertently stirred up. In the process they applauded gender transformations and replaced a legal discourse of nuisance and criminality with the promise of entertaining performances and harmless family fun.[1]

These entertainment venues had a complex but ultimately complementary relationship with cross-dressing law. As we have seen, the law produced its own displays of gendered problem bodies in courtrooms, police photographs, and crime reports. Additionally city amusements offered strategies of containment that could circumscribe entertainers and audiences alike. In particular, entertainment venues regulated performers, manipulated audiences, and represented cross-dressing in highly specific ways that perpetuated its marginality and ensured a profitable show. Ultimately city entertainment venues provided popular forums that publicized, dramatized, and democratized the normative gender boundaries that cross-dressing law produced.

Gender and Illusion

Given the punitive forces impinging on cross-dressing bodies in nineteenth-century San Francisco, their concurrent display in entertainment venues across the city is striking. Nowhere is this more apparent than on the vaudeville stage. During the final decades of the nineteenth century vaudeville developed as a wildly popular form of family entertainment that took San Francisco—and the nation—by storm. Adopting the variety-show format of the English music hall, vaudeville productions featured multiple acts, including acrobats, magicians, comedians, singers, and "blackface" minstrel performers. However, the stars of vaudeville were female impersonators—and occasionally male impersonators—who commanded the highest salaries, received top billing, and drew the biggest crowds. Unlike earlier cross-dressing theatrics in the English pantomime and U.S. minstrel show, vaudeville female impersonators did not don women's clothing, wigs, and makeup for comedic purposes; they did so in order to convincingly portray the imitated sex. Audiences thus packed the vaudeville houses to see beautiful women in the latest fashions, fully aware that the objects of their admiring gaze were men. Female impersonators were not only popular with the usual crowd of young, male theatergoers but were also marketed as wholesome family entertainment that was particularly suitable for middle-class women and children.[2]

Since the early years of the gold rush, San Francisco had embraced female impersonation as entertainment. The city's very first theatrical performance, in June 1849, featured a man named Stephen Massett, who "imitated . . . Madame Anna Bishop," as well as "an elderly lady and German girl" auditioning as "soprano and alto singers in one of the churches in Massachusetts."[3] While Massett's impersonations were probably humorous parodies, by the early 1870s more convincing impersonators drew large, appreciative crowds. In July 1871, for example, one of the nation's most famous female impersonators, William Horace Lingard, made his San Francisco debut, impersonating a high-society fashionable belle, complete with fan and corset. Also in 1871 the male impersonator Ella Wesner appeared in San Francisco for the first time, performing at the Barbary Coast music hall Bella Union. At that time the Bella Union was an all-male venue, leading reviewers to lament the fact that "ladies can't go to the Bella Union, they would all fall in love with Ella Wesner."[4]

As audiences packed vaudeville theaters and local newspapers published glowing reviews of female and male impersonators, people who cross-dressed on San Francisco streets continued to be arrested and thrown in jail. For example, in October 1897—a month when the San Francisco police made eleven separate arrests for cross-dressing offenses—the press failed to publish any reports on the arrests but ran a celebratory article on the male impersonator Vesta Tilly, complete with an artist's sketch of "Vesta the Johnny" looking dapper in a sharp suit, bow tie, and short hair.[5] In 1879— the year with the highest number of cross-dressing arrests of the century— the San Francisco Chronicle published an admiring front-page article on the recently deceased circus performer Omar Kingsley, who had performed as a woman, Ella Zoyara, to enhance audience perceptions of his equestrian skills. Kingsley had lived and performed in San Francisco in the 1860s and 1870s, and audiences rarely knew that Zoyara was his creation. Remembering these shows, the Chronicle praised Kingsley's skills as an equestrian and female impersonator and fondly recalled his ability to "impersonate female character in a manner that almost defied detection." Even though Kingsley's "deception" attracted many "would-be lovers and husbands," the Chronicle embraced the act with good humor, remarking that "few of those who have witnessed the graceful performance of the beautiful Zoyara dreamed that the performer was a man."[6] Reporters who wrote such stories were aware of cross-dressing law and occasionally noted the disjuncture between stage acclaim and street harassment, although not with any critical insight. During a 1911 interview with the female impersonator Lew Sully, a Chronicle reporter compared the theatrical value of male and female impersonation while noting, in passing, that "off the stage, to be sure, both misdemeanors are equally reprehensible in the eyes of the law."[7]

Perhaps the starkest illustration of the disconnect between cross-dressing's illegality on the street and its wide acclaim on the stage is found in the scrapbook collections of San Francisco's chief of police Jesse Brown Cook, who worked for the police department from the 1890s to the 1930s. Cook was an avid fan of theatrical drag, and his scrapbooks contain a large collection of theater memorabilia, including promotional postcards of male and female impersonators who performed in his city in the nineteenth century. These include postcards of the actress Adah Isaacs Menken in dashing male drag, as well as William Horace Lingard, the female impersonator who dazzled city audiences in 1871. Even more striking, Cook took part in an acrobatic troupe that included drag performances; when he was chief of police the department used a cartoon illustration of him wearing women's clothing to advertise their annual Valentine's Day ball. The cartoon is remarkable for its easy play with cross-gender and homoerotic symbolism; wearing drag and his chief's hat, Cook asks the mayor to dance, since it is leap year, and the mayor coyly replies, "Well if you insist." However, despite Cook's clear and open appreciation for theatrical drag, he worked for and led a police force that persistently harassed and arrested people for cross-dressing on the city streets. These arrests continued when he was chief of police (1908–10), and alongside his lovingly preserved collection of theatrical postcards, his scrapbooks contain crime scene photos and mug shots of people arrested for breaking cross-dressing law.[8]

Scholars of theater and gender history have explained the disjuncture between cross-dressing's adoration on the stage and its abjection on the street in terms of vaudeville's conservative nature. According to Marybeth Hamilton, vaudevillian female impersonation purposefully pursued middle-class respectability by distancing itself from the raunchy humor and parodies of pre-1860s minstrelsy and promoting a genuine celebration of female modesty and grace. Moreover performers were billed as female "illusionists," in the same league as Houdini, who achieved a remarkable magical feat: crossing the unbridgeable divide between separate male and female spheres. In framing gender crossings as magical illusions, female impersonators ultimately confirmed rather than threatened the ostensibly natural and immutable gender divide.[9]

For the frame of illusion to hold, female and male impersonators had to emphasize their gender normativity and sexual propriety off-stage, or else their on-stage transformation would conjure up a different set of associations—not an awe-inspiring act of magic but the grotesque display of a freakish self. The nation's top female impersonator, Julian Eltinge, was probably the most accomplished at these dual performances, affecting a virile off-stage masculinity with as much style and sincerity as he displayed femininity on-stage. Vaudevillian male impersonators similarly strove to project a gender-normative identity off-stage; one newspaper reporter, for example, was impressed with Vesta Tilly's "utter femininity," underscored by her conventional marriage to a man who was rightly proud of "his talented little wife."[10]

The simultaneous worship of cross-dressing on the vaudeville stage and its criminalization on the city streets points to the multiple meanings of cross-dressing practices rather than a paradoxical relationship between theatrical display and legal control. In particular the context of vaudeville transformed cross-dressing from a dangerous, freakish act of marginality to an admirable, temporary act of magic. Moreover by emphasizing gender normativity and sexual propriety and through a strict stage/street divide, vaudeville impersonations reinscribed the gender boundaries that the law policed.

Of course, the boundary between stage and street was never completely impermeable, and in many cities a burgeoning underground theater movement existed alongside mainstream vaudeville, featuring performances that blurred the line between stage and street. These included female dancers who gave bawdy performances to indicate an off-stage involvement in prostitution and female impersonators whose dresses and gestures did not indicate a magical transformation from virile man to convincing woman but an off-stage, cross-gendered self. In San Francisco this demimonde was centered in the Barbary Coast, where raunchy cross-gender performers played in all-male concert saloons in the 1860s and 1870s and where "degenerate" female impersonators held forth in Pacific Street bars in the 1890s and early 1900s. Respectable vaudeville theater experienced its own fall from grace in the early twentieth century, as, despite their best efforts to the contrary, female and male impersonators were increasingly associated with sexual and gender transgressions on the street. However, during the nineteenth century the vaudeville stage successfully contained gender transgressions, providing a space for gender-normative audiences to gain pleasure from beautiful men in stunning gowns and handsome women in dashing suits, while blissfully ignoring the plight of gender-variant people in the city around them.[11]

The Bogus Man

In vaudevillian theater the social distance between stage and street enabled female and male impersonators to become major stars, while cross-dressers on the city street were thrown in jail. However, for those who appeared on a different city stage—the freak-show stage—the social distance between cross-dressing performers and cross-dressing offenders evaporated. As freak shows featured cross-dressing characters as star attractions, the performer was, quite literally, the person criminalized on the streets. As with vaudevillian theater, this points to a complex relationship between entertainment venues and the law, as the former placed cross-dressing bodies on display for public amusement, while the latter outlawed their appearance as a public nuisance. However, unlike vaudevillian theater, the freak show's exhibition of cross-dressing bodies cannot be explained by a framework of illusion or a clear performer/criminal divide. Instead it points to a complex interplay between regulation, fascination, and the containment of gender transgressions.

Dime museum freak shows emerged in most major U.S. cities after the Civil War and peaked in popularity in the 1890s. The dime museum had its institutional roots in the anatomical museum, a place of medical and moral education that featured models and preserved body parts displayed in glass cabinets, with frequent emphasis on fetuses, diseased genitalia, and the dissected organs of notorious criminals and "freaks of nature." Dime museums built upon the anatomical museum tradition by adding two categories of live performers: sideshow circus artists and freaks. Dime museums also appealed to a wider audience, often breaking from the gentlemen-only admission policy of anatomical museums to attract anyone who could pay the low one-time admission price of a dime. Most studies of dime museums and freak shows have focused on East Coast institutions, with particular emphasis on P. T. Barnum's American Museum in New York. San Francisco, however, boasted numerous freak shows of its own, ranging from the short-lived Museum of Living Wonders that operated out of a "leaky tent on Kearny street" in the early 1870s, to the grand exhibitions held at Woodward's Gardens, an expansive family amusement resort that occupied two city blocks in the Mission district from 1866 to 1891. Most of the city's freak shows were clustered along Market Street, operating out of small, seedy, rented storefronts. Market Street was also home to the Pacific Museum of Anatomy and Science, the city's longest running dime museum, which claimed to be the "largest anatomical museum in the world."[12]

In San Francisco, as elsewhere, dime museum entertainment centered on performances of bodily difference and paid particularly close attention to bodies that challenged gender, racial, and national boundaries or that ostensibly revealed the somatic penalties of immorality through spectacles of disease or deformity. For example, freak shows typically featured a Bearded Lady or Half-Man/Half-Woman character, while the Pacific Museum of Anatomy and Science displayed "a beautiful dissection" of a hermaphrodite cadaver that featured "the internal arrangements and dissections of this wonderful freak of nature." Another staple attraction was the popular Missing Link or What-Is-It? exhibit, which usually featured an African American or white man in blackface who was presented as the "missing link" between man and animal. Many dime museums also featured pathology rooms that contained displays of diseased sexual organs and other body parts, damaged by syphilis, gonorrhea, and "the filthy habit of self-abuse." Dime museums regularly staged performances of racialized national dominance that corresponded to contemporary wars. One of the first crowd-drawing exhibits at the Pacific Museum of Anatomy and Science, for example, was the preserved head of Joaquin Murietta, the notorious Mexican "bandit" who fought against Anglo dominance and violence in the southern mines before being killed by state-sponsored rangers in 1853. Murietta was a popular symbol of Mexican resistance, and the display of his severed head, "preserved in vinegar," graphically dramatized a narrative of Anglo dominance and Mexican defeat against the backdrop of the Mexican-American War. Occasionally dime museum exhibits explicitly linked gender and national boundary transgressions, as when Barnum's American Museum displayed a waxwork figure of Jefferson Davis, the defeated leader of the Confederacy, wearing women's clothing, at the close of the Civil War. This exhibit dramatized rumors that Davis had disguised himself in hoopskirts when trying to escape his Northern captors, deploying cultural anxieties about cross-gender practices to emasculate the defeated South, fortify territorial boundaries, and reconsolidate the postwar nation.[13]

In 1890s San Francisco cross-dressing performers joined this cast of characters when Milton Matson was offered a job as a freak-show exhibit. Matson came to public attention in January 1895, when he was arrested in San Francisco in the room of his fiancée, Ellen Fairweather, on charges of obtaining money under false pretenses. Following his arrest, Matson was taken to San Jose County Jail and locked up in a cell with several other men, where he remained for two weeks, until the jailer received a bank telegraph addressed to Miss Luisa Matson and identified Matson as female. After complicated legal wrangling, charges against Matson were dropped, and he walked free from the jail in men's clothing, returning to San Francisco the following month.[14]

The exposure of Matson's "true sex" generated a mass of newspaper coverage; the San Francisco dailies ran numerous stories on the "male impersonator" and "pretender." In these stories the press excitedly debated the possibility of Matson's apprehension under cross-dressing law and reported that he publicly dared the police to arrest him: "Arrest! . . . I'd like to see anyone arrest me for wearing men's clothes. Why, I have been wearing this style of costume for the last twenty-six years . . . and I wouldn't wear any other." Before this could happen Matson was approached by a local dime museum manager, Frank Clifton, and offered work sitting upon a museum platform in men's clothing for the public to view. In need of employment and money, particularly since the press had undermined his ability to live as a man, Matson accepted Clifton's offer and appeared on stage for five weeks as "The Bogus Man." The strangeness of this transition—"from a cell in the San Jose prison to the electric brilliancy of an amusement resort"—was not lost on Matson, who commented, "Funniest thing . . . I'm getting letters from all sorts of showmen offering good salaries if I will exhibit myself. It amuses me very much. . . . I'm beginning to think it pays to be notorious. It certainly does not seem to be a detriment to people in America." The appeal of Matson's notoriety proved so popular that several other local freak shows began featuring cross-dressing performers in men's clothing, deceptively advertised as "the only genuine Miss Martson [sic] in male attire."[15]

Local newspapers ran dozens of sensationalized reports on Matson's "strange story," creating a readymade audience for his freak-show exhibition. These reports expressed moral outrage and prurient fascination with Matson's gender "fraud," framing him as a fast-talking swindler who nonetheless "truly makes a fine-looking man." In particular, newspapers focused on his engagement to Fairweather, framing her as a respectable if naïve schoolteacher who "has learned that her betrothed is a woman." Matson protested reporters' harassment but also toyed with them in lengthy published interviews, explaining that he was "always more of a boy than a girl" and deeming it "outrageous . . . that a man cannot have any peace, but must be badgered to death by reporters." Matson also defended Fairweather and provided tantalizing descriptions of his relationships with women: "Yes, I like the ladies and in my earlier days was quite a beau. I was a good dancer and I guess I pretty thoroughly understand all about the female weaknesses. I have been made a confidante by the fair ones more than once and have had some interesting experiences. It was lots of fun carrying on flirtations with the ladies and a real joy to make love to them." In full-length interviews, artists' sketches, and sensationalized stories, newspapers exploited Matson's legal troubles to produce the ready-to-exhibit "Bogus Man" freak (see figures 5.1 and 5.2).[16]

As Matson's case suggests, the relationship between cross-dressing law and freak-show entertainment was complex.[17] At first glance they appeared to operate through very different logics. The law imprisoned, the freak show displayed; the law administered a fine as punishment, the freak show offered a salary as inducement; the law disapproved and condemned its subject's deviance, the freak show was fascinated by and exaggerated and increased it. Additionally, unlike the female and male impersonators on the vaudeville stage, the freak-show performer and the cross-dressing criminal were not separated by real or imagined social distance; they were the very same person.

On closer examination, however, cross-dressing law and the freak show clearly performed similar work. In part this was because the law also displayed problem bodies, in courtrooms and police photographs, as criminal nuisances and sensational freaks. It was also because freak-show entertainment had its own normalizing effects with explicit connections to criminal law. After all, Matson was recruited into freak-show entertainment directly from a jail cell, following a path that other San Francisco performers had walked before him. In 1888, for example, two freak-show managers recruited an accused con-woman named Bertha Stanley directly from jail, paying the 280-pound woman's bail to exhibit her as "Big Bertha the Queen of Confidence Women" in their Market Street show. Matson's participation in a freak-show exhibition regulated his off-stage behavior in a very direct way; his contract forbade him to wear men's clothing on San Francisco's streets so as to preserve the mystique—and profitability—of his show. Consequently the law and the freak show were not autonomous institutions, and showmen sometimes utilized the law to maintain and control a steady supply of novel bodies that were exhibited as freaks.[18]

In addition to its effects on performers, the freak show paralleled cross-dressing law as a normalizing discourse that communicated to audiences, in starkly visual terms, the parameters of acceptable behavior and the penalties for violating these norms. After all, freak shows did much more than

LOUISA E. B. METSON, WHO WAS BETROTHED TO MISS FAIRWEATHER AND IS NOW IN JAIL.
[From a sketch made recently in Los Gatos.]

secure and display nonnormative bodies; they actively transformed these bodies into one-of-a-kind curiosities that ultimately reinforced the norm. For example, freak shows exaggerated the corporeal differences of the people they displayed through costuming, props, and narrative techniques. The Bearded Lady was never simply a woman with facial hair but a hyperfeminized "lady," "madame," or "princess" who appeared in long Victorian gowns and extravagant jewelry to highlight the "freakishness" of her masculine beard. Freak-show managers also carefully arranged the exhibition space, placing performers on small roped-off platforms, so as to stage social distance between the freak and the audience and to create a fantasy of permanent inherent difference between the normal and the abnormal. Finally, the freak show enhanced the abnormality of individual performers through a dual process of specification and generalization, which isolated individual bodily differences, only to then group these differences together again into the amorphous category "freak." This process suggested to audiences, as they moved through the show from body to body, that those marked by sexual and gender ambiguity, by racial and national difference, and by disease and disability all shared a common existence outside of the normal. There was, of course, no original freak whose essence tainted those sharing the freak-show stage, but a circular process through which specific techniques of racialization, sexualization, and dehumanization bled into and fed off one another.[19]

While there are few historical records that speak to the disciplinary impact of cross-dressing performers on freak-show audiences, a dime novel that was popular at the time of Matson's performance is highly suggestive of possible effects. In Archibald Gunter and Fergus Redmond's 1891 novel, *A Florida Enchantment*, a wealthy white woman, Lillian Travers, purchases a box of African sex-change seeds from a dime museum in Florida. Following an argument with her fiancé, she swallows a seed and transitions

FIGURE 5.1. (*opposite above*) Newspaper sketch of Milton Matson, 1895. Caption reads, "Louisa E. Metson [*sic*], who was betrothed to Miss Fairweather and is now in jail. [From a sketch made recently in Los Gatos.]" *San Francisco Examiner*, January 30, 1895.

FIGURE 5.2. (*opposite below*) Newspaper sketch of Milton Matson, 1895. Caption reads, "Louise Elizabeth Merton Blaxton Matson, dressed in two of her best suits of clothes. [Sketched last week from life.]" *San Francisco Examiner*, February 10, 1895.

into a man named Lawrence Talbot. Realizing that a wealthy man needs a male valet rather than a female maid, Lawrence forces his "mulatto maid," Jane, to also swallow a seed and become a man named Jack. Lawrence later realizes with "fearful horror" that dime museums would love to exhibit him as a freak, and he has a nightmare in which the city is covered in gigantic dime museum posters, advertising him as "The Freak of All Ages" and "The Woman Man," appearing alongside "The Living Skeleton" and "The Missing Link" (see figure 5.3). Although doubly fictional (appearing in both a novel and a dream), this scene illuminates the operations of the freak show in two specific ways.[20]

First, by illustrating Lawrence's "fearful horror" of being displayed as a freak, the nightmare suggests that freak-show visibility could have disciplinary effects, operating as a threat against gender transgression and an inducement to conform. Moreover the context of Lawrence's nightmare within the novel suggests that the disciplinary effects of freak-show visibility were informed by racialized anxieties rather than by a universal fear of being labeled "freak." Specifically Lawrence's nightmare occurs after he has already entered a dime museum to purchase sex-change seeds from Africa and after he has learned that his former "mulatto maid," now Jack, has begun working at a dime museum as "the greatest freak on earth." Additionally the poster from his nightmare suggests that part of the horror of being displayed as "The Woman Man" is being displayed alongside and in association with the racialized "Missing Link" character and the "Living Skeleton." Indeed throughout the novel the dime museum appears as a racialized site that serves as both the source of gender transgression (i.e., sex-change seeds from Africa) and the space of its containment. This suggests that the potential disciplinary effects of freak-show visibility were intricately connected to its association with imperial exoticism and racialized difference.

Second, the appearance of freak-show characters in a popular novel such as *A Florida Enchantment* suggests that these characters had cultural resonance outside of the freak-show exhibition space. Consequently their disciplinary effects could extend to those who had never attended a show. This is similarly indicated by newspaper articles that relied upon readers' familiarity with freak-show characters when they criticized cross-dressing practices. For example, an 1895 article in the *Call* newspaper referenced the freak show's What-Is-It? and Half-Man/Half-Woman characters in its critique of women's dress reform clothing:

FIGURE 5.3. Dime museum poster from the 1890s novel *A Florida Enchantment*. Archibald Clavering Gunter and Fergus Redmond, *A Florida Enchantment: A Novel* (New York: Hurst, 1891).

Surely among all the fertile brains which have put their energies into this subject something could be evolved other than the hybrid costumes which have appeared in the public prints, half man, half woman, and wholly detestable. . . . Some years ago an animal was exhibited called "whatisit." This must be something of the same species, or perhaps it is the "new woman" there is so much talk about—certainly it is not the old one. . . . If in a hundred years time some archeologist rummaging through the British Museum should come across one of these relics of refined civilization, surely he would innocently remark, "What is it?"

Two years later, in nearby Stockton, a local newspaper relied upon the same freak-show characters to disparage cross-dressing practices, describing a person named Babe Bean, who wore men's clothing on a body classed as female, as "the mysterious girl-boy, man-woman, or what-is-it?" These articles indicate the popular cultural currency of freak-show characters and hence the potential for freak shows to have diffuse disciplinary effects.[21]

In addition to producing disciplined audiences, schooled in the dangers of gender transgressions, freak shows worked in tandem with cross-dressing law to produce vigilant audiences trained in the pleasures of suspicion. The possibility of being duped was central to dime museum entertainment, and showmen encouraged audiences to gain pleasure from suspecting, confronting, and unmasking frauds. Performances of sexual and gender ambiguity were particularly susceptible to this suspicion. For example, the Bearded Lady's combination of feminine dress and masculine facial hair confronted audiences with a fascinating gender dilemma: Was this a woman who pushed the female body beyond recognizable femininity, or was it a man in drag? Visitors sought to resolve this dilemma by prodding at flesh, tugging at beards, and demanding to know the Bearded Lady's marital and maternal status. Freak-show managers encouraged this questioning and occasionally brought in experts to heighten the drama. At New York's American Museum Barnum instigated a confrontation that ended in court, in which a freak-show visitor accused a Bearded Lady of being male, only to be rebuffed by the Lady's husband, father, and numerous doctors who testified that she was indeed female. Back in San Francisco, Matson's manager also went to court to sue his rivals who allegedly featured "fake" Miss Matsons in their shows; apparently there could be just one authentic

Bogus Man. Far from resolving the gender confusion at hand, such events merely reminded audiences of their susceptibility to being duped. As such, freak shows not only reproduced the boundary between permissible and criminal gender displays that was policed by cross-dressing law; they also popularized and democratized it, turning audiences into aware and vigilant judges of possible gender fraud.[22]

Seeing the Sights

The disparate bodies gathered on the freak-show stage eerily mirrored the bodies targeted by municipal law: the sexually ambiguous, the indecent, the racialized, and the diseased. Given these consistent parallels, the absence of the intensely policed Chinese body from San Francisco freak-show exhibitions is striking. However, this does not mean that the Chinese body was not an object of fascination in San Francisco's entertainment economy; rather its display occurred in a different site, as one of the central attractions on the city's commercial slumming tours.

The commercial slumming tour was popular in San Francisco—and other U.S. cities—from the 1870s until at least the century's end. These standardized tours guided a wide range of visitors through Chinatown and the Barbary Coast to glimpse the bodies that the law sought to conceal (see figure 5.4). Chinatown and the Barbary Coast were spatially contiguous, at times overlapping, and many slumming tours traversed both, each offering its own set of ostensibly authentic pleasures. Usually led by off-duty police officers or official licensed guides, commercial slumming tours included brothels, gambling saloons, opium dens, and dive bars, as well as the local jail and sick rooms housing Chinese patients who were denied access to the city's hospital. Far from marginal expeditions enjoyed by the adventurous few, slumming tours were a central part of the city's tourist trade, forming a staple part of visitors' itineraries, including those of notable celebrities, war heroes, and religious leaders.[23]

Far more explicitly than vaudeville theater and dime museum freak shows, the appeal of slumming tours rested on their promised encounter with bodily sights and practices that existed against the law. Guidebooks and travel narratives frequently emphasized mysterious underground passages and labyrinths that contained "some of the most dangerous places and secrets

FIGURE 5.4. Sketch of a slumming tour in San Francisco's Chinatown. "California—An Evening in the Chinese Quarter of San Francisco," *Frank Leslie's Illustrated Weekly*, August 24, 1878, 420.

of Chinatown." In these labyrinths, the guidebooks promised, tourists could encounter any number of crimes and vices as they stumbled across gambling rings, opium dens, and enclaves of murderous hatchet men. Somewhat ironically the desire to witness authentic crime fueled the popularity of police guides, particularly among tourists who saw off-duty officers as experts in the geography of vice. Other tourists, however, worried that a police guide would inhibit their ability to experience the "the true criminal flavor" of the neighborhood and boasted of venturing into Chinatown's "labyrinths of dirt and darkness" alone.[24]

Slumming tours promised not only access to hidden urban landscapes of crime and vice but also close-up encounters with the problem bodies that lurked in, lured to, and threatened from the labyrinth's darkness. As such their entertainment value rested on the voyeuristic pleasures of gazing at bodily difference, mirroring the appeal of freak-show displays. One advertisement for a licensed Chinatown tour guide, for example, listed opium dens, dive bars, and lodging houses as the tour's main "attractions," but also "lepers," a "one-arm miner," and a "little feet family." Other guidebooks promised more sexualized sights, describing Chinatown as "a panoptican [*sic*] of peepshows," where tourists could gaze at female sex workers on display. Tourists rarely, if ever, documented the sex they had on slumming tours, instead lingering on the visuals of the "depraved" and "helpless" women subjected to the advances of even more depraved men. However, one slumming tourist, who claimed to be a studious man, took advantage of the rooms of prostitution on Washington Street to subject a Chinese woman to a physical examination so as to debunk an ostensibly common belief that white and Chinese women had different sexual anatomies. Although the man concluded "that there are no physical differences between the Chinese and American women, their configuration being identical," his investigation nonetheless reveals the extent to which European Americans positioned Chinese women's bodies outside of legible male/female distinctions.[25]

In this context of dehumanizing scrutiny, even the body of the healthy, moral, gainfully employed Chinese man was transformed into a spectacle for tourist consumption by a focus on his ostensibly feminine appearance. One writer described a waiter in a local restaurant: "As your eye studies the figure before you, the dress and the physiognomy, you do not fail to notice the long pigtail, the Chinaman's glory, as a woman's delight in her long hair." Another tour guide described an archetypical Chinese aristocrat who "carries [his queue] looped about his hand as he walks, with the grace of [a] woman with a light hold upon her skirts." Further mirroring the logic of the freak show, observers frequently framed racial and gender difference as less than human, describing the Chinese men they gazed at as "pig-tailed Orientals" and "creature[s] of the queue."[26]

In addition to taking in these sights on the streets, slumming tours stopped at theaters and dive bars where participants perhaps saw female or male impersonation on stage. Tour guides regularly described visiting Chinese theaters where male actors performed in women's roles and clothing in scenes of love, marriage, and childbirth. As the historian Daphne Lei explains, San Francisco's Chinatown theaters predominantly staged regional Cantonese operas that were rooted in Guangdong Province. Although male and female actors shared the stage through much of China's theater history, exclusively male casts dominated Cantonese opera during the nineteenth century and, by extension, Chinese theater in San Francisco. As early as 1852 San Francisco's Chinese residents flocked to these theaters to watch troupes from Canton perform familiar national stories and facilitate affective connections between migrants and homeland. Individual theater companies employed multiple male actors who played women's roles, and some achieved significant fame.[27] In the 1880s Lee Hoo was particularly popular, commanding a high salary and thrilling large crowds, as s/he performed in "silk dresses, satin materials [and] fur cloaks."[28]

As slumming tours grew in popularity, increasing numbers of white tourists visited Chinese theaters, viewing the acting, music, and even the audience through a lens of incomprehensible difference. Male actors performing in women's roles were particular enigmas; some observers admired the skill of actors who played "their parts so perfectly that one cannot detect the deception," although others mocked the performers, claiming that they "skip about in wanton abandon" and "speak in a most distressing, squeaky falsetto."[29] Willfully ignoring the historical and cultural context of Cantonese opera and refusing to draw parallels with female impersonation on the minstrel or vaudeville stage, slumming tour theatergoers reduced the all-male, cross-gender casting of Chinese theater to a racialized spectacle.

Slumming tours may also have stopped at Barbary Coast dive bars that hired female impersonators to perform on stage or work the bar. In the 1890s Bottle Meyer's bar on Pacific Street employed performers like Bert Larose to increase their liquor sales, and by 1908 a Pacific Street bar called The Dash employed a full staff of "degenerate female impersonators" who entertained "the most depraved type of men." Both bars offered sexual services on the premises, in booths where patrons could indulge in semiprivate pleasures with bar staff. These bars existed in uneasy tension with cross-dressing law. In 1907, for example, police arrested a Pacific Street female impersonator named Charles Harrington after s/he stepped down from the stage to join two sailors in the audience. The judge released Harrington without penalty but clarified the criminality of cross-dressing within the semipublic space of the saloon. Harrington could perform on stage, the judge granted, but to avoid arrest under cross-dressing law, he ordered, "You must confine yourself strictly to the footlights." Published tour guides do not mention these bars, and it is not known whether they were included on slumming tour itineraries. However, an early San Francisco historian remembered Bottle Meyer's as an institution "as famous as the Cliff House," while The Dash was embedded in a vice district economy that increasingly catered to sightseers in the postearthquake years. Consequently the San

FIGURE 5.5. Newspaper sketch of two women arrested on a slumming tour of Chinatown for wearing men's clothing. "Inspiration Comes from a Stage Play," *San Francisco Examiner*, May 25, 1903.

Francisco historian Nan Alamilla Boyd describes The Dash as a tourist venue that anticipated the cross-gender entertainments that became a central part of the city's tourist economy in the 1930s.[30]

Although slumming tours probably offered some cross-gender entertainments to their customers, tourists were perhaps even more likely to encounter cross-dressing practices within their own tour parties. When the police arrested Mrs. Dubia and Mrs. Dessar in 1903, the two women were enjoying a guided tour of Chinatown in men's clothes (see figure 5.5). Mrs. Dubia explained her actions to a local reporter: "We wanted to see Chinatown, of course. . . . We were told that the best way would be to go in men's clothes, that lots of women went like that, that it would be better in every way—climbing up and down ladders, and that sort of thing." Ultimately let off with a warning, the women first endured a "lecture" from the chief of police, who "pointed out the folly of their course, as women may see all of Chinatown, that is open for any one to see." However, Dubia's explanation suggests that slumming tour guides often encouraged female tourists to dress as men, in direct violation of cross-dressing law, to see the neighborhood's seediest sights. Such accounts were not limited to San Francisco. In an investigative government report on Chinese prostitution in Sacramento, for example, a police officer testifying on the age of white boys who visited prostitutes stated, "I have also known cases where young girls, dressed up as boys, went to these places—out of curiosity perhaps."[31]

Similar to freak shows, slumming tours had a complex relationship to the law. On the one hand, they thrived on the existence of crime and vice and strove to uncover the problem bodies and criminal acts that local laws tried to hide from "general" public view. Additionally slumming tours promised or threatened to incite illegality by directing tourists to places where they could indulge in criminal pleasures and encouraging them to engage in public cross-dressing, opium smoking, and gambling, in direct violation of local law. On the other hand, slumming tours were led by off-duty police officers who moonlighted as popular guides, and they sometimes featured police raids on criminal dens as exciting sights. Moreover slumming tours worked through strategies of surveillance that supported law enforcement, constructing racialized and gendered knowledge of city space.[32]

Although slumming tours were directly advertised to visiting tourists, they were also popular among state investigators, journalists, and moral crusaders, who made explicit the connections between a desire to see and a desire to control. Most immediately, information gathered on slumming tours could be used to guide criminal prosecutions that were brought by grand juries or individual citizens. In 1891 the city's grand jury convened the Committee on Dives and Schools of Vice. Preparing a crackdown on urban indecency, committee members took a police-guided slumming tour of Chinatown and the Barbary Coast to "thoroughly inspect" dive bars, dance halls, opium dens, and "lewd houses." In 1895 two religious leaders from a local Methodist church went on a guided slumming tour of the Barbary Coast, where they witnessed an "indecent exhibition" performed in a house on Dupont Street. They subsequently persuaded the district attorney to indict for indecent exposure the six French women they had observed. Local newspapers publicized these prosecutions and pursued their own antivice agendas, sending reporters on slumming tours and publishing lurid reports. Consequently slumming tours could dovetail with the law by providing local officials with eyewitness information to be used in subsequent police crackdowns.[33]

The information gathered on slumming tours also formed the basis of multiple government reports that investigated and condemned Chinatown in the name of public health. According to the San Francisco historian Nayan Shah, local government officials first toured Chinatown with the aid of police in 1854, and subsequent governments adopted the police-guided tour as a central method of investigation. In 1871, for example, Thomas Logan, secretary of the California State Board of Health, conducted a "midnight visit" to San Francisco's Chinatown, accompanied by the city's medical officer and a police guide. Similar to recreational slumming tourists, Logan's party visited opium dens, places of prostitution, and gambling saloons; they also entered "private premises," observed seminaked women, and speculated on the "frequent epilatory condition of the genital organs" in relation to "sexual appetite." In 1885 the San Francisco Board of Supervisors issued a report on conditions in Chinatown, which again featured a midnight journey, a police guide, and an official report that mirrored the lurid style of slumming tour travelogues. Throughout these reports government investigators emphasized the need for eyewitness evidence to uncover the truth of Chinese depravity, thus securing the relationship between slumming tours and local law.[34]

In the second half of the century recreational and official slumming tours became a central mechanism for generating knowledge of Chinese people and space. As Barbara Berglund argues, slumming tour guidebooks provided visitors with "templates of meaning" through which to understand Chinatown and its residents. In particular, guidebooks depicted Chinatown as a foreign and dangerous place that was inhabited by an "alien race." Such depictions stood in stark contrast to residents' own understandings of their neighborhood and overlooked the multiple ethnicities that called Chinatown home. Staging encounters between predominantly European American visitors and predominantly Chinese residents, slumming tours participated in the production of racial meanings, allowing visitors to consolidate claims to whiteness in distinction from Chinese culture. Slumming tours also presumed that discrete racial territories existed and imposed a homogeneous racial identity on Chinatown, shaping its existence as both a real and an imagined space.[35]

Although slumming tours brought tourists and residents into close proximity, these commercial encounters confirmed rather than challenged the social distance between viewer and viewed. In part this was because slumming tours transformed human bodies into racialized tourist locations and offered them up as sights to be consumed. However, it was also because these tours were carefully managed events that were designed to confirm visitors' fantasies and fears about the residents of the racialized slums. After all, slumming tours were commercial enterprises, and to guarantee their success many licensed tour guides employed local Chinese actors to carefully stage the vice and violence that tourists craved. These business practices were publicly exposed in 1904, when the Chinese consul general filed a formal complaint with the Police Commission, alleging that white tour guides were staging indecent exhibitions and constructing fake opium dens in Chinatown. Slumming tours of the Barbary Coast similarly relied on staged vice, particularly during the postearthquake years. Indeed, according to Herbert Asbury, an early historian of the Barbary Coast, the district became a "veritable slummers' paradise," where wealthy tourists could watch sham knife fights and indecent dancing from the safety of "slummers' balconies" installed in dance halls and bars. By confirming tourists' expectations, slumming tours transformed the relationship between slum resident and city tourist from one of incomprehension into one of perceived knowledge, giving tourists a new sense of mastery over those they viewed. Consequently these tours not only located problem bodies on a tourist grid of intelligibility and brought them into the commercial order of the city but also neutralized their potential and actual political threat.[36]

Staging Desire

Despite their immediate concern with bodily displays, vaudevillian theater, freak-show exhibitions, and commercial slumming tours performed cultural work similar to that of cross-dressing law, operating as techniques of normalization that strove to produce clear, recognizable boundaries between normative and deviant bodily displays. Also similar to cross-dressing law, their preoccupation with cross-dressing bodies did not occur in a vacuum but as one part of a broader set of cultural concerns about the public visibility of problem bodies, particularly those marked by sexual immorality, race, and disease or disability. Ultimately the cultural effects of displaying such bodies as entertainment were similar to the effects of criminalizing them as nuisance, producing discourses of abnormality or "not belonging" through the manipulation of bodies and space. Instead of pointing to a contradictory relationship between legal regulation and cultural fascination, these entertainments reveal their overlaps and reinforcements, with regulation inciting interest and a desire to see, and fascination having disciplinary effects that circle back to law.

In drawing these conclusions, however, I also want to leave open the possibility that institutions of display had ironic or unintended consequences that cannot be fully explained in terms of discipline. In particular I want to imagine the multiple responses that audiences may have had to cross-dressing entertainments, including recognition and desire. To be clear, there is scant evidence of such responses, as the voices of those who may have appropriated entertainment discourse in this manner have not made their way into the archive. Neglecting the possibility owing to insufficient evidence, however, may be more problematic than raising it unsupported, as it replicates the structure of the archive, amplifying some voices and silencing others.

In vaudeville, freak shows, Chinese theater, and Barbary Coast saloons, audiences clamored to see male and female impersonators on stage. Some audience members were drawn by the strangeness of these performances, but others perhaps were attracted by a different set of pleasures. These pleasures could have been fueled by a shared sense of gender difference and a longing for connection. Perhaps people with gender identifications that diverged from their legal sex visited freak shows to befriend Matson, for example, or attended Chinese theaters to meet Lee Hoo backstage. They could also have been fueled by an erotic desire for the cross-dressing star on stage. After all, theater reviewers predicted that women would fall for Ella Wesner, Lee Hoo was reportedly stunning on stage, and sailors happily fondled Charles Harrington when s/he stepped into the audience. The freak show's interactive format seemed particularly supportive of alternative pleasures, as a reporter acknowledged when describing Matson's dime museum exhibit: "Her part will not be a difficult one. She will be faultlessly attired in patent leathers, a handsome dress suit, embroidered linen and a white tie. She will recline in an easy-chair on a little platform and chat with the socially inclined, but whether she will divulge any of the interesting secrets connected with her numerous love episodes is not definitely known."

Although cross-dressing entertainments were shaped by legal and cultural prohibitions, we can imagine different ways that different audiences may have interacted with performers—with fascination and titillation, perhaps; with discomfort and disdain; but also with identification, attraction, and desire.[37]

Problem Bodies, Nation-State

On December 9, 1910, a Japanese ship named the *Chiyo Maru* arrived in San Francisco from Hong Kong. Immigration and customs house officials boarded the liner to search for stowaways and discovered five Chinese men hiding throughout the ship. Officials took the men to the city prison, where the prison matron reported that one of them had a female body. Immigration officials transported the nineteen-year-old Wong Ah Choy to the newly constructed Angel Island immigration station, where s/he was interrogated by immigration inspectors (see figure 6.1). Wong initially insisted that s/he had stowed away on his/her own accord but later "confessed" that Yow On, a member of the crew, had been of assistance. Federal marshals arrested Yow On for "unlawfully bringing a Chinese girl into this country" and locked him up in the Alameda County jail to await trial. As the key witness against him, Wong was detained on Angel Island for three months. Eventually the U.S. District Court found Yow On not guilty, accepting Wong's claim that he simply supplied food during the journey. Nonetheless both were denied entry to the United States as undesirable aliens.[1]

As Wong sailed into San Francisco Bay wearing men's clothes on a body the law deemed female, s/he participated in a clothing practice that had been common among migrants since at least gold rush days. Additionally,

FIGURE 6.1. Newspaper image of Wong Ah Choy, detained at Angel Island, 1910. *San Francisco Examiner*, December 11, 1910.

as a person who wore "a dress not belonging to his or her sex," Wong engaged in a criminal act that local law had targeted for over forty-five years. San Francisco police, however, did not arrest Wong for violating the city's cross-dressing law, nor did they hold him/her in prison as an annoying nuisance who disturbed urban order. Instead federal agents arrested Wong for violating immigration law, triggering a lengthy detention on Angel Island and expulsion from the nation.

This chapter examines the conditions that created a distinct fate for Wong and for other immigrants who engaged in multiple cross-dressing practices in the late nineteenth century and early twentieth. From 1875 onward the federal government used immigration law to shape the nation's population by determining the terms of entry and exclusion. Immigration law did not target cross-dressing as a specific practice, but proponents of exclusion deployed cross-dressing imagery in their constructions of national belonging, linking Chinese immigrants in particular to gender deviance and deceit. Federal immigration law also created considerable hardships for people who wore clothing that "did not belong" to their sex. Some of these people engaged in cross-dressing to evade immigration inspectors, as did Chinese women who stowed away in men's clothing during the exclusion era. Others engaged in cross-dressing because it was their preferred mode of dress and were excluded at the border as undesirable. Still more established lengthy residences in the United States but were subsequently deported following arrest or institutionalization for cross-dressing crimes. By the early twentieth century federal immigration laws had joined cross-dressing laws in the policing of normative gender and excluded multiple problem bodies from the nation-state. In the process it established gender normativity as a precondition for full national belonging.

Passages

In 1910 Wong encountered a dense web of immigration controls that structured the experience of new arrivals in racially specific and gendered ways. These included federal immigration laws that dictated the terms of entry and exclusion, federal inspectors who boarded and surveyed arriving ships, detention facilities that housed suspect passengers, and U.S. marshals who pursued people charged with related crimes. This marked a significant contrast with the legal vacuum that accompanied gold rush mass migrations decades earlier and signaled a new era of using immigration policy to shape the nation-state. From its inception U.S. immigration law promoted an exclusionary vision of the nation that restricted multiple problem bodies on the grounds of gender, sexuality, race, and ability. Supporters of this vision did not target cross-dressing practices directly, but they did mobilize cross-dressing imagery in pursuit of a gender-normative nation.[2]

Until 1875 the federal government expressed little interest in policing the nation's borders, and California developed its own system for administering and regulating immigration. In 1870 the state legislature passed a racially specific antiprostitution law that banned the entry of "Mongolian, Chinese and Japanese females" who were not "of correct habits and good character." In 1874 twenty-two excluded women and their representatives challenged the law. During the subsequent trial their supporters argued that immigration officials had wrongly denied entry to respectable women, while opponents claimed that the women were recognizable as prostitutes because of their distinct and sometimes masculine clothing, as well as their tendency to "play the men" aboard ship. Although sympathetic to California's interest in Chinese exclusion, the U.S. Circuit Court overturned the law on jurisdictional grounds. Two years later the U.S. Supreme Court found all state immigration laws unconstitutional.[3]

In 1875 the federal government adopted a more direct role in immigration policy by adopting the Page Law. Similar to California's 1870 Act, the 1875 Page Law banned Asian women from entering the United States for "lewd and immoral purposes," alongside contract laborers and felons. On paper the law denied entry to Chinese prostitutes, but in practice immigration inspectors suspected sexual immorality of virtually all Chinese women, creating a much broader barrier to admission. The Page Law also operated as "a blueprint for exclusion" that established the principle of selective immigration and set the stage for multiple additional prohibitions.[4] Seven years later, in 1882, Congress passed the Chinese Exclusion Act, which prevented almost all Chinese immigration, with limited class-based exceptions for diplomats, merchants, teachers, students, and tourists. Initially passed for a ten-year period, the Exclusion Act was renewed twice, in 1892 and 1902, before Congress extended it indefinitely in 1904. It remained in force until its repeal in 1943.[5]

Centered in San Francisco, West Coast anti-Chinese activism exerted a crucial influence on the development of federal immigration policy. San Francisco had long sought to exclude and remove its Chinese residents through the powers granted by nuisance laws. Problems of jurisdiction and constitutionality often hampered local efforts, however, prompting federal officials to take up the task of managing problem bodies through exclusionary immigration laws. Supporters of exclusion mobilized multiple tropes of danger that positioned Chinese immigration as a direct threat to white labor, public health, and family life. These campaigns did not target cross-dressing practices as objects of control, but they did rely upon political narratives of nonnormative gender to mobilize public support. These narratives took several different forms but primarily centered on the stereotypical figure of the hyperfeminized Chinese male domestic. Most notably political cartoons that mobilized popular support for Chinese exclusion regularly featured caricatures of hyperfeminized Chinese men.

Efforts to mobilize and maintain support for Chinese exclusion quickly homed in on the figure of the feminized Chinese male domestic. For example, the Workingmen's Party of California argued that the Chinese male servant had a competitive edge in the domestic labor market as a direct result of his lack of masculinity: "You cannot discern that he is a man. . . . He has no tell-tale blush for indelicate sights or sounds. He cleanses the baby with the same indifference that he washes the dishes. He can lace Madam's corsets, or arrange the girls' petticoats, smooth their pillows, or tuck in their feet as calmly as he can set the table for breakfast. In an emergency he is called into the bedroom, or the bathroom without a thought. Why, bless you, he is not a man!" Against this emasculated Chinese servant, argued the WPC, white domestic laborers were destined to fail "because they have sex, and shame, and sense of propriety."[6] Moreover anti-Chinese agitators alleged that unlike the Chinese railroad worker, the Chinese domestic servant did not compete directly with white men but with white women, who were "compelled to work at starvation prices" or were driven out of the domestic labor market and into prostitution.[7] Thomas Magee, publisher of the anti-Chinese periodical *San Francisco Real Estate Circular*, wrote, "Men from China come here to do laundry work. . . . Every one doing this work takes bread from the mouths of our women."[8] Anti-Chinese discourse thus constructed the feminized Chinese male domestic as a potent and dangerous figure, who threatened not only normative gender relations but also the economic well-being of white workers in general, and white women workers in particular.

Political cartoons featured caricatures of Chinese men that centered on their ostensibly feminine appearance, using visual cues such as long hair, rich, billowing gowns, and ornate fans. When violence broke out against Chinese laborers in Wyoming in 1885 a political cartoon in *Harper's Weekly* depicted two feminized Chinese men watching the brutal scene, simpering behind ornate fans and declaring, "Here's a Pretty Mess!" (see figure 6.2). Even more starkly, in 1887 the national magazine *Wasp* published a cartoon that featured Chinese men, wearing women's clothing and clutching baby dolls, passing through immigration control into the United States (see figure 6.3). This cartoon commented on provisions in federal alien contract acts that banned employers from paying to import laborers but exempted several categories of workers, including domestic servants. In depicting men in feminine apparel, such cartoons framed Chinese immigrants not only as deceptive interlopers, sneaking into the country in disguise, but also as effeminate, deviant men, unable to perform normative masculinity and hence unworthy of inclusion in the nation.[9]

Although the interplay of anti-Chinese politics and cross-gender discourses primarily focused on the figure of the feminized Chinese man, other cross-gender figures were discursively produced. For example,

FIGURE 6.2. "Here's a Pretty Mess!" political cartoon. *Harper's Weekly*, September 19, 1885. Courtesy of Bancroft Library, University of California, Berkeley, MTP/HW: vol. 29: 623.

masculinizing accounts of Chinese women joined feminizing accounts of Chinese men to produce an image of Chinese gender as utterly illegible. In a scathing book-length critique of social life in California, Hinton Helper dedicated an entire chapter to the "problems" of Chinese immigration, including the difficulty of interpreting Chinese gender. "You would be puzzled to distinguish the women from the men," Helper instructed his readers, "so inconsiderable are the differences in dress and figure." Another visitor to San Francisco's Chinatown claimed that the "women are not easily distinguishable from the men by the difference of their toilettes," and a local newspaper reported, "In China the men wear skirts and the women trousers." In these representations Chinese immigrants

FIGURE 6.3. "Another Bar Down" political cartoon. *Wasp* 18 (January–June 1887).
Courtesy of Bancroft Library, University of California, Berkeley, F850.W18.

disrupted the natural order of binary gender through a gender indeterminacy that was inextricably connected to racial distinctiveness.[10]

Anti-Chinese politics and cross-gender discourse also came together in the figure of the besieged white male laborer, threatened with emasculation by Chinese immigration. The American Federation of Labor presented its call for Chinese exclusion in gendered high-stakes terms—"American Manhood against Asiatic Coolieism, Which Shall Survive?"—while the San Francisco Board of Health represented Chinese immigrants as a three-pronged threat to the "morals, the manhood and the health of our people."[11] Given these ostensible threats to white masculinity, it is perhaps unsurprising that white men who failed to support anti-Chinese measures were sometimes represented in feminized forms. For example, in 1882 *Wasp* magazine published a political cartoon featuring President Chester Arthur, who had just refused to sign the first version of the Chinese Exclusion Act (see figure 6.4).[12] This cartoon depicts Arthur in women's clothing, perhaps as a domestic servant, entertaining a white child (identified as the Pacific States) as a literally monstrous Chinese character moves in closer. As this cartoon suggests, the figure of the feminized Chinese man was embedded in a broader discourse that linked Chinese immigration to multiple cross-gender threats and called for a specifically gender-normative white masculinity to "protect" the nation through Chinese exclusion.

The relationship between cross-gender discourses and anti-Chinese politics did not begin in the 1870s. During the early gold rush years many white migrants from the eastern states and Europe framed Chinese men as inherently feminine to naturalize the effects of discriminatory laws and violence that led to their concentration in domestic service occupations marked as "women's work." However, by the 1870s anti-Chinese agitators deployed cross-gender narratives with a different goal: not to rationalize Chinese men's disproportionate incorporation into a particular segment of the labor market but to justify their total exclusion from the city, the state, and ultimately the nation. Animated by numerous cultural anxieties, efforts to pass exclusionary immigration laws deployed the boundary between normative and nonnormative gender to produce and police the racialized borders of the nation-state. In the process they linked Chinese migration to multiple cross-gender threats, against which gender-normative white masculinity could be defined.

FIGURE 6.4. "Amusing the Child" political cartoon. *Wasp* 8 (January–June 1882).
Courtesy of Bancroft Library, University of California, Berkeley, F850.W18.

The rhetorical linkage of Chinese immigrants to gender deviance and deception animated efforts to police the border, attaching to the bodies of Chinese women in particular. By the end of the nineteenth century federal immigration laws severely restricted Chinese immigration in gender-specific ways. As numerous scholars have detailed, Chinese men and women developed multiple strategies for navigating these obstacles.[13] Fabricating membership in an exempt class was perhaps the most common; a man might claim to be a merchant or native-born U.S. citizen, for example, while a woman could claim to be a merchant's or citizen's wife. These strategies carried considerable risk, as officials conducted extensive investigations that triggered lengthy detentions at the Angel Island immigration station. Women who traveled alone came under particular suspicion, as officials scrutinized their relationship claims and searched for signs of immorality. Consequently some people took a different route, seeking to circumvent immigration officials altogether. Traveling to the United States as stowaways, they avoided identification on the ship's manifest and hoped to disembark undetected once the ship docked. Several Chinese women in men's clothes pursued this path.[14]

It is unlikely that cross-dressing would have helped a Chinese woman enter the United States through official channels. Immigration officials interrogated Chinese men about their business ties if they sought entry as a merchant or their history of residence if they asserted U.S. citizenship. Moreover beginning in the 1890s officials required Chinese men to disrobe at the border, for bathing and disinfection under quarantine protocols or for medical examination under immigration law.[15] Dressing as a man, however, might improve a woman's chance of sidestepping official controls and entering the nation unnoticed.

Cross-dressing could help women stowaways survive their voyage undetected. Wong Ah Choy recalled how men's clothing facilitated his/her stowaway experience, enabling him/her to live as a man among men on ship and to "mingle with the crew at night."[16] Cross-dressing could also help stowaways to disembark undetected, either escaping on rowboats before their ship reached land or hiding during the ship's inspection and then creeping ashore after dark. The week before Wong's capture a group of fifteen stowaways left the ship *Manchuria* in two rowboats as it entered San Francisco's harbor at night; immigration officials intercepted the boats and discovered seven women in men's clothes.[17] Some women even used these tactics to escape custody when they were denied entry and held for deportation aboard ship—the typical site of detention before the Angel Island immigration station opened in 1910. In October 1885 a woman named Ah Choi donned a man's sailor outfit and brazenly walked ashore from the *Oceanic* steamship, where she had been held for two weeks on the grounds that she lacked the documentation required for landing.[18] Ah Choi's escape was ultimately unsuccessful; she was captured by customs officials who "laid violent hands" on her and returned her to the ship. If she had successfully vanished into the crowd, she would also have disappeared from the historical record, and her cross-dressing practices would today be unknown.

Because stowaways went to great lengths to avoid detection, it is difficult to assess the frequency of their cross-dressing practices; newspapers document a handful of cases that failed but tell us nothing of those that succeeded. Shipping companies and Christian missions that had contact with Chinese communities, however, sometimes acknowledged their existence. In 1877 a representative of the Oriental and Occidental Steamship Company testified to Congress of rumors that "twenty or thirty" Chinese women had been placed aboard a vessel "in male attire."[19] San Francisco missionaries who sought to "rescue" Chinese women from prostitution issued similar claims. In 1897 a Methodist missionary named Mrs. Lake reported that she had "discovered a celestial trick" of dressing girls in boys' clothes to "hoodwink the United States officials" and sneak unwitting girls into the country for the purpose of prostitution. Apparently Lake had discovered two young women wearing men's clothes in a Chinatown brothel; she was "positive that the discovery thoroughly accounts for the hitherto inexplicable manner in which female children have been smuggled into this country past the eyes of the customs officers."[20]

White officials and newspapers too viewed these practices as evidence of an organized prostitution ring that trafficked in helpless cross-dressing girls. Certainly organized prostitution existed in Chinatown, structured by extreme poverty in China's Guangdong Province and economic opportunities in the United States. According to Lucie Cheng Hirata, Chinatown crime syndicates, or "tongs," exploited these conditions and brought young women to the United States to work as prostitutes through a complex system of procurement, transportation, and bribery.[21] In representing immigrant women's cross-dressing practices, however, official reports and newspapers did far more than recognize the institutional structure of Chinatown prostitution and the specific sufferings it could generate. Instead these reports framed all Chinese women as prostitutes and all of their travels as forced importation. The possibility that women were active participants in their "disguise" or wore men's clothing for other reasons was ignored.

Immigration officials and city newspapers viewed Wong's cross-dressing as the work of a "gigantic smuggling ring" that sought to "import" Chinese "slave girls" to work as prostitutes.[22] Wong resisted this framing, claiming that s/he had migrated to San Francisco on his/her own initiative. According to Wong, s/he had attempted to land in San Francisco the previous year as a merchant's wife, but immigration officials rejected the claim and deported him/her as "destined for an immoral life." S/he then decided to return as a stowaway and donned men's clothes to facilitate the journey. Newspapers reported these claims and acknowledged that Wong "wanted to come back, so not a great deal of persuasion on the part of the smugglers was necessary to get her to stow away on the vessel." Nonetheless the framework of smuggling persisted, denying Wong's agency or alternative narratives of Chinese women's migration.[23]

Alternative narratives are difficult to uncover, of course, particularly since the voices of turn-of-the-century deportees were generally recorded during official investigations only.[24] This doesn't negate the possibility, however, of imagining different contexts for Wong's clothing and travel. Perhaps, as immigration officials conjectured, Wong did wear men's clothing as a disguise that facilitated border-crossing during the era of exclusion. Perhaps, however, s/he also preferred men's clothing, identifying as a masculine woman or as a man. Certainly at the time of Wong's migration women in men's clothing were achieving new cultural visibility in China, associated with morally suspect classes, such as prostitutes and actresses, as well as respectable women, such as students and soldiers. We do not know whether Wong associated with any of these groups before his/her voyage to the United States, but it is certainly unlikely that s/he encountered cross-dressing practices for the first time aboard the ship.[25]

We can also imagine different possibilities for Wong's interest in San Francisco residency: perhaps s/he traveled to work as a prostitute, or perhaps to pursue the economic opportunities that attracted migrant men, or to join family and friends. Whatever the combination of motivation, pressure, constraint, and desire that informed Wong's travel, we can imagine him/her as an active participant in the experience, planning the stowaway voyage, sailing as a man, enduring arrest and detention, and disputing the meanings that officials imposed. Certainly Wong's agency was limited, as s/he no doubt reflected upon during the long journey back to Hong Kong. Nonetheless Wong's actions spotlight the resiliency of at least some Chinese migrants as they navigated and challenged the gendered dynamics of exclusion.

Expansions

Chinese exclusion laws persisted for over sixty years and had profound effects on Chinese communities in the United States, shaping the contours of economic, political, social, and cultural life.[26] These laws also formed the bedrock of an exclusionary immigration control apparatus, and every few years new grounds for exclusion were added and new processes of control developed. By the time Congress passed the 1917 Immigration Act, the list of excluded persons was long, specifying that convicts, idiots, lunatics, imbeciles, the feeble-minded, prostitutes, paupers, anarchists, epileptics, alcoholics, beggars, vagrants, the mentally and physically "defective," and those afflicted with "a loathsome or dangerous contagious disease" be denied entry. Persons of constitutional psychopathic inferiority, persons guilty of moral turpitude, persons with a history of insanity, and persons deemed likely to become a public charge were also excluded, with particular consequence for people engaging in cross-dressing practices. Policing problem bodies through spatial regulation had become a federal preoccupation.[27]

People who engaged in multiple cross-dressing practices became entangled in this web of immigration control, even as it passed over cross-dressing as a specific offense. In late April 1907 immigration officials launched an investigation of a "woman-man of mystery" who arrived in San Francisco from Australia aboard the ship *Ventura*. The "mysterious" person had traveled under the name George Pepper, lodging in the men's quarters with his brother John and passing time on the long journey by working as the ship's doctor. Once the ship docked in San Francisco, Pepper changed into women's clothing and presented himself/herself as Marpha Mittig, the wife of John Pepper. It is unclear exactly why Pepper donned a dress upon arrival, particularly since s/he had traveled under a man's name, in men's clothing, which s/he continued to wear after arrival. Possibly s/he knew there was little chance of entering the country via San Francisco if s/he continued to present as a gender (man) that diverged from his/her legal sex (female).[28]

Following the 1891 Immigration Act, officials conducted medical examinations of all people arriving in the United States. According to Nayan Shah, different ports of entry developed different procedures to meet this mandate. San Francisco's were particularly invasive, requiring an initial examination aboard the ship, followed by a more thorough inspection and disrobing at the Angel Island Quarantine Station.[29] As Erica Rand argues, these disrobings were not designed to search for sex or gender incongruities, but they nonetheless functioned as such, requiring immigrants to strip and reveal the body beneath their clothes. Certainly immigration officials paid close attention to the naked bodies before them, searching for visible differences, including atypical genitalia. Margot Canaday and Douglas Baynton document multiple cases of immigration officials denying entry to men with a small or "defective" penis, worrying that their "lack of sexual development" would lead to unemployment, economic dependency, and sexual perversity. Had Pepper tried to enter the country as a man, immigration officials would likely have discovered and interpreted his/her body as female, which could have constituted grounds for exclusion.[30]

Unfortunately for Pepper, however, appearing as a woman created problems of its own, particularly since s/he appeared on the ship's manifest under the name George. Immigration officials were alarmed by Pepper's gender transformation and launched an insanity investigation of the "woman disguised in male attire" who "would have no difficulty passing for a man anywhere." City newspapers fanned the flames of the insanity charge, reporting that Pepper claimed to be a Russian countess, related to the czar, who had fled Moscow after being falsely accused of murder. The Board of Special Inquiry found Pepper to be sane but nonetheless denied him/her entry as an "undesirable" who was likely to become a public charge. After three weeks' detention aboard the *Ventura*, Pepper was deported, setting sail for Canada in men's clothing.

On paper the category "likely to become a public charge" (LPC) was concerned with economic risk, as lawmakers excluded people whom they predicted would become dependent on the state. At first glance it is striking that immigration officials would exclude Pepper on these grounds, particularly since s/he was a practicing doctor carrying over $800 in gold. According to the historian Martha Gardner, however, the LPC designation operated as "a catchall category of exclusion," which marked thousands of would-be immigrants as ineligible for entry; indeed more people were denied entry under the LPC ban than any other category.[31] In large part its popularity stemmed from its effectiveness; by referring to future potential rather than current status, an LPC exclusion was very difficult to contest. Women who flouted traditional gender roles were particularly susceptible, appearing economically vulnerable as well as morally suspect. Immigration officials clearly viewed Pepper through this lens; they found that that s/he lacked the medical license required to practice in the United States, and they did not expect John Pepper to support his masculine spouse. Consequently, although city journalists viewed the case as particularly "strange," it ended in a most conventional way, with Pepper excluded as a likely public charge.[32]

While some people who engaged in cross-dressing were excluded at the border, others were removed after they had entered the nation, as the United States adopted new powers of deportation in the late nineteenth century. Initially deportation laws facilitated the removal of people who crossed the border without authorization or who violated a specific condition of entry. The 1891 Immigration Act, for example, allowed the government to deport people within one year of entry if it was later determined that they "should" have been excluded at the border, and to deport those who became a public charge within one year if the cause of their dependency had existed when they had entered the country. These laws signaled a relatively straightforward extension of border control powers by allowing officials to fix any "mistakes" they made at the time of entry.[33]

In 1894 officials viewed Henry Pohlmann as one of these mistakes. Born and raised in Germany, Pohlmann had moved to California nine years earlier and worked as a music teacher in San Francisco. In June 1894 a city resident named George Kammerer called the police to report that Pohlmann, his friend, was acting strangely; Pohlmann had "shaved off his moustache, powdered and pasted his cheeks, [and] wishe[d] to appear in girl's clothes," insisting "that he [was] a woman." Pohlmann had been institutionalized the previous month, after Kammerer had testified that his friend experienced "hallucinations" and tended to "tear off all his clothes." Doctors had released Pohlmann after three weeks, but were now concerned that the "disease [was] increasing." The Insanity Commission heard Pohlmann's case, declared her insane, and sent her to the Stockton

Asylum. Identifying masturbation as the cause of insanity, the doctors detained Pohlmann in the asylum for two months before deporting her to Germany in August 1894.[34]

During the 1890s the federal government would have lacked the power to deport Pohlmann through formal channels. Asylum records indicate that Pohlmann had experienced insanity in Germany, so officials could claim that she had been LPC when she arrived in the United States. Her arrival, however, occurred nine years previously, which far exceeded the time frame for deportation established by federal law. According to Ji-Hye Shin, individual state governments sidestepped such problems by developing their own procedures to remove the "alien insane." Seeking to reduce the costs of institutionalization, California's government negotiated directly with foreign governments and persuaded friends or family to transport asylum patients "home." By taking matters into its own hands, California could remove Pohlmann from the state and the nation, even though her deportation was not authorized by federal law.[35]

Federal deportation powers were limited in the 1890s because they operated within a framework of extended border control. In the early twentieth century, however, Congress adopted a second form of deportation law that triggered a significant extension of federal power by regulating resident immigrants' conduct within the United States. A 1907 immigration law allowed the government to deport any resident immigrant woman who engaged in prostitution within three years of landing, regardless of her status at entry. Concerned that women would lie about their date of entry to avoid deportation, the 1910 Immigration Act removed the three-year time limit, rendering a resident immigrant perpetually deportable for prostitution. The 1917 Immigration Act expanded these powers by swelling the list of deportable offenses and removing time limits for certain cases. In doing so the Act established the foundations of a formidable system of "post-entry social control."[36]

In 1917 a young Mexican woman named Geraldine Portica fell victim to this new system of control. Classified as male at birth, Portica had lived and dressed as a woman for many years. In the winter of 1917 she lived in San Francisco and worked as a chamber maid on Sixth Street. Under circumstances that have been lost to history, police arrested Portica for violating the city's cross-dressing law when she appeared in public in women's clothing. A police photographer recorded her image (figure 4.3), with the following caption handwritten beneath: "This is not a girl, but a boy, who was reared by his mother as a girl and has always dressed as a girl and went to school as a girl and has never associated with any one else but girls and was employed as a chamber maid on 6th St. when arrested, he is a native of Mexico and speaks several languages, his English with the Spanish accent, he is now waiting to be deported to Mexico by the U.S. Gov. Dec. 27th, 1917."[37] With a dense web of immigration controls and deportation powers now in place, cross-dressing laws triggered a new form of spatial control: not exclusion from city space but expulsion from the nation.

According to the legal scholar William Eskridge, sexual and gender non-conformists could be deported on multiple grounds in the early twentieth century, and immigration officials would have had several options when contemplating Portica's removal. In late 1917 officials may have ruled on the grounds of "constitutional psychopathic inferiority," a new category of exclusion added by the 1917 Immigration Act. The U.S. Public Health Service viewed the category as applicable to "sexual perverts," as well as to those who "because of eccentric behavior, defective judgment, or abnormal impulses are in constant conflict with social customs and constituted authorities."[38] Margot Canaday argues that in practice, however, this provision was rarely used against gender nonconformists, who were more likely to be deported under the LPC provision or for committing a crime of moral turpitude.[39]

In part immigration officials relied upon the LPC provision when investigating sexual and gender deviance for the same reasons they used it in other investigations: it was particularly effective and difficult to dispute. Additionally, as Canaday argues, notions of economic dependency and immorality were deeply entwined during this period, and immigration officials imagined multiple scenarios in which sexual degenerates and gender nonconformists would drain state resources. In Portica's case, officials may have argued that her cross-dressing practices would lead to an arrest or insanity charge, both of which required detention at the state's expense. Alternatively they may have argued that her gender deviance, once publicly known, would lead to unemployment and state dependency, pursuing the same logic that officials used when excluding people at the border for "lack of sexual development." Immigration officials may also have expelled Portica on the grounds of "moral turpitude." This was a particularly vague and variable category that incorporated a wide range of crimes in different jurisdictions, including misdemeanor offenses. By the time of Portica's cross-dressing arrest, a person who committed a crime of moral turpitude within five years of entry could be deported, as could a person who committed more than one crime of moral turpitude at any time after entry. If Portica was arrested for cross-dressing within five years of her arrival in the United States, or on multiple occasions, she could have been deported on these grounds.[40]

....

In the mid-nineteenth century a San Francisco journalist described immigration to gold rush California as a "sweeping wave of desire" that brought fresh energy, resources, and initiative to the region.[41] By the end of the century, however, a new national vision of immigration had emerged that imagined a "sweeping wave of undesirables." The federal government crafted immigration laws to stem this wave, banning multiple problem bodies from the nation, including those who wore clothing that "did not belong" to their sex. According to Canaday, the federal response to gender nonconformity was sluggish, as the government lacked a clear framework for conceptualizing these bodies.[42] Nonetheless immigration officials based in San Francisco expelled multiple people who engaged in cross-dressing practices, and supporters of exclusion deployed cross-dressing imagery in their campaigns. By the turn of the century cross-dressing laws intersected with immigration laws to create new networks of control. Undoubtedly local cross-dressing laws and federal immigration laws operated on vastly different scales, with political effects that cannot be read as equivalent. Nonetheless both sets of laws positioned gender normativity as a precondition for full belonging, denying access to the city and nation to those who fell outside its bounds.

Against the Law

In this book I have employed a new critical approach termed "trans-ing analysis" to assemble a wide range of cross-dressing practices that are rarely considered alongside one other, thereby facilitating a series of juxtapositions that expose the workings of cross-dressing laws. Viewing the cross-dressing slumming tourist who avoided prosecution alongside the freak-show star who received jail time or situating the celebrated vaudeville performer alongside the institutionalized asylum patient makes clear that not all cross-dressing practices faced the same legal fate. Instead cross-dressing laws operated by sifting through multiple clothing practices to mark some as harmless or entertaining and condemn others as criminal or insane. Reaching beyond its surface concern with the types of clothing that "belonged" to a particular sex, cross-dressing laws primarily dictated the types of people who "belonged" in public city space and the types of bodies that "belonged" in the categories of man and woman. San Francisco's cross-dressing law did not simply police normative gender but actively produced it.

Local law is a distinct terrain in these productions. In particular, local law had the power to define cross-dressing practices as criminal and the ability to write these definitions onto city space. By regulating access to public space, cross-dressing laws pushed visible gender difference into private realms and pressured people to modify their public appearance under threat of arrest. This drained gender difference from the urban landscape and made it virtually impossible for gender-variant people to fully participate in everyday city life. Thus cross-dressing laws significantly impacted the urban environment, imposing gender normativity onto city space.

Although I have focused on cross-dressing laws, my close attention to local government and city space brings a broader legal matrix into view that targets the visibility of multiple problem bodies, particularly those of sex workers, Chinese immigrants, and those identified as maimed or diseased. The cross-dressing criminal appears alongside these problem bodies in multiple sites: the municipal codebook, the city police court, urban entertainments, and federal immigration law. This analysis reveals particularly close connections between cross-dressing and commercial sex work, ranging from the dress practices of female sex workers during the gold rush years to representations of Chinese women stowaways during the exclusion era and the sexualized performances of "degenerate" female impersonators in turn-of-the-century bars. These associations drove the criminalization of cross-dressing as part of a broader effort to police prostitution through indecency law.

In *Arresting Dress* I have also used trans-ing analysis to bring multiple cross-dressing representations into the framework of study. Legal and popular representations played a crucial role in the operations of cross-dressing laws, displaying offenders under the sign of criminality as public nuisances or fascinating freaks. City newspapers, however, depicted white and Chinese cross-dressing crimes in significantly different terms. Newspapers focused almost exclusively on white cross-dressing crimes, framing offenders as aberrant individuals who strayed from normative gender because of personal failings and flaws. In stark contrast, they represented Chinese cross-dressing as evidence of a pathological culture that threatened the nation. From rare reports on cross-dressing arrests to full-blown investigations of immigration cases, city newspapers framed Chinese cross-dressing in terms of organized prostitution, gang warfare, and systematic deceit. Mobilizing a wealth of discordant representations, cross-dressing laws sharpened lines between white and Chinese San Franciscans and established gender normativity as exclusively white.

Cross-dressing representations also played a crucial role in efforts to mobilize support for federal immigration laws that excluded Chinese migrants from the nation. Animated by multiple cultural anxieties, efforts to pass such laws frequently represented Chinese men as hyperfeminine, deploying the boundary between normative and nonnormative gender to produce and police the racialized borders of the nation-state. Cross-gender narratives worked politically because the stigma of male femininity had already been established, constructed in large part by cross-dressing laws. In turn these narratives deepened societal investments in normative gender as a precondition for national belonging. After all, cross-gender narratives mobilized support for Chinese exclusion by presenting a particular image of Chinese gender consisting of cross-dressing, deception, and an uncontainable national threat. However, feminine men (and masculine women) were not only figments of a reactionary imagination but also actual cultural figures on San Francisco streets. By treating female masculinities and male femininities as inherently contemptible, cross-gender narratives vilified Chinese immigration and demonized nonnormative gender and made these gender identities difficult to occupy. Cross-gender discourses consolidated the normative boundaries produced by cross-dressing laws, operating as a punitive force and an inducement to conform.

By magnifying the visibility of cross-dressing, however, legal and popular representations could have ironic effects, advertising the practices that the law strove to contain. Moreover this visibility could incite cultural fascination with bodies that transgressed gender boundaries, by inviting city audiences to scrutinize cross-dressing in particularly intimate ways. Popular entertainments exploited this fascination, featuring cross-dressing performers in vaudeville, freak shows, and slumming tours. Certainly fascination could perpetuate marginalization by framing cross-dressing as an abnormal spectacle. At the same time, however, it could destabilize such processes by introducing spaces for identification and desire. I have highlighted the circuits of regulation and fascination as the former seeped into voyeurism and the latter incited its own set of controls. Although cross-dressing laws played a central role in producing new definitions of gender marginality, their normalizing effects were never fully complete.

....

As this book has documented, San Francisco's cross-dressing law could have dire consequences for those arrested, including heavy fines, imprisonment, psychiatric institutionalization, and deportation. The law, however, did more than exert intense pressure to conform; it also impelled considerable opposition and resistance. Opportunities for collective opposition were limited, owing in large part to the restrictions on public association that cross-dressing law incited. Nonetheless individual protests abounded, both in spontaneous refusals to bend to police power and in deliberate challenges to the logic of the law.

Some people simply defied government orders, refusing to comply with cross-dressing law even after multiple encounters with the police. In the 1870s, for example, newspapers reported that Jeanne Bonnet had been arrested over twenty times for "wearing male attire." Despite heavy fines and jail time, Bonnet was defiant, declaring to the police court judge, "You may send me to jail as often as you please but you can never make me wear women's clothing again." Two decades later Dick/Mamie Ruble was similarly bold. While most cross-dressing offenders appeared in court wearing gender-"appropriate" clothing, Ruble wore men's clothing, "walked with a swagger up to the witness stand," and claimed the right to wear men's clothing as a person who was "as much a man as a woman."[1] Certainly not all cross-dressing offenders were as vocal as Bonnet and Ruble, and their courtroom protests appear relatively rare. Nonetheless police court proceedings did not deter all cross-dressing offenders; some people laughed while their charges were read, while others were rearrested for the same offense.[2]

Cross-dressing offenders also engaged in spontaneous protests at the moment of arrest. Some people challenged the police's authority by disputing their underlying suspicions of criminal dress. During separate arrests in the early 1900s, both So Git and Charles Merrel informed the police that they were women and hence permitted to wear women's clothing in public.[3] Other cross-dressing arrests triggered physical resistance. When city police attempted to arrest Mabel McCarthy and May Nelson as they left a Barbary Coast saloon in men's clothes, a nearby sailor assaulted the arresting officer because he "thought the police had no right to interfere."[4] Even those who did modify their clothing in public were far from submissive, creating and defending private spaces where they resisted the law's disciplinary work. After her first arrest, Ferdinand Haisch not only continued to wear women's clothing at home but also hosted numerous visitors and fought back when groups of young men harassed her, throwing water, bricks, and wood at those who gathered beneath her window.[5] As such cases demonstrate, cross-dressing laws not only facilitated the regulation of nonnormative gender but also incited considerable opposition.

Cross-dressing law was a local innovation enforced by city officials. By the end of the nineteenth century, however, it crossed paths with federal immigration controls that focused on the port of San Francisco. Immigrants targeted for exclusion resisted state power in multiple ways, including those who engaged in cross-dressing practices. Some people contested the dominant meanings that immigration officials ascribed to their clothing. Wong Ah Choy argued tenaciously with immigration inspectors who viewed his/her clothing as evidence of an organized smuggling ring; produced in the face of considerable pressure, Wong's testimony helped to secure Yow On's release from criminal charges. George Pepper also quarreled forcefully with immigration inspectors, challenging the accusations of insanity that his/her clothing practices had triggered. When officials denied Pepper permission to enter the United States, s/he physically resisted the exclusion order, threatening an immigration inspector with violence and refusing to board the *Ventura* to await deportation.[6] While cross-dressing practices put immigrants at risk of exclusion and deportation, they also facilitated some attempts to evade immigration inspectors, as when Chinese women donned men's clothing to enter the country as stowaways. Engaging in local struggles with federal officials, cross-dressing immigrants challenged their classification as undesirable and refused to accept their fate as spelled out by law.

In addition to defying police power, some people directly challenged the binary gender logic that underwrote cross-dressing law. After all, this law rested on two problematic assumptions: first, that clothing could be easily identified as "belonging" to one of two discrete sexes; second, and more fundamentally, that people could be similarly neatly classified. From the 1860s onward cross-dressing law was challenged on both of these grounds by individuals who claimed ownership of clothing that ostensibly did not "belong" to their sex and by those who asserted self-identification with a sex that ostensibly did not "belong" to their body. These challenges rarely succeeded in establishing the defendant's innocence, but they did succeed in publicly contesting and politicizing the boundaries of normative gender.

The first of these assumptions was challenged by feminist dress reformers who brought court cases that asserted women's right to wear clothing that ostensibly belonged to men. In early May 1866 Eliza DeWolf appeared in the police court with a defense team to challenge her cross-dressing arrest. DeWolf argued that cross-dressing law was invalid because the California State Legislature had not granted the Board of Supervisors the authority to regulate dress, nor was any such power found in common law. Her defense recognized the supervisors' power to regulate indecent behavior, but her clothing, they argued, was "decent and becoming . . . far beyond that usually worn by ladies in this city."[7] The defense also argued that even if cross-dressing law were valid, it would not apply in DeWolf's case because her dress reform clothing was not "male attire" nor worn with the intent to conceal her sex. Indeed, according to the defense, DeWolf's dress had prompted social outcry only because she was instantly recognizable as a woman.[8] Initially found guilty, DeWolf challenged her conviction and won a rare victory against cross-dressing law, with the charges against her eventually dismissed. The case generated a wealth of local publicity and even received cross-country coverage in the *New York Times*.[9]

When DeWolf and other dress reformers challenged their arrests, courtrooms and newspapers became vehicles for public debate on the parameters of cross-dressing law and its applicability to different types of clothing practices. Admittedly these debates could take a conservative turn. DeWolf's defense, for example, rested on the claim that she was a proper woman in decent dress. This defense would have been far less tenable for Barbary Coast denizens such as John Roberts (who was arrested drunk in the dress of a "pretty waiter girl") or Jeanne Bonnet (who befriended prostitutes). It would also have been less plausible if asserted by people arrested for wearing women's clothing. As the *Bulletin* newspaper wryly noted, "If a gentleman had been arrested for walking down Montgomery street in his wife's apparel—although he might have defended its neatness, propriety and convenience with convincing logic—he would have received no sympathy."[10] Similarly the defense's claim that DeWolf's clothing did not disguise her sex had little relevance for those who wore gender-specific clothing to communicate a gender identity that diverged from their legal sex, such as Dick/Mamie Ruble and Ferdinand Haisch. In presenting their case, DeWolf's legal team thus combined a sweeping attack on the validity of cross-dressing law with a conservative dissociation from other offenders who wore clothing that challenged the boundaries of decency or that conflicted with their legal sex.

At the same time, however, DeWolf's case shone a critical spotlight on the instability of cross-dressing law. The law prohibited a person from appearing in public in "a dress not belonging to his or her sex," but the question of whose dress belonged to whom was a social one and open to contestation and change. This imbued cross-dressing law with the flexibility to police a shifting sartorial boundary, but it also made the law inherently unstable, targeting a practice that was never quite fixed. Exploiting the visibility that law conferred, DeWolf's case brought this confusion into public view.

When DeWolf sought an appeals court judge to review her case, she encountered different legal opinions on the validity of the law. In the county court Judge Cowles refused to hear DeWolf's appeal, ruling that the California State Legislature had clearly given the Board of Supervisors the authority to regulate dress when it extended their powers to police all practices that are "against good morals." Cowles ruled that this authority could be found in common law, which made it "a misdemeanor for a woman to appear on the street in male attire . . . because [it] is an act contrary to decency and good morals." The following week, however, Judge Dwinelle of the Fifteenth Circuit agreed to hear the case and interpreted matters very differently, immediately overturning DeWolf's conviction on the grounds that the Board of Supervisors lacked the authority to regulate dress.[11] Judicial disagreement hinged on the perceived relationship between dress and decency. If cross-dressing was judged to be indecent (as in Cowles's ruling), it fell within the city's policing powers; if it was not (as in Dwinelle's ruling), it was beyond the city's reach. In bringing this legal uncertainty into the pages of the city press, DeWolf not only won her own case but also interrupted the smooth, commonsense operations of cross-dressing law.

Judge Dwinelle's ruling did not set a legal precedent, and feminist dress reformers continued to be arrested through at least the century's end. As had DeWolf, some of these arrestees challenged their criminalization and highlighted the confusion that lay at the heart of cross-dressing law. Thirty years after DeWolf's successful appeal, for example, a young, wealthy "society" woman named May Smith appeared in police court following her arrest for wearing men's clothes. Reporters described Smith as "more defiant than demure," as she argued that changing fashions had blurred the lines between men's and women's clothing such that "it was a questionable assumption upon the part of a police judge to decide what was man's and what was woman's dress." The judge rejected Smith's logic and insisted that the line between legal and criminal clothing could be found in the difference between bloomers (legal) and pants (criminal). When pushed to clarify what made a garment bloomers rather than pants, Judge Low stated that bloomers were baggy, pants were tight, and hence the amount of material used in production was crucial. City newspapers mocked Low's efforts to police gender normativity through fabric measurements, jeering that he "did not know exactly how many yards of cloth it takes to keep a woman on the legal side of propriety, but he insisted, nevertheless, that there is a dividing line." Such cases did not lead to the dissolution of cross-dressing law, but they did destabilize its operations by highlighting the instability and incoherence at its core.[12]

The second assumption of cross-dressing law was also challenged in court, in the late nineteenth century and early twentieth, by people who asserted a gender identity that could not be contained by rigid binary sex or gender categories. In 1890 Ruble disrupted the foundational logic of cross-dressing law by asserting, "I am neither a man nor a woman and I've got no sex at all."[13] Similarly in 1903 Milton Matson appeared in police court after his arrest for public cross-dressing and obtaining money under false pretenses. At the time of his arrest, Matson had lived as a man for several decades, and he called for the law to recognize that gender identity could diverge from anatomy. Matson took the stand in court to insist that he was a man, demanding that the state recognize his manhood, even as the police insisted that "the prisoner was a woman."[14] In both cases the judges were unimpressed. Ruble was sent to the state insane asylum indefinitely, and Matson was sentenced to sixty days in the women's jail, where, reporters suggested, wearing women's petticoats would add to his punishment. Even though Ruble and Matson lost in court, they successfully used courtroom and newspaper venues to narrate different gender identities that could not be contained by discrete binary gender categories. Consequently, although cross-dressing law facilitated the regulation of nonnormative gender through constructions of criminality, it also facilitated their public articulation and politicization.

Despite nineteenth-century protests, cross-dressing law persisted, remaining in force for more than one hundred years. San Francisco's Board of Supervisors did not remove the law from the municipal codebook until July 1974, and police continued to make arrests well into that decade. As late as May 1974 city police arrested ten people in the Tenderloin district for wearing women's clothing on bodies the law classified as male. When asked to comment, a police spokesperson stated that such arrests were common: "If I tried to track down every drag arrest that is all I would be doing."[15] By the end of the 1970s, however, cross-dressing law ceased to operate as a central mechanism of exclusion, marking the end of a remarkably durable strategy of gender policing and governance. Histories of the law's twentieth-century enforcement and eventual repeal remain to be written. *Arresting Dress* has laid the conceptual and historical groundwork for those inquiries by documenting the depth and complexity of nineteenth-century investments in normative gender.

Of course, the formal demise of cross-dressing law did not mean that transgender and gender-variant people would be granted full participation in public life, and the law's exclusionary effects continue to reverberate today. Questions of who can lay claim to public space, for example, reemerge in police actions that profile poor transgender women as sex workers and frame homeless queer and transgender youth as public nuisances. Questions of who can successfully lay claim to a gender identity that diverges from legal sex similarly structure multiple transgender and intersex experiences, with particular consequence for those incarcerated in sex-segregated jails, prisons, and immigration detention centers.[16] Policing strategies used in contemporary queer and transgender communities have complex genealogies that extend far beyond the history of cross-dressing laws. Nonetheless San Francisco's cross-dressing law put in motion new presumptions of cross-gender criminality and a gender-normative public that continue to haunt us today.

Introduction

1 "Ad Captandum Vulgas," *Alta*, May 9, 1866; "A Question of Dress," *Evening Bulletin*, May 12, 1866.

2 "A Man in Woman's Attire," *Call*, December 14, 1874; "Jottings about Town," *San Francisco Chronicle*, December 15, 1874.

3 "In Female Attire," *San Francisco Call*, April 16, 1895; "Masqueraded as a Woman," *San Francisco Examiner*, April 16, 1895; "The Female Impersonator," *San Francisco Call*, April 17, 1895.

4 San Francisco Board of Supervisors, *Revised Orders of the City and County of San Francisco*.

5 See Eskridge, *Gaylaw*, 338–41; Eskridge, "Law and the Construction of the Closet."

6 See "California Penal Code Section 185," *Statutes of California* (1873–74), chapter 614, section 15; *New York Laws* (1845), chapter 3, section 6. The absence of federal or state cross-dressing laws is perhaps not surprising, as during the nineteenth century municipal law played a far more central role than federal or even state law in regulating everyday social and sexual life. See Friedman, *A History of American Law*; McDonald, *The Parameters of Urban Fiscal Policy*.

7 See Kennedy and Davis, *Boots of Leather, Slippers of Gold*; Boyd, *Wide-Open Town*; Feinberg, *Stone Butch Blues*; Nestle, *A Restricted Country*; Cain, "Litigating for Lesbian and Gay Rights"; Eskridge, "Challenging the Apartheid of the Closet"; Whisner, "Gender Specific Clothing Regulation"; Silverman and Stryker, *Screaming Queens*; Duberman, *Stonewall*. Although I have not found any specific reference in legal documents to the rule requiring three items of clothing, nineteenth-century cross-dressing laws were still on the books in the 1950s and 1960s, and police appear to have used the rule as an enforcement guideline. See Duberman, *Stonewall*.

8 The legal historian William Eskridge is the only scholar to have published significant information on cross-dressing laws, documenting the wave of local orders that swept the country during the second half of the nineteenth century. See Eskridge, *Gaylaw*, 338–41.

9 For criticism of San Francisco's privileged position in U.S. queer historiography, see Tongson, *Relocations*, 47–49.

10 Feinberg, *Transgender Warriors*; Katz, *Gay American History*; San Francisco Lesbian and Gay History Project, "'She Even Chewed Tobacco'"; Sullivan, *From Female to Male*.

11 For examples of these debates, see Califia, *Sex Changes*; Sullivan, *From Female to Male*. For analysis of these debates, see Boag, "Go West Young Man, Go East Young Woman"; Rand, *The Ellis Island Snow Globe*, 80–92; Boyd, "Bodies in Motion."

12 See Halberstam, *Female Masculinity*; Vicinus, "'They Wonder to Which Sex I Belong.'"

13 For example, see Chauncey, "From Sexual Inversion to Homosexuality"; Halperin, *One Hundred Years of Homosexuality*; Foucault, *The History of Sexuality*; Katz, *The Invention of Heterosexuality*; Weeks, *Sex, Politics, and Society*. For rich primary sources on cross-gender practices and same-sex sexualities in U.S. history, see Katz, *Gay American History* and *Gay/Lesbian Almanac*.

14 Butler, *Gender Trouble*; Garber, *Vested Interests*.

15 For criticism of queer theory's neglect of transgender lives, see Chapman and Du Plessis, "'Don't Call Me *Girl*'"; Namaste, *Invisible Lives*; Prosser, *Second Skins*. For general discussion of the relationship between queer theory and transgender studies, see Prosser, "Transgender"; Stryker, "Transgender Studies"; Stryker, "(De)Subjugated Knowledges."

16 For a comprehensive introduction to transgender studies, see Stryker and Whittle, *The Transgender Studies Reader*. For discussion of scholarship that seeks to queer history, see Sullivan, *A Critical Introduction to Queer Theory*.

17 In identifying trans-ing as a distinct process, I am indebted to conversations with Susan Stryker and to a paper delivered by Joanne Meyerowitz, "A New History of Gender."

18 See Terry and Urla, *Deviant Bodies*.

19 Omi and Winant, *Racial Formation in the United States*; Goldberg, *Racist Culture*; Almaguer, *Racial Faultlines*.

20 For studies that examine the intersections of sexuality, gender, race, nationality, and class in western U.S. history, see Casteñada, "Women of Color and the Rewriting of Western History"; Hurtado, *Intimate Frontiers*; Johnson, *Roaring Camp*; Pérez, *The Decolonial Imaginary*; Sánchez, *Telling Identities*.

21 Leong, *The China Mystique*; Leong, "'A Distinct and Antagonistic Race'"; Shah, *Contagious Divides*. Also see Eng, *Racial Castration*; McClintock, *Imperial Leather*.

22 See Welke, *Law and the Borders of Belonging in the Long Nineteenth Century United States*; Gross, *What Blood Won't Tell*; Pascoe, *What Comes Naturally*; López, *White by Law*.

23 See Mohl, *The New City*; Monkkonen, *America Becomes Urban*; Gluck and Meister, *Cities in Transition*. The first comprehensive zoning law was not passed until

1916, in New York City. However, early technologies of zoning were adopted by local governments, including San Francisco's, from the 1850s onward, operating under the power granted by nuisance law. See Lotchin, *San Francisco*, 11–13.

24 This argument builds upon historical analyses of San Francisco's antiprostitution ordinances as early forms of zoning law, specifically Shumsky and Springer, "San Francisco's Zone of Prostitution"; Ryan, *Women in Public*, 91–92; Lotchin, *San Francisco*, 206–7.

25 See Coombe, "Contingent Articulations"; Sarat and Kearns, "The Cultural Lives of Law"; Moran, Monk, and Beresford, *Legal Queeries*.

26 For this study I collected and analyzed documents from the Bancroft Library, the California Historical Society, the California State Archives, the California State Library, the Gay, Lesbian, Bisexual and Transgender Historical Society of California, the Library of Congress American Memory National Digital Archive, the San Francisco History Center, the San Francisco Public Library Magazines and Newspaper Center, and the San Francisco Public Library Government Center.

27 See Burton, *Dwelling in the Archive*; Derrida, *Archive Fever*; Dirks, "Annals of the Archive"; Foucault, *The Order of Things*; Steedman, *Dust*.

28 Jennifer Terry has similarly noted about derogatory historical accounts of lesbian and gay men, "These sources are ripe for the destabilizing strategies of reading for difference. They constitute the hegemonic discursive field for watching the conflictual interplay between scientists, doctors, police and clergy on the one hand, and deviants on the other" ("Theorizing Deviant Historiography," 59).

29 The unavailability of police court records is made particularly frustrating by references to extensive record-keeping practices. For example, the 1864–65 *Municipal Report* notes that the year's Police Court records amounted to 869 pages, while the 1868–79 *Municipal Report* includes a request from the county clerk for more storage space for the vast amount of court records.

30 For a description of these registers, see San Francisco Board of Supervisors, *General Orders of the Board of Supervisors*, 1866.

31 Arrest statistics contained in *Municipal Reports* do not provide any information about the person arrested or the place of arrest. The absence of demographic data is particularly frustrating, as it is impossible to identify the legal sex of those arrested under cross-dressing laws. In one year, 1867–68, arrests were reported separately for "wearing female attire" and "wearing male attire," and consequently arrestees' legal sex can be inferred: four people were arrested for "wearing female attire" on a body judged to be male and two for "wearing male attire" on a body judged to be female (*Municipal Reports*, 1867–68). In subsequent years, however, arrests were reported for the single offense "wearing attire of other sex," making it impossible to disaggregate by legal sex.

32 I did not locate any evidence of African Americans or Native Americans arrested under San Francisco's cross-dressing law during the nineteenth century. Such

arrests may have occurred, but they are not documented in available historical records.

33 "She Wanted to Be a Man," *San Francisco Examiner*, October 3, 1890.

34 Almaguer, *Racial Faultlines*, 9–12.

35 I use the term *legal sex* to refer to the institutional classification of bodies as male or female on the basis of anatomy. Determination of legal sex was essential for the enforcement of cross-dressing law. Sometimes this classification occurred after a jailhouse medical examination, although it often occurred through police suspicion alone.

Chapter 1. Instant and Peculiar

1 Dornin, *Thirty Years Ago*, 20–21.

2 Issel and Cherney, *San Francisco*.

3 Lotchin, *San Francisco*, xix.

4 Sánchez, *Telling Identities*.

5 Casteñada, "Women of Color and the Rewriting of Western History."

6 For a comprehensive cultural analysis of female masculinities, see Halberstam, *Female Masculinity*. For historical studies of female masculinities, male femininities, and transgender subjectivities during the nineteenth century, see Rand, *The Ellis Island Snow Globe*; Boag, "Go West Young Man, Go East Young Woman"; Romesburg, "Don't Fence Me In."

7 Senkewicz, *Vigilantes in Gold Rush San Francisco*, 33.

8 "The Gold Excitement," *Alta*, April 19, 1849.

9 "Private Lodgings," *Alta*, December 22, 1849.

10 Lotchin, *San Francisco*, 45.

11 George Kent's diary, quoted in Altrocchi, *The Spectacular San Franciscans*, 45; Soulé, Gihon, and Nisbet, *The Annals of San Francisco*, 244.

12 William McCollum, 1850, quoted in Gentry, *The Madams of San Francisco*, 29.

13 Helper, *The Land of Gold*, 37.

14 "Mrs. Farnham," *Alta*, December 14, 1849. See also "A New Adventure," *Alta*, May 24, 1849; Taylor, *California Life Illustrated*, 205–10.

15 Hurtado, *Intimate Frontiers*.

16 Casteñada, "The Political Economy of Nineteenth Century Stereotypes of Californianas."

17 William Bullard to Dear Cousin, quoted in Hurtado, *Intimate Frontiers*, 97.

18 Bancroft, *History of California*, 232n33; Borthwick, *Three Years in California*, 262–63. For an excellent account of men's cross-dressing dance practices in the southern mines, see Johnson, *Roaring Camp*, 172–74.

19 Wilson, "Luzena Stanley Wilson, 49er," 80.

20 Margo, *Taming the Forty-Niner*, 151.

21 Derbec, *A French Journalist in the California Gold Rush*, 168.

22 Soulé, Gihon, and Nisbet, *The Annals of San Francisco*, 248. For a similar description of the city's masquerade balls, see de Russailh, *Last Adventure*, 31.

23 Borthwick, *Three Years in California*, 77.

24 "California Correspondence," *Alta*, July 19, 1849.

25 Boessenecker, *Against the Vigilantes*, 18.

26 Lott, *Love and Theft*; Hudson, "Entertaining Citizenship."

27 Hikozō Hamada later became the first Japanese American naturalized citizen and changed his name to Joseph Heco. His recollections appear in Heco, *The Narrative of a Japanese*; see 2: 93–95 for his account of the masquerade ball. For newspaper coverage of the masquerade ball, see "Something New," *Daily Alta California*, March 18, 1851; "Masquerade Ball," *Daily Alta California*, March 19, 1851; "The Japanese at the Ball," *Daily Alta California*, March 20, 1851. Also see Hsu, "Personality, Race, and Geopolitics in Joseph Heco's Narrative of a Japanese"; Oaks, "Golden Gate Castaway."

28 Bennett, *The Miners' Pioneer Ten Commandments of 1849*.

29 "Humors of the Ball," *San Francisco Examiner*, Inaugural Ball Supplement, January 29, 1895.

30 For a similar argument concerning the cross-dressing practices of elite white men, see Garber, *Vested Interests*, 59–66.

31 Farnham, *California Indoors and Out*, 28.

32 Fairchild, *California Letters of Lucius Fairchild*, cited in Johnson, *Roaring Camp*, 119.

33 *Alta*, July 2, 1849.

34 *Alta*, June 21, 1849.

35 See Almaguer, *Racial Faultlines*.

36 Takaki, *Strangers from a Different Shore*.

37 Richardson, *Beyond the Mississippi*, 390.

38 See Helper, *The Land of Gold*, 53.

39 "Metamorphose Extraordinary," *Alta*, January 21, 1850. Similarly, in 1852 a soon-to-depart sailor was arrested in New York City as a female in men's clothing. When brought into court, the sailor, identified as Lydia Ann Puyfer, stated that "she had stolen her cousin's clothing with the intention of shipping as a seaman, and that she was bound for California." See *New York Daily Tribune*, October 31, 1854, cited in Katz, *Gay American History*, 601n29.

40 "Stranger than Fiction," *San Francisco Chronicle*, January 2, 1880.

41 Richardson, *Beyond the Mississippi*, 200. Richardson provides another account of women dressing as men to live and work in the California gold mines (172).

42 "Stranger than Fiction," *San Francisco Chronicle*, January 2, 1880; "Metamorphose Extraordinary," *Alta*, January 21, 1850.

43 Stephens, *Life Sketches of a Jayhawker of '49*, 65.

44 I am grateful to Jennifer Watts for bringing this photograph and its history to light. See Watts, "From the Photo Archive." See also Johnson, *Roaring Camp*, 175.

45 Bates, *Incidents on Land and Water*, 63. See also Ryan, *Personal Adventures in Upper and Lower California*; Taylor, *Eldorado*.

46 Dame Shirley, *The Shirley Letters from California Mines in 1851–52*, 268.

47 Seacole, *Wonderful Adventures of Mrs. Seacole in Many Lands*, 20. Also see Farnham, *California Indoors and Out*, 297–99. For analysis of Seacole's travel writings, see Mercer, "I Shall Make No Excuse."

48 "Pants," *Alta*, December 14, 1849.

49 See "The Costume of the Day," *Alta*, March 14, 1850; "Boston Notions and Bloomer Fashions," *Alta*, July 7, 1851; "Retrenchment and Reform," *Alta*, July 11, 1851.

50 See Soulé, Gihon, and Nisbet, *The Annals of San Francisco*, 259; Farnham, *California Indoors and Out*, 22–23; Bancroft, *History of California*, 232n35. These descriptions correspond with accounts of female prostitutes in New Orleans who sometimes adopted men's names when they advertised in the city's Blue Book guide to commercial sex services. See Friedman, *Strapped for Cash*, 27n88.

51 "Boston Notions and Bloomer Fashions," *Alta*, July 7, 1851.

52 *Sunday Varieties*, June 8, 1856.

Chapter 2. Against Good Morals

1 See "Usurping the ____," *Bulletin*, November 20, 1857; "Case Dismissed," *Alta*, November 21, 1857. I am grateful to Anne Parsons for pointing me toward this case.

2 My discussion of law and government in early San Francisco draws from Roger W. Lotchin's indispensable book, *San Francisco, 1846–1856: From Hamlet to City*. For a broader analysis of San Francisco's nineteenth-century political history, see Ethington, *The Public City*; Issel and Cherney, *San Francisco*; McDonald, *The Parameters of Urban Fiscal Policy*; Shumsky, *The Evolution of Political Protest and the Workingmen's Party of California*.

3 San Francisco Board of Supervisors, *Revised Orders of the City and County of San Francisco*.

4 Ruling of Judge Cowles, printed in "Eliza A. Hurd DeWolf Released on Habeas Corpus," *California Police Gazette*, August 11, 1866.

5 Soulé, Gihon, and Nisbet, *The Annals of San Francisco*, 259; Farnham, *California Indoors and Out*, 22–23; Bancroft, *History of California*, 232n35.

6 In 1850, for example, a small group of "respectable" churchgoing women evicted a parlor-house madam named Irene McCready from a social event that they had organized. One of the women, Sarah Royce, celebrated her victory, claiming that McCready's lover had "previously boasted that he could introduce 'Irene' anywhere in San Francisco, but the events of that evening proved . . . that while Christian women would forego ease and endure much labor . . . they would not

welcome into friendly association any who trampled upon institutions which lie at the foundation of morality and civilization" (Royce, *A Frontier Lady*, 114).

7 San Francisco Board of Supervisors, *Revised Orders of the City and County of San Francisco*.

8 See San Francisco Board of Supervisors, *Ordinances of the City of San Francisco*; San Francisco Board of Supervisors, *Ordinances and Joint Resolutions of the City of San Francisco*.

9 San Francisco Board of Supervisors, *General Orders of the Board of Supervisors*, 1866, 1869, 1874, 1878, 1884, 1894, 1898.

10 "Enlargement of Society," *Alta*, May 7, 1850; *Pacific News*, October 23, 1850.

11 Almaguer, *Racial Faultlines*. As Almaguer notes, historical processes of racialization took radically different forms for different groups.

12 See Soulé, Gihon, and Nisbet, *The Annals of San Francisco*, 555.

13 For analysis of the racialized gold rush sex work economy, see Barnhart, *The Fair but Frail*; Chan, "The Exclusion of Chinese Women," 75; Hurtado, *Intimate Frontiers*, 87; Johnson, *Roaring Camp*, 76–77; Yung, *Unbound Feet*, 31–32.

14 San Francisco Board of Supervisors, *Ordinances and Joint Resolutions of the City of San Francisco*.

15 "Recorder's Court," *Alta*, April 5, April 7, April 20, 1854; "The Chinese Case," *Alta*, April 26, 1854.

16 For Mary Blane's prosecution, see "Recorder's Court," *Alta*, May 7, May 10, 1854. For the police marshal's instructions to the Board of Supervisors, see "Common Council," *Alta*, June 13, 1854. For subsequent cases that followed a similar pattern, see "Law Report," *Alta*, December 21, 1854; "Arrest of Females," *Alta*, November 24, 1855; "Recorder's Court," *Alta*, November 28, 1855; "Equality of Punishment in San Francisco," *Alta*, November 29, 1855; "A New Dodge," *Alta*, December 10, 1855.

17 For discussion of these shifts in San Francisco's gender demographics, see Ethington, *The Public City*, 47. For similar transformations in the southern mines, see Johnson, *Roaring Camp*, 279–80.

18 "Home Influence—Ladies in California," *Alta*, January 13, 1853; "Influx of Females," *Alta*, June 27, 1851.

19 See Mohl, *The New City*, 27; Gluck and Meister, *Cities in Transition*; Lotchin, *San Francisco*, 16–17.

20 Lotchin, *San Francisco*, 206, 256–57.

21 "Report of the Special and Judiciary Committee, upon Houses of Ill Fame," *Alta*, November 27, 1855; "Disreputable Houses," *Bulletin*, November 26, 1855; "Nuisances," *Alta*, September 11, 1855; "Houses of Infamy on Clay Street," *Bulletin*, January 16, 1856.

22 See "City Reforms," *Alta*, March 31, 1854; "Disgraceful Nuisances," *Alta*, June 1, 1855; "The Report of the Grand Jury," *Bulletin*, December 2, 1856; "Last Session of the Recorder's Court," *Alta*, July 2, 1855.

23 For example, see "A Letter from the Mines" and "The Eastern Press and Califor-
     nia Politics," *Alta*, August 31, 1849.

24 Geary's inaugural address, 1849, reprinted in Soulé, Gihon, and Nisbet, *The An-
     nals of San Francisco*, 230.

25 "San Francisco—Her Prospects," *Alta*, February 1, 1849.

26 Vigilance Committee of San Francisco, *Proclamation of the Vigilance Committee
     of San Francisco*.

27 For general analysis of San Francisco's 1856 Vigilance Committee, see Senke-
     wicz, *Vigilantes in Gold Rush San Francisco*; Ethington, *The Public City*, 86–169;
     Ethington, "Vigilantes and the Police." For a specific focus on gender and San
     Francisco's Vigilance Committee, see Jolly, "The Price of Vigilance"; Jolly, "Sex,
     Vigilantism and San Francisco in 1856"; Ryan, *Women in Public*, 104–7; Ryan,
     Civic Wars; Lotchin, *San Francisco*, 245–75. For broader discussions of vigi-
     lante justice in the United States, see Friedman, *A History of American Law*, 367;
     Adrian and Griffith, *A History of American City Government*.

28 Ethington, *The Public City*, 81–83.

29 Senkewicz, *Vigilantes in Gold Rush San Francisco*, 33.

30 "Hang Billy Mulligan," *Bulletin*, November 22, 1855; "To the Vigilance Commit-
     tee," *Bulletin*, May 26, 1856; "Another Word for This Belle Cora," *Bulletin*, May 29,
     1856; "A Word to Those Who Stare at Ladies," *Bulletin*, May 24, 1856. For detailed
     analysis of these letters to the press, see Jolly, "The Price of Vigilance."

31 "Opening of the Second Seal," *Alta*, June 15, 1856. Also see "Banner Presentation—
     The Vigilance Committee Endorsed by the Ladies," *Alta*, July 19, 1856; "Events of
     Yesterday," *Alta*, August 19, August 22, 1856.

32 "A Woman on the Crisis," *Bulletin*, May 19, 1856; "Women in the Crisis No. 4,"
     Alta, June 19, 1856. These articles are referenced in Ryan, *Women in Public*, 72.

33 "To the Proprietors of the Evening Bulletin," *Bulletin*, May 15, 1856; "Citizens of
     San Francisco," *Bulletin*, May 15, 1856; "An Appeal to the Citizens of San Fran-
     cisco," *Bulletin*, May 20, 1856; *Bulletin*, editorial, October 13, 1855; "Federal Office
     Holders in San Francisco," *Bulletin*, February 12, 1856; "Murder, Gambling, Etc,"
     Bulletin, November 19, 1856; "Theatres and Ladies," *Bulletin*, November 21,
     1855. For additional associations between the Vigilantes and normative mas-
     culinity, see "The Cora Jury," *Bulletin*, January 4, 1856; "Woman in the Crisis,"
     Alta, June 8, 1856; *Bulletin*, editorial, October 13, 1855; "Justice," *Bulletin*, May
     15, 1856; "California—San Francisco—Their Condition—The Remedy," *Bul-
     letin*, April 16, 1856.

34 See Ethington, *The Public City*, 153, 159; "From Alfred Clarke to Executive Com-
     mittee, May 17, 1856," Files of the Vigilantes Investigative Committee, Records
     of the San Francisco Committee of Vigilance 1856, Box 2, Huntington Library,
     San Marino, California. Also see "Thomas Maguire, June 28, 1856," "Charles Wal-
     deier, June 9, 1856," and "Character of Judge Murray, from Mr. Dempster, July 28,

1856," Records of the San Francisco Committee of Vigilance 1856. The Vigilantes also investigated people for various sexual improprieties, including seduction, indecency, and operating a dance house. See files of Calico Pete, Isaiah Merritt, Tom Malloy and Sophia McInnes, Jack Story, John L. Colby, Edward Nouville, Louis Newman, and W. Willis, Records of the San Francisco Committee of Vigilance 1856.

35 Jolly, "The Price of Vigilance," 547; "Dame Partington in California," *California Lettersheets from the Robert B. Honeyman Jr. Collection of Early Californian and Western American Pictorial Material*, Bancroft Library, University of California, Berkeley. For newspaper approval of this caricature, see "Dame Partington in California," *Alta*, June 19, 1856. For newspaper accounts of unmanly opponents, see "Where Will It End?," *Alta*, June 13, 1856.

36 The People's Party championed an "antiparty" ideology that sought to keep local politics separate from state and national affairs. This ideology became increasingly untenable after the Civil War, marking the People's Party demise. Historians debate the exact duration of the People's Party rule. Philip Ethington, for example, claims its direct rule ended at the close of the Civil War, but Terrence McDonald argues that it continued to operate under different names (the Union Party and the Taxpayer's Party) until 1873. See Ethington, *The Public City*, 167; McDonald, *The Parameters of Urban Fiscal Policy*, 92.

37 Decker, *Fortunes and Failures*.

Chapter 3. Problem Bodies, Public Space

1 Asbury, *The Barbary Coast*, 254–55.

2 Most years between 1865 and 1900 witnessed at least one cross-dressing arrest, and some witnessed considerably more; there were seventeen in 1878–79 and twelve in 1898–99. Across the same thirty-five-year period police made fewer arrests for lewd acts (n = 29), indecent exhibitions (n = 68), and sodomy (n = 96), but arrest for using vulgar language was a daily occurrence, with nearly twenty thousand recorded. See San Francisco Board of Supervisors, *Municipal Reports*, 1865–1900.

3 "Ad Captandum Vulgas," *Alta*, May 9, 1866.

4 For analysis of the gender and sexual politics of spiritualism, see McGarry, "Spectral Sexualities." For DeWolf's personal account of adopting dress reform clothing in the early 1850s on her way to gold rush California, see "The DeWolf Lecture," *California Police Gazette*, May 26, 1866, 2.

5 "Disguised in Male Apparel," *Daily Alta California*, March 9, 1869; "Chinese Love and Elopement," *San Francisco Chronicle*, March 9, 1869; "Police Court," *San Francisco Chronicle*, March 10, 1869. I discuss newspaper coverage of this case in chapter 4.

6 Beginning in the mid-1870s the San Francisco Board of Supervisors passed a series of orders, known as "dive laws," to restrict women's presence in bars. These prohibited women from being in bars at night (between 6 p.m. and 6 a.m.) and from working in bars at any time, targeting working-class women. By limiting the recreational spaces that women could occupy, dive laws sought to disrupt an alleged relationship between barroom heterosociality, indecency, and crime, in which women's bodies attracted men in search of commercial sex, who then fell victim to petty thefts. See San Francisco Board of Supervisors, *General Orders of the Board of Supervisors*, 1875; "In the Matter of Mary Maguire," *California Reports* 57 (January 1881): 604–12.

7 For a report on young women dressing as men to do the town, see "San Francisco Women," *California Police Gazette*, May 12, 1866, 2. For a report of Nellie and Lizzie Brown's arrest, see "In the Garb of Jeanne Bonnet," *Call*, September 18, 1876, press clipping from the Edward Byram Scrapbooks, vol. 4, California Historical Society. I am grateful to Estelle Freedman for directing me to these scrapbooks. The San Francisco luminary Lily Hitchcock Coit was also rumored to dress as a man for a night on the town during this period. See Longstreet, *The Wilder Shore*, 233; Beebe and Clegg, *San Francisco's Golden Era*, 236.

8 See "Masqueraded as a Woman," *San Francisco Examiner*, April 16, 1895; "In Female Attire," *San Francisco Call*, April 16, 1895; "The Female Impersonator," *San Francisco Call*, April 17, 1895.

9 Although strangers and distant acquaintances sometimes related to Bonnet as a man, her closest friends referred to her as a woman, and I follow their lead throughout this book.

10 "The Last Tragedy," *San Francisco Chronicle*, September 17, 1876; "Tired of Women's Clothing," *Call*, July 11, 1876, press clipping from Edward Byram Scrapbooks, vol. 4, California Historical Society. For further discussion of the Bonnet case, see San Francisco Lesbian and Gay History Project, " 'She Even Chewed Tobacco.' "

11 "Two Women in Male Attire," *San Francisco Examiner*, May 24, 1903; "Comic Opera Does Not Convince the Police," *San Francisco Examiner*, May 25, 1903. Dubia and Dessar were not the only cross-dressing women who received lenient treatment following a slumming tour arrest. Also see "Jailed through Cashing Check," *San Francisco Call*, April 4, 1905; "A School Girls Lark Winds Up in Prison," *San Francisco Chronicle*, August 2, 1909; "Pretty Girl Repents of Midnight Escapade," *San Francisco Chronicle*, August 3, 1909; "Pretty Masqueraders in Very Penitent Mood," *San Francisco Chronicle*, March 24, 1910. I discuss slumming tours in more detail in chapter 5.

12 "Too Funny by Half," *San Francisco Call*, December 23, 1890; "Masquerading in Woman's Attire," *Bulletin*, December 22, 1890; "What He Got for Wearing Women's Clothes," *Bulletin*, December 23, 1890; "Freak of Verdant Youth," *San Francisco Chronicle*, December 23, 1890; "Bent on No Good Purpose," *San Fran-*

cisco Call, December 24, 1890; "Six Months for Masquerading," *San Francisco Examiner*, December 24, 1890.

13 For Sullivan and McCarthy's case, see "Girl Maskers Are Severely Lectured," *San Francisco Call*, March 24, 1910; "Pretty Masqueraders in Very Penitent Mood," *San Francisco Chronicle*, March 24, 1910. For Salas's case, see "Judge Lets Trousered Wife Go," *San Francisco Call*, November 22, 1913; "Arrest Yacht Owner's Wife Discovered Dressed as Man," *San Francisco Chronicle*, November 22, 1913.

14 See Ryan, *Women in Public*, 59–62; Schweik, *The Ugly Laws*, 25.

15 See "An Act to Confer Further Powers upon the Board of Supervisors of the City and County of San Francisco," *Statutes of California*, 1863, 540. For further discussion of San Francisco's use of nuisance law in the nineteenth century, see Shah, *Contagious Divides*, 45–76.

16 "Nuisances under the Plea of Charity," *Daily Evening Bulletin*, April 9, 1863.

17 Schweik, *The Ugly Laws*, 17, 163.

18 *People v. Hall* 4 Cal. 399 (1854), quoted in Almaguer, *Racial Faultlines*, 162.

19 For analysis of anti-Chinese politics in the nineteenth century, see McClain, *In Search of Equality*; Saxton, *The Indispensable Enemy*; Shah, *Contagious Divides*; Takaki, *Strangers from a Different Shore*, 79–131; Yung, *Unbound Feet*, 21–24.

20 For analysis of the WPC, see Shumsky, *The Evolution of Political Protest and the Workingmen's Party of California*.

21 Merry, "Spatial Governmentality and the New Urban Social Order."

22 San Francisco Board of Supervisors, *Revised Orders of the City and County of San Francisco*, italics mine; San Francisco Board of Supervisors, *General Orders of the Board of Supervisors*, 1869, 1872. For a detailed analysis of laws that prohibited "diseased, maimed or mutilated" people from appearing in public, see Schweik, *The Ugly Laws*.

23 Shumsky and Springer, "San Francisco's Zone of Prostitution."

24 San Francisco Board of Supervisors, *General Orders of the Board of Supervisors*, 1890, 1892, 1898; "To Remove an Evil," *Call*, January 29, 1898; "Berry Place to Be Cleared of Shame," *Call*, August 28, 1898; "Barbary Coast Harpies Seek to Settle among Homes of Pacific Heights," *Call*, September 15, 1906; "Biggy Marks Deadline for Tenderloin Women," *Call*, January 12, 1908. Also see "Closing of Bacon Place," *Call*, November 26, 1898. See Shumsky and Springer, "San Francisco's Zone of Prostitution."

25 San Francisco Board of Supervisors, *Municipal Reports*, 1865–66.

26 See Yung, *Unbound Feet*, 31–32; Chan, "The Exclusion of Chinese Women," 75; San Francisco Board of Supervisors, *General Orders of the Board of Supervisors*, 1866; San Francisco Board of Supervisors, *Municipal Reports*, 1865–66; "The Chinese Prostitutes," *San Francisco Examiner*, May 30, 1866.

27 "Board of Assistant Alderman," *Daily Alta California*, August 22, 1854; Committee of the Senate of the State of California, *The Social, Moral and Political Effect of*

Chinese Immigration, 45; San Francisco Board of Health, "The Board of Health," 6. For a detailed analysis of these efforts, see Shah, *Contagious Divides*, 45–76.

28 For excellent historical examples of these intersections, see Alexander, *Pedagogies of Crossing*; Craddock, *City of Plagues*; McClintock, *Imperial Leather*; Shah, *Contagious Divides*; Somerville, *Queering the Color Line*; Stern, *Eugenic Nation*.

29 Friedman, *A History of American Law*, 585. For similar analysis of San Francisco's prostitution laws as a form of urban zoning, see Ryan, *Women in Public*, 91–92; Shumsky and Springer, "San Francisco's Zone of Prostitution"; Lotchin, *San Francisco*, 206–7.

30 "Crazy on Female Attire," *Call*, July 3, 1895; Jenny O. quoted in Hirschfeld, *Transvestites*, 84.

31 For newspaper reports on John Wilson's jail sentence, see "The Police Court," *San Francisco Chronicle*, September 27, 1878. For Bonnet's fines and jail sentences, see "The Police Court," *Call*, May 16, 1874; "Police Intelligence," *Bulletin*, December 16, 1875; and *Call*, May 12, 1876, press clippings compiled in the Edward Byram Scrapbooks, vol. 4, California Historical Society. Also see "The Last Tragedy," *San Francisco Chronicle*, September 17, 1876. For Livernash's sentence, see "Editor Livernash's Lark," *San Francisco Chronicle*, October 3, 1891. For Matson's sentence, see "Masquerading Woman Is Brought to Time," *Call*, November 28, 1903. For Portel's sentence, see "Six Months for Masquerading," *San Francisco Examiner*, December 24, 1890; "What He Got for Wearing Women's Clothes," *Daily Evening Bulletin*, December 23, 1890; "Bent on No Good Purpose," *San Francisco Call*, December 24, 1890.

32 See "A Man in Woman's Attire," *Call*, December 14, 1874; "Louisa Matson Fails to Move Judge Mogan," *Call*, November 29, 1903.

33 California's commitment rate soared between 1870 and 1920, surpassing that of every state in the nation. Indefinite detention was standard practice, and asylums primarily served a custodial rather than therapeutic function. For an excellent history of California's insane asylums, see Fox, *So Far Disordered in Mind*.

34 For Ruble's insane asylum commitment and death, see Stockton State Hospital Commitment Registers, 10: 138, and Stockton State Hospital Register of Deaths, 1862–1921, 350. S/he appears in these records under the name Nicolina Ruble. For newspaper coverage of Ruble's courtroom appearance and insanity hearing, see "To the Asylum," *Evening Post*, October 4, 1890; "Dressed as a Man," *Evening Post*, October 2, 1890; "She Wanted to Be a Man," *San Francisco Examiner*, October 3, 1890; "She Denied Her Sex," *San Francisco Chronicle*, October 3, 1890; "A Strange Delusion," *Evening Bulletin*, October 2, 1890; "In Male Attire," *Morning Call*, October 3, 1890; "She Wanted to Be a Man," *Morning Call*, October 5, 1890; "Court Notes," *San Francisco Chronicle*, October 5, 1890.

35 For Maria Rogers's insanity hearing, see "Mrs. Rogers Dismissed," *San Francisco Call*, May 27, 1891; "She Followed Him," *San Francisco Chronicle*, May 26,

1891. For the outcome of insanity hearings in 1891, see Fox, *So Far Disordered in Mind*, 48. For Henry Pohlmann's commitment, see Stockton State Hospital Commitment Registers, 10: 683. For Sophie Lederer's commitment and death, see Stockton State Hospital Commitment Registers, 13: 15, and Stockton State Hospital Register of Deaths, 1862–1921, 348. Also see "Odd Fish of the Public Law Library," *San Francisco Chronicle*, June 14, 1903, describing an unnamed "German inventor" who was locked up in the state insane asylum after wearing women's clothing in public. As early as 1877 at least some doctors identified cross-dressing as a psychiatric disorder, proposing the term *gynomania* to "refer to the passion that some young people have for the dress and manner of the opposite sex." According to these doctors, gynomania was comparable to kleptomania and required psychiatric treatment rather than legal punishment. See "Gynomania and Other Manias," *Scientific American* 36, no. 3 (1877): 41.

36 This argument builds on the work of Mary Ryan, who mapped the gender contours of public space in nineteenth-century San Francisco, finding the city to be "crisscrossed with real and imaginary gender boundaries: the categories of proper and improper womanhood, the segregated territories of the ladies, the places for polite heterosociality, and the spatial restrictions on prostitution" (*Women in Public*, 92). I bring another set of gender boundaries into dialogue with those articulated by Ryan: the boundaries between normative and nonnormative gender in relation to the boundaries between public and private space.

37 Habermas, *The Structural Transformation of the Public Sphere*; Fraser, "Rethinking the Public Sphere." For further discussion of the concept of the public sphere, see Negt and Kuge, *Public Sphere and Experience*; Black Public Sphere Collective, *The Black Public Sphere*.

Chapter 4. A Sight Well Worth Gazing Upon

1 The photographs of Jenny O. appear in an illustrated supplement to Hirschfeld's text. See Hirschfeld and Tilke, *Der erotische Verkleidungstrieb (Die Transvestiten), illustrierter Teil*. The illustrated supplement is rare, and I am extremely grateful to Gerard Koskovich for granting me access. For an English translation of Hirschfeld's book, without the accompanying illustrations, see Hirschfeld, *Transvestites*.

2 For example, see arrests of Mary Jones in "Caution to Truant Husbands and Suspicious Wives," *Daily Alta California*, January 23, 1869; William Thomas in "A Jolly Joker," *Daily Alta California*, September 21, 1874; Mamie Baldwin in "Masquerading in Men's Attire," *San Francisco Call*, July 7, 1896; Jennie Wallace in "Out for a Lark," *San Francisco Call*, September 27, 1898.

3 "A Man in Woman's Attire," *Call*, December 14, 1874; "Jottings about Town," *San Francisco Chronicle*, December 15, 1874; "In Female Dress," *Daily Alta California*, December 14, 1874.

4 For reports on Ruble's arrest, see "In Male Attire," *Morning Call*, October 3, 1890; "Dressed as a Man," *Evening Post*, October 2, 1890. For Baldwin's arrest, see "Masquerading in Men's Attire," *San Francisco Call*, July 7, 1896.

5 "In the Garb of Jeanne Bonnet," *Call*, September 18, 1876, press clipping from the Edward Byram Scrapbooks, vol. 4, California Historical Society.

6 For police surveillance of Haisch, see "Masqueraded as a Woman," *San Francisco Examiner*, April 16, 1895; "Wore Female Attire," *San Francisco Chronicle*, April 16, 1895. For reports of police removing suspects' veils and wigs, see arrest of John Roberts in "A Man in Woman's Attire," *Call*, December 14, 1874; "Masquerades in Wife's Dress and Is Jailed," *San Francisco Call*, December 11, 1909.

7 For Ruble's medical exam, see "She Denied Her Sex," *San Francisco Chronicle*, October 3, 1890. For Castle, see "Carries with Her Proof of Sex," *San Francisco Chronicle*, July 22, 1909; "Queer Attire Compels Woman to Prove Sex," *San Francisco Chronicle*, July 23, 1909; "Clever with Fists Is 'Miss Castle' of Boston's Elect," *San Francisco Call*, July 23, 1909. For additional examples of San Francisco police using medical exams to determine a suspect's sex, see the case of Andrew Salverson in "A Queer Freak," *Daily Alta California*, July 8, 1888; "He Wore Corsets," *San Francisco Chronicle*, July 8, 1888.

8 For Dick/Mamie Ruble's arrest, see "A Strange Delusion," *Evening Bulletin*, October 2, 1890; "She Wanted to Be a Man," *San Francisco Examiner*, October 3, 1890. For May Smith's arrest, see "Her Bifurcates Too Scant," *San Francisco Chronicle*, September 7, 1895.

9 "Disguised in Male Apparel," *Daily Alta California*, March 9, 1869; "Police Court Items," *Daily Alta California*, March 10, 1869; "Disguised Chinese May Be Tong's Lure," *San Francisco Call*, July 24, 1908; "Chinese Arrested in Female Dress," *San Francisco Examiner*, July 23, 1908; "Masquerading Boy Stirs Up Chinese," *San Francisco Examiner*, July 24, 1908.

10 For newspaper calls for cross-dressing arrests, see "Ad Captandum Vulgas," *Alta*, May 9, 1866; "Why Is This Thus?," *Call*, December 5, 1873. For newspapers mistakenly describing a man as a cross-dressing woman, see "The Park Girl a Boy," *San Francisco Chronicle*, April 4, 1895.

11 For Bert Larose's arrest and prosecution, see "Will Wear Stripes," *San Francisco Chronicle*, September 2, 1894; "A Queer Young Man," *San Francisco Chronicle*, August 4, 1894; "Hugged by a Boy," *Morning Call*, August 3, 1894. For additional newspaper stories of people who failed to detect cross-dressing practices, see "Irene Wore His Clothes," *San Francisco Examiner*, July 28, 1897; "Will Again Don Woman's Garb," *San Francisco Examiner*, January 30, 1895.

12 For Roberts's jailhouse disrobing, see "A Man in Woman's Attire," *Daily Morning Call*, December 14, 1874. For Stallcup, see "Sorority Girl Dons Trousers and Is Jailed," *San Francisco Call*, August 2, 1909.

13　Most histories of crime photography begin with the work of Alphonse Bertillon, the Parisian police officer who invented a standardized system of physical measurement and mug-shot photography to identify repeat offenders in the 1870s. However, Lees's personal rogues' gallery predates this by some fifteen years and is believed to be the earliest collection of crime photography in the United States. The collection was apparently sold to a private collector for $6,000 when he died. See "Biographical Note," Lees Family Papers, 1851–1948, Bancroft Library, University of California, Berkeley.

14　For Larose's prison photographs, see Department of Corrections San Quentin Prison, Inmate Photographs, no. 15950-16201, California State Archives. For San Francisco Police Department photograph collections that remain accessible to the public, see the Criminal Descriptions File, 1890–1902, San Francisco History Center, San Francisco Public Library; Police Criminal Photos, 1897–98, San Francisco History Center, San Francisco Public Library; Jesse Brown Cook Scrapbooks Documenting San Francisco History and Law Enforcement, Bancroft Library, University of California, Berkeley; Criminal Photographs: Photograph Album, 1875–1915, California History Room, California State Library.

15　Jesse Brown Cook Scrapbooks, vol. 4, Unit ID 184. This collection also contains two photographs of Ernest Long, arrested in San Francisco in 1922 for "impersonating a woman." Cook's caption notes that Long is a "chief engineer on the steamship Rose City" but provides no other detail about the arrest. See Jesse Brown Cook Scrapbooks, vol. 12, Unit ID 161a and 161b. For a detailed discussion of Portica's photograph, see Edwards, "Archives of Uncertainty."

16　Mark Twain, "San Francisco Letter, December 29, 1865. The Black Hole of San Francisco. Printed in Territorial Enterprise, January 1866," in Taper, Mark Twain's San Francisco, 171–73. Twain presumably based his comments on his experiences working as a police court reporter for the Daily Morning Call between 1863 and 1864.

17　Established by the 1856 Consolidation Act, the police court had jurisdiction over vagrancy, petit larceny (less than $50 stolen), misdemeanors punishable by six months or less, and all violations of city and county ordinances. See San Francisco Board of Supervisors, The Consolidation Act.

18　For cases processed on the same day as Roberts's, see "Before His Honor," Call, December 15, 1874. For Stallcup's hearing in the judge's chambers, see "Saved from Facing Crowd in Courtroom," San Francisco Call, August 3, 1909; "Pretty Girl Repents of Midnight Escapade," San Francisco Chronicle, August 3, 1909.

19　"The Police Court," San Francisco Chronicle, September 27, 1878.

20　For a description of Livernash's arrest and the accompanying artist's sketch, see "In Female Attire," San Francisco Chronicle, September 27, 1891.

21　For a description and artist's sketch of Mamie Baldwin's courtroom appearance, see "Masquerading in Men's Attire," San Francisco Call, July 7, 1896; "Carried the New Woman Fad Too Far," *San Francisco Chronicle*, July 7, 1896. For Judge Campbell's ruling, see "Mamie Not on Mischief Bent," *San Francisco Call*, July 9, 1896; "City News in Brief," *San Francisco Call*, July 9, 1896.

22 City newspapers occasionally reported on arrests that are not reflected in official statistics, indicating that the total number of nineteenth-century cross-dressing arrests exceeded one hundred.

23 Geraldine Portica's 1917 arrest was documented in a police photograph. See Jesse Brown Cook Scrapbooks, vol. 4, Unit ID 184. So Git's San Francisco arrest was referenced in a subsequent newspaper report when he was arrested in Oakland the following year. See "Masquerading Boy Stirs Up Chinese," *San Francisco Examiner*, July 24, 1908.

24 "Disguised in Male Apparel," *Daily Alta California*, March 9, 1869; "Chinese Love and Elopement," *San Francisco Chronicle*, March 9, 1869; "Police Court," *San Francisco Chronicle*, March 10, 1869.

25 Lei, "The Production and Consumption of Chinese Theater in Nineteenth-Century California," 298.

26 For So Git's courtroom appearance, see "Chinese Arrested in Woman's Dress," *San Francisco Call*, July 23, 1908; "Chinese Arrested in Female Dress," *San Francisco Examiner*, July 23, 1908.

27 "Chinese Arrested in Woman's Dress," *San Francisco Call*, July 23, 1908; "Chinese Arrested in Female Dress," *San Francisco Examiner*, July 23, 1908; "Disguised Chinese May Be Tong's Lure," *San Francisco Call*, July 24, 1908; "Masquerading Boy Stirs Up Chinese," *San Francisco Examiner*, July 24, 1908.

28 "The Female in Pantaloons Case," *Alta*, May 13, 1866; "Bloomerism," *Bulletin*, August 23, 1866.

Chapter 5. Indecent Exhibitions

1 Although there were important differences between vaudeville, freak shows, and slumming tours, they were all components of the new mass entertainment industry that developed in the United States during the mid-nineteenth century, with similar roots in the technological, demographic, and economic changes that led to an unprecedented rise in leisure time among working-class and middle-class city residents. See Adams, *Sideshow USA*; Peiss, *Cheap Amusements*. In turn these entertainment venues were part of a broader institutional culture of display that also encompassed the ostensibly educational sites of the medical museum and world's fair.

2 See Senelick, "Boys and Girls Together"; Hamilton, "'I'm the Queen of Bitches'"; Stryker and Van Buskirk, *Gay by the Bay*; Ullman, *Sex Seen*.

3 Stephen C. Massett Concert Program, reproduced in Soulé, Gihon, and Nisbet, *The Annals of San Francisco*, 656.

4 For analysis of Lingard's performances, see Durden, "Not Just a Leg Show." For a review of Ella Wesner's San Francisco debut, see *San Francisco Figaro*, August 9, 1871.

5 "A Real 'Johnnie' for New Yorkers," *San Francisco Examiner*, October 10, 1897.

6 "Death of Omar Kingsley," *San Francisco Chronicle*, May 19, 1879.

7 "Lew Sully, Alice Lloyd's Double," *San Francisco Chronicle*, January 15, 1911.

8 See Jesse Brown Cook Scrapbooks Documenting San Francisco History and Law Enforcement, vols. 4, 12, and 25, Bancroft Library, University of California, Berkeley. These scrapbooks contain police photographs of two people arrested under cross-dressing law in San Francisco: Geraldine Portica, arrested in 1917, and Ernest Long, arrested in 1922. They also include four Los Angeles Police Department photographs of cross-dressing arrests from 1927.

9 Hamilton, "'I'm the Queen of Bitches,'" 109–11; Toll, *On with the Show!*, 243–45.

10 See "A Real 'Johnnie' for New Yorkers," *San Francisco Examiner*, October 10, 1897; Hamilton, "'I'm the Queen of Bitches,'" 115–17; Ullman, *Sex Seen*, especially chapter 3.

11 Senelick, "Lady and the Tramp," 33; Boyd, *Wide-Open Town*, 25–26; Hamilton, "'I'm the Queen of Bitches,'" 113–18.

12 For descriptions of San Francisco's freak shows and dime museums, see "A Shocking Exhibition," *Call*, December 17, 1873; "Visit Dr. Jordan's Great Museum of Anatomy," *Call*, September 11, 1902; Asbury, *The Barbary Coast*; Cowan, *Forgotten Characters of Old San Francisco*. For analysis of East Coast institutions, see Dennett, *Weird and Wonderful*; McNamara, "'A Congress of Wonders'"; Bogdan, *Freak Show*.

13 As with the local nuisance laws that criminalized multiple problem bodies, there were important differences between freak-show characters and the power struggles they dramatized. Nonetheless I bring them together here—as they were brought together under the dime museum roof—to foreground the preoccupations with race, disease, and nation that contextualized freak-show performances of cross-dressing. For descriptions of exhibits at the Pacific Museum of Anatomy and Sciences, see Jordan, *Handbook of the Pacific Museum of Anatomy and Science*; Berglund, *Making San Francisco American*, 80–94; Asbury, *The Barbary Coast*, 47–48. For analysis of racialized freak-show performances, see Cook, "Of Men, Missing Links, and Nondescripts"; Fausto-Sterling, "Gender, Race, and Nation"; Lindfors, "Ethnological Show Business." For analysis of the Jefferson Davis exhibit, see Silber, "Intemperate Men, Spiteful Women, and Jefferson Davis." Thanks to Susan Stryker for pointing me to this reference.

14 For newspaper coverage of Matson's case, see "Posed as Her Brother," *San Francisco Chronicle*, January 27, 1895; "A Secret for Years," *Call*, January 27, 1895; "Louisa Has Her Say," *Call*, January 28, 1895; "Her Betrothed Is a Woman," *San Francisco Examiner*, January 28, 1895; "The Woman in Man's Clothes," *San*

Francisco Examiner, January 29, 1895; "Denies the Impeachment," *Call*, January 29, 1895; "Will Again Don Woman's Garb," *San Francisco Examiner*, January 30, 1895; "Has No Love for Petticoats," *San Francisco Examiner*, February 7, 1895; "She Has Been a Man of the World for over Twenty-Six Years," *San Francisco Examiner*, February 10, 1895. In addition to substantial coverage in the San Francisco press, Los Angeles newspapers also reported on Matson's case. See "Flashes from the Wires," *Los Angeles Times*, February 6, 1895.

15 "Louisa Has Her Say," *Call*, January 28, 1895; "Will Again Don Woman's Garb," *San Francisco Examiner*, January 30, 1895; "Miss Matson May Be a Freak," *San Francisco Chronicle*, February 6, 1895; "Miss Matson Goes Cityward," *San Francisco Examiner*, February 6, 1895; "Has No Love for Petticoats," *San Francisco Examiner*, February 7, 1895; "Louisa Matson's Double Sued," *Call*, February 15, 1895; "News from All Parts of the Slope," *San Francisco Chronicle*, September 2, 1895.

16 "A Secret for Years," *Call*, January 27, 1895; "Her Betrothed Is a Woman," *San Francisco Examiner*, January 28, 1895; "Louisa Has Her Say," *Call*, January 28, 1895; "Has No Love for Petticoats," *San Francisco Examiner*, February 7, 1895.

17 A similar tension has been noted by Eric Fretz, who argues that the simultaneous rise of the freak show (which displayed aberrant bodies) and the penitentiary and asylum (which hid them from view) "illustrates one of the paradoxes of the tension-filled nineteenth century" ("P. T. Barnum's Theatrical Selfhood and the Nineteenth-Century Culture of Exhibition," 102).

18 For coverage of Bertha Stanley's freak-show performance, see "Madame Stanley," *Call*, June 11, 1888; "Bertha Stanley," *Call*, June 12, 1888; "Big Bertha," *Call*, June 14, 1888; Criminal Descriptions File, 1890–1902, San Francisco History Center, San Francisco Public Library; Asbury, *The Barbary Coast*, 133–37; Longstreet, *The Wilder Shore*, 138–39. For details on Matson's freak-show contract, see "She Has Been a Man of the World for over Twenty-Six Years," *San Francisco Examiner*, February 10, 1895.

19 For analysis of the cultural process of producing freaks, see Thomson, *Extraordinary Bodies*; Hevey, *The Creatures Time Forgot*, 53; Thomson, *Freakery*, 4–10; Bogdan, *Freak Show*, 225–26.

20 Archibald Clavering Gunter and Fergus Redmond, *A Florida Enchantment: A Novel* (New York: Hurst, 1891). My discussion of this novel draws upon and extends the earlier analysis by Somerville, *Queering the Color Line*.

21 "Fashion Plates," *Call*, January 6, 1895; untitled article, *Stockton Evening Mail*, August 27, 1897, cited in Sullivan, *From Female to Male*, 31–32.

22 For descriptions of gender "frauds" in freak shows, see Wood, "Dime Museums"; Bogdan, *Freak Show*, 226; Dennett, *Weird and Wonderful*, 28–29. For analysis of fraud's centrality to freak-show entertainment, see Frost, "The Circassian Beauty and the Circassian Slave"; Harris, *Humbug*; Reiss, *The Showman and the Slave*.

23 Evans, *A la California*, chapter 12; photograph of unidentified alley, Chinatown, ca. 1906, San Francisco Chinese Community and Earthquake Damage collection, Bancroft Library, University of California, Berkeley.

24 Buel, *Metropolitan Life Unveiled*, 275; Fletcher, *Ten Drawings in Chinatown*, 14. See also Stoddard, *A Bit of Old China*, 5; Lloyd, *Lights and Shades in San Francisco*, 257.

25 "See the Sights of Chinatown" advertisement, published in DeWitt, *DeWitt's Guide to San Francisco*, 30; Higgins, *To California and Back*; Buel, *Metropolitan Life Unveiled*, 276.

26 Carey, *By the Golden Gate*, 194; Doxey, *Doxey's Guide to San Francisco and the Pleasure Resorts of California*, 121–22; Johnson, *Edith*, 23.

27 See Lei, "Can You Hear Me?"; Lei, "The Production and Consumption of Chinese Theater in Nineteenth-Century California." For in-depth analysis of cross-dressing in Chinese theater, see Li, *Cross-Dressing in Chinese Opera*.

28 See "A Dishonest Chinese Actor," *Morning Oregonian*, October 20, 1889; "Lee Hoo in Limbo," *Morning Oregonian*, October 24, 1889. Lee Hoo's performance is discussed in Boag, *Redressing America's Frontier Past*, 66.

29 DeWitt, *DeWitt's Guide to San Francisco*, 32; Buel, *Metropolitan Life Unveiled*, 288; Doxey, *Doxey's Guide to San Francisco*, 117. For other descriptions of slumming tour visits to Chinese theaters, see Carey, *By the Golden Gate*, 204; Fletcher, *Ten Drawings in Chinatown*, 17.

30 For a description of a female impersonator working at Bottle Meyer's, see "Hugged by a Boy," *Morning Call*, August 3, 1894. For female impersonators working at The Dash, see "Dive Men Officials for Cook," *Call*, October 20, 1908. For Charles Harrington's arrest, see "Fooled by Man Wearing Skirts," *Oakland Tribune*, November 15, 1907. For accounts of these bars' probable popularity with tourists, see Morphy, *San Francisco's Thoroughfares*, 3; Boyd, *Wide-Open Town*, 28.

31 "Comic Opera Does Not Convince the Police," *San Francisco Examiner*, May 25, 1903; "Two Women in Male Attire," *San Francisco Examiner*, May 24, 1903; "Would See the Sights," *Los Angeles Times*, May 25, 1903; Farwell, *The Chinese at Home and Abroad*, 99. For additional reports of women arrested under cross-dressing law while slumming in Chinatown, see "Donned Male Attire," *San Francisco Call*, October 12, 1898; "Jailed through Cashing Check," *San Francisco Call*, April 4, 1905; "A School Girls Lark Winds Up in Prison," *San Francisco Chronicle*, August 2, 1909; "Pretty Girl Repents of Midnight Escapade," *San Francisco Chronicle*, August 3, 1909; "Pretty Masqueraders in Very Penitent Mood," *San Francisco Chronicle*, March 24, 1910; "She Was from Missouri," *San Francisco Call*, December 23, 1912.

32 For a first-person account of a slumming tour police raid on a Chinese gambling den, see Robert Howe Fletcher's description of police officers "armed with axes, crow-bars and sledges . . . smashing the furniture and interior fittings of

the room and making kindling wood of the presiding Joss" (*Ten Drawings in Chinatown*, 8). Police chiefs were aware that their officers doubled as slumming tour guides and apparently did not object. For example, in 1877 the son of a local newspaper editor wrote to the chief of police, seeking to procure the services of an officer who could lead a tour through Chinatown (Letter to Chief Ellis from Frederick Marriott Jr., April 2, 1877, Henry H. Ellis Papers, Bancroft Library, University of California, Berkeley).

33 "Among Dives and Dance Halls," *San Francisco Call*, October 25, 1891; "Ministers before the Grand Jury," *Call*, February 28, 1895. For a journalist's account of a Barbary Coast slumming tour, undertaken "for the purpose of obtaining statistics and taking a general view of the volcano of crime that rages in its subterranean passages," see "The Crusade," *Call*, January 15, 1874.

34 Shah, *Contagious Divides*, 20–44; California State Board of Health, *Biennial Report of the State Board of Health of California*, 46; San Francisco Board of Supervisors, *Report of the Special Committee of the Board of Supervisors of San Francisco on the Condition of the Chinese Quarter and the Chinese in San Francisco*. Also see San Francisco Board of Health, "The Board of Health," 12.

35 Berglund, *Making San Francisco American*, 98. For a comparable argument about slumming, racialization, and African American culture in Chicago, see Heap, *Slumming*.

36 "Asks That Police Enforce Opium Laws," *San Francisco Chronicle*, September 21, 1904. Also see Longstreet, *The Wilder Shore*, 162; Asbury, *The Barbary Coast*, 171–72, 284–85.

37 "Has No Love for Petticoats," *San Francisco Examiner*, February 7, 1895.

Chapter 6. Problem Bodies, Nation-State

 1 The National Archives hold approximately 100,000 immigration case files of Chinese people who migrated to the United States via San Francisco. Unfortunately these records are not complete, and Wong's is not among them. My discussion of the case is based on the following newspaper reports: "Five Chinese Found Secreted on Chiyo Maru," *San Francisco Chronicle*, December 10, 1910; "Steamer Raid Yields Five Orientals," *San Francisco Examiner*, December 10, 1910; "Keep Close Watch Today on Liner," *San Francisco News*, December 10, 1910; "Schultz Was in Plot to Land Chinese," *Bulletin*, December 10, 1910; "Slave Girl Tells of Voyage Two Days without Food," *San Francisco Examiner*, December 11, 1910; "Confederates of Schultz Watched," *San Francisco Chronicle*, December 12, 1910; "Longshoreman Slips from Fingers of Federals," *San Francisco Examiner*, December 18, 1910; "Steward's 'Boy' Is Put under Arrest," *San Francisco Call*, December 18, 1910; "Marshal Arrests Schultz and Chinese," *San Francisco Chronicle*, December 18, 1910; "Schultz's Lips Are Sealed on Smuggling," *San Francisco Examiner*,

December 19, 1910; "Accused Smugglers Appear in Court," *Bulletin*, December 19, 1910; "Three Chinese Smuggled in Arrested," *San Francisco Examiner*, December 20, 1910; "Yow On Arraigned," *San Francisco Chronicle*, December 20, 1910; "Habeas Corpus Asked for Slave Smuggler," *San Francisco Chronicle*, January 13, 1911; "Alleged Smuggler of Woman Freed after Jury Trial," *San Francisco Chronicle*, March 23, 1911. City newspapers occasionally referred to Wong Ah Choy as Wong Sun Shee and to Yow On as On Ah, On Gon, and You On.

2 For analysis of nation-making through immigration law, see Gardner, *The Qualities of a Citizen*; Lee and Yung, *Angel Island*; Lowe, *Immigrant Acts*; Luibhéid, *Entry Denied*.

3 For reports on the clothing and masculine demeanor of the excluded women, see "The Twenty-Two Chinese Maidens," *Daily Alta California*, August 28, 1874; "A Cargo of Infamy," *San Francisco Chronicle*, August 28, 1874; "Stemming the Foul Tide," *San Francisco Chronicle*, August 27, 1874. For discussion of the case's legal trajectory, see Chan, "The Exclusion of Chinese Women," 98–105; Shah, *Contagious Divides*, 84–85.

4 Luibhéid, *Entry Denied*, 31.

5 Chan, "The Exclusion of Chinese Women"; Gardner, *The Qualities of a Citizen*; Lee and Yung, *Angel Island*.

6 Workingmen's Party of California, *The Chinese Must Go*, 25.

7 Mechanics' State Council San Francisco, *Communication from the Mechanics' State Council of California in Relation to Immigration*, 3. Also see Workingmen's Party of California, *The Chinese Must Go*, 19; American Federation of Labor, *Some Reasons for Chinese Exclusion*, 8.

8 Letter to *Forum* magazine, October 1890.

9 "Here's a Pretty Mess!," *Harper's Weekly*, September 19, 1885, 623; "Another Bar Down," *Wasp* 18 (January–June 1887). For further analysis of the relationship between normative gender and Chinese exclusion, see Leong, " 'A Distinct and Antagonistic Race.' "

10 See Helper, *The Land of Gold*, 89; Lloyd, *Lights and Shades in San Francisco*, 221–22; "Spirit of the Press," *Call*, February 24, 1895. Also see "Mrs. Cheng Tsao Ju," *San Francisco Chronicle*, August 19, 1883. Similar claims about gender indeterminacy were frequently made in gold rush mining districts and on migration journeys, focusing on the ostensible difficulty of distinguishing indigenous men and women. See Perkins, *William Perkins' Journal of Life at Sonora*; Derbec, *A French Journalist in the California Gold Rush*, 154–55; Richardson, *Beyond the Mississippi*, 145, 229.

11 American Federation of Labor, *Some Reasons for Chinese Exclusion*; San Francisco Board of Health, "The Board of Health," 12.

12 "Amusing the Child," *Wasp* 8 (January–June 1882).

13 Gardner, *The Qualities of a Citizen*, 9. Also see Shah, *Contagious Divides*, 181; Lee and Yung, *Angel Island*, 76.

14 For a broader discussion of unauthorized Chinese immigration during the exclusion era, see Lee, *At America's Gates*.

15 Shah, *Contagious Divides*, 183.

16 "Slave Girl Tells of Voyage Two Days without Food," *San Francisco Examiner*, December 11, 1910.

17 "Chinese Girls' Pitiful Story of Kidnapping," *San Francisco Call*, December 7, 1910; "Chinese Captives Tell Tale of Horror," *San Francisco Chronicle*, December 7, 1910; "Smugglers' Boatman Is Arrested," *San Francisco Call*, December 9, 1910.

18 "A Few More Chinese," *Daily Alta California*, October 4, 1885; "Chinamen Held," *Daily Alta California*, October 7, 1885.

19 U.S. Congress, Joint Special Committee to Investigate Chinese Immigration, *Report* (Washington, D.C.: Government Printing Office, 1877), 599. This report is referenced in Hirata, "Free, Indentured, Enslaved."

20 "Chinese Girls Dressed as Boys," *San Francisco Chronicle*, July 25, 1897. For an excellent analysis of the relationship between Chinese women and white Christian missionaries, see Pascoe, *Relations of Rescue*.

21 For a detailed description of Chinese organized prostitution, see Hirata, "Free, Indentured, Enslaved."

22 "Confederates of Schultz Watched," *San Francisco Chronicle*, December 12, 1910; "Keep Close Watch Today on Liner," *San Francisco News*, December 10, 1910; "Schultz Was in Plot to Land Chinese," *Bulletin*, December 10, 1910; "Steamer Raid Yields Five Orientals," *San Francisco Examiner*, December 10, 1910; "Slave Girl Tells of Voyage Two Days without Food," *San Francisco Examiner*, December 11, 1910; "Accused Smugglers Appear in Court," *Bulletin*, December 19, 1910; "Three Chinese Smuggled in Arrested," *San Francisco Examiner*, December 20, 1910.

23 For Wong's own account, see "Habeas Corpus Asked for Slave Smuggler," *San Francisco Chronicle*, January 13, 1911; "Slave Girl Tells of Voyage Two Days without Food," *San Francisco Examiner*, December 11, 1910.

24 Some people held at the Angel Island immigration center wrote poetry on the barrack walls, expressing anger, loneliness, and frustration with their detention. See Lai, Lim, and Yung, *Island*.

25 Finnane, *Changing Clothes in China*, 191–92.

26 Lee, *At America's Gates*, 223–43.

27 Luibhéid, *Entry Denied*; Lee and Yung, *Angel Island*; Gardner, *The Qualities of a Citizen*.

28 Unfortunately records of the immigration service's examination of George Pepper no longer exist. City newspapers, however, reported widely on the case. See "Special Board Will Examine 'Princess,'" *San Francisco Call*, April 23, 1907; "Melodrama Fills Mind of Bogus 'Countess,'" *San Francisco Call*, April 24, 1907; "Brainstorm of Czar's Princess," *San Francisco Chronicle*, April 24, 1907;

"Pretended Countess Not Allowed to Land," *San Francisco Call*, April 26, 1907; "Countess Still under Suspense," *San Francisco Chronicle*, April 26, 1907; "Landing Denied the 'Countess,'" *San Francisco Chronicle*, May 1, 1907; "Woman of Many Names Must Take Ship Again," *San Francisco Call*, May 1, 1907; "Countess in Trousers Resists Two Officers," *San Francisco Call*, May 3, 1907; "Countess Ordered Sent to Vancouver," *San Francisco Chronicle*, May 8, 1907; "Countess Convalinsky Departs for Victoria," *San Francisco Call*, May 8, 1907.

29 Before the Angel Island Immigration Station opened in 1910, it operated as a quarantine station for twenty years. See Shah, *Contagious Divides*, 183–84.

30 For medical examinations and disrobing at the border, see Rand, *The Ellis Island Snow Globe*, 73–80; Baynton, "Defectives in the Land"; Canaday, *The Straight State*, 32–39.

31 Gardner, *The Qualities of a Citizen*, 89.

32 See, for example, "Keeping Out Undesirables," *San Francisco Chronicle*, February 21, 1909.

33 For a detailed discussion of U.S. deportation laws, see Kanstroom, *Deportation Nation*.

34 See Stockton State Hospital Commitment Registers, 10: 673.

35 Shin, "Insanity on the Move."

36 Kanstroom, *Deportation Nation*, 6.

37 Jesse Brown Cook Scrapbooks Documenting San Francisco History and Law Enforcement, vol. 4, Bancroft Library, University of California, Berkeley, Unit ID 184.

38 Public Health Service, *Manual for the Mental Examination of Aliens* (Washington, D.C.: Government Printing Office, 1918), quoted in Eskridge, *Gaylaw*, 36.

39 Canaday, *The Straight State*, 21.

40 For a general discussion of the "likely to become a public charge" and "moral turpitude" provisions, see Kanstroom, *Deportation Nation*, 134–35. For discussion of their specific use in cases concerning sexual or gender deviance, see Rand, *The Ellis Island Snow Globe*, 78; Canaday, *The Straight State*, 24–25; Eskridge, *Gaylaw*, 35–36; Baynton, "Defectives in the Land." Portica was not the only San Franciscan deported to Mexico during these years following a police investigation of nonnormative gender. According to Canaday, immigration officials also deported Marcos Cervellos in 1916, after city police conducted a sodomy investigation that uncovered evidence of unconventional gender, reporting that Cervellos "was powdered and perfumed the way a woman would do" (*The Straight State*, 41–42).

41 "The Gold Excitement," *Daily Alta California*, April 19, 1849.

42 Canaday, *The Straight State*, 3, 21–22.

Conclusion

1 For Bonnet, see "Tired of Women's Clothing," *Call*, July 11, 1876, press clipping from Edward Byram Scrapbooks, California Historical Society. For Ruble, see "Dressed as a Man," *Evening Post*, October 2, 1890.

2 For people laughing in court at cross-dressing charges, see "Young Women Don Male Attire and Are Jailed," *San Francisco Call*, November 20, 1902. For people rearrested, see "Jottings about Town," *San Francisco Chronicle*, December 15, 1874; "The Last Tragedy," *San Francisco Chronicle*, September 17, 1876; "Masquerading Boy Stirs Up Chinese," *San Francisco Examiner*, July 24, 1908.

3 "Chinese Arrested in Woman's Dress," *San Francisco Call*, July 23, 1908; "Hairdresser Tries to Play a Joke on Wife," *San Francisco Chronicle*, December 11, 1909; "Masquerades in Wife's Dress and Is Jailed," *San Francisco Call*, December 11, 1909.

4 "Masqueraded as Men," *San Francisco Chronicle*, January 3, 1900. Also see the case of Rose Driscoll: "Unruly Child Removed from Juvenile Home," *San Francisco Call*, April 19, 1911; "Battles Fiercely to Retain Pretty Dress," *San Francisco Chronicle*, April 19, 1911.

5 Unfortunately Haisch's vigilant neighbors used this incident to have her rearrested for "offensive conduct." See "Hirsch Again Arrested," *San Francisco Chronicle*, July 3, 1895; "Crazy on Female Attire," *San Francisco Call*, July 3, 1895.

6 "Brainstorm of Czar's Princess," *San Francisco Chronicle*, April 24, 1907; "Countess in Trousers Resists Two Officers," *San Francisco Call*, May 3, 1907; "Titled Woman Makes Trouble," *San Francisco Chronicle*, May 3, 1907.

7 "A Question of Dress in a San Francisco Court," *New York Times*, June 11, 1866.

8 "A Question of Dress," *Bulletin*, May 12, 1866; "A Question of Dress in a San Francisco Court," *New York Times*, June 11, 1866; "An Enlightened Discussion," *Dramatic Chronicle*, August 10, 1866.

9 "Who Shall Wear the Breeches?," *Alta*, May 16, 1866; "Ad Captandum Vulgas," *Alta*, May 9, 1866; "A Question of Dress in a San Francisco Court," *New York Times*, June 11, 1866.

10 "Bloomerism," *Bulletin*, August 23, 1866.

11 See California State Legislature, "An Act to Confer Further Powers upon the Board of Supervisors of the City and County of San Francisco," *Statutes of California*, 1863, 540. Ruling of Judge Cowles, printed in "Eliza A. Hurd DeWolf Released on Habeas Corpus," *California Police Gazette*, August 11, 1866.

12 See "Her Bifurcates Too Scant," *San Francisco Chronicle*, September 7, 1895. Debates concerning the scope of cross-dressing law continued in the city press well into the twentieth century. In 1915, for example, the arrest of the Oakland police chief's daughter under the law prompted the *Chronicle* to raise the question "How far is a woman legally entitled to go in the matter of wearing male attire?

At what precise point does she cross the sartorial boundary, supposed to separate the sexes in street costume?" ("In Male Attire," *San Francisco Chronicle*, October 18, 1915).

13 "Dressed as a Man," *Evening Post*, October 2, 1890, 2.

14 "Masquerading Woman Is Brought to Time," *Call*, November 28, 1903; "Supposed Man Proves Woman," *Call*, November 27, 1903.

15 For removal of cross-dressing law from the San Francisco municipal codebook, see San Francisco Board of Supervisors, *Journal of Proceedings*, 771, 788. The supervisors' vote to remove the law is also briefly described in "Linda Lee's Drag Scene," *Drag* 4, no. 16 (1974): 26. For the May 1974 arrests, see "Street Sweep Nets 40," *Advocate*, May 22, 1974, 39; "Female Impersonators" clippings file, Allan Bérubé Papers, Gay, Lesbian, Bisexual and Transgender Historical Society of California, San Francisco; "San Francisco Arrests 40 Drags," *Drag* 4, no. 15 (1974): 7–8.

16 For excellent analysis of policing in recent transgender and queer communities, see Mogul, Ritchie, and Whitlock, *Queer (In)justice*; Spade, *Normal Life*; Hanhardt, *Safe Space*.

Primary Sources

GOVERNMENT DOCUMENTS

California State Board of Health. *Biennial Report of the State Board of Health of California*. Sacramento, 1870–71.

Committee of the Senate of the State of California. *The Social, Moral and Political Effect of Chinese Immigration*. Sacramento: State Printing Office, 1876.

Farwell, William B. *The Chinese at Home and Abroad Together with the Report of the Special Committee of the Board of Supervisors of San Francisco on the Condition of the Chinese Quarter of That City*. San Francisco: A. L. Bancroft, 1885.

New York Laws. 1845.

San Francisco Board of Health. "The Board of Health: Resolutions of Condemnation Adopted." Reprinted in Workingmen's Party of California, *Chinatown Declared a Nuisance!* San Francisco: Workingmen's Party of California, 1880.

San Francisco Board of Supervisors. *Codified Ordinances of the City and County of San Francisco*. San Francisco, 1861.

——. *The Consolidation Act, or Charter of the City and County of San Francisco with Other Acts Specially Relating to San Francisco and of General Interest Within; and the General Orders of the Board of Supervisors*. San Francisco, 1866.

——. *General Orders and Ordinances of the Board of Supervisors*. San Francisco, 1904.

——. *General Orders of the Board of Supervisors*. San Francisco, 1866–98.

——. *General Ordinances of the Board of Supervisors*. San Francisco, 1907–15.

——. *Journal of Proceedings: Board of Supervisors, City and County of San Francisco*. San Francisco: Board of Supervisors, 1974.

——. *Municipal Reports*. San Francisco: Board of Supervisors, 1859–1918.

——. *Ordinances and Joint Resolutions of the City of San Francisco*. San Francisco, 1854.

——. *Ordinances of the City of San Francisco*. San Francisco, 1850.

————. *Report of the Special Committee of the Board of Supervisors of San Francisco on the Condition of the Chinese Quarter and the Chinese in San Francisco.* San Francisco, 1885.

————. *Revised Orders of the City and County of San Francisco.* San Francisco, 1863.

Statutes of California. 1863–1953.

COURT CASES

Ex Parte Delaney, 43 Cal. 478 (1872).

Ho Ah Kow v. Matthew Nunan, 12 F. Cas. 252 (1879).

In the Matter of Mary Maguire, 57 California Reports (January 1881), 604–12.

People v. Hall, 4 Cal. 399 (1854).

NEWSPAPERS/PERIODICALS

Alta (also published as *Daily Alta California*)

Bulletin (also published as *Daily Evening Bulletin* and *San Francisco Bulletin*)

California Police Gazette

The Call (also published as *San Francisco Morning Call*)

Drag

Harper's Weekly

Los Angeles Times

New York Times

San Francisco Chronicle (also published as *Dramatic Chronicle*)

San Francisco Examiner

Scientific American

Sunday Varieties

The Wasp

ARCHIVAL COLLECTIONS

Bancroft Library, University of California, Berkeley

   Burke, Martin J. *The San Francisco Police.* Unpublished manuscript, 1887.

   Henry H. Ellis Papers

   Jesse Brown Cook Scrapbooks Documenting San Francisco History and Law Enforcement

   Lees Family Papers, 1851–1948

   Robert B. Honeyman Jr. Collection of Early Californian and Western American Pictorial Material

   San Francisco Chinese Community and Earthquake Damage Collection

California Historical Society, San Francisco

   Edward Byram Scrapbooks

California State Archive

   Stockton State Hospital Commitment Registers

Stockton State Hospital Register of Deaths
California State Library
    Criminal Photographs: Photograph Album, 1875–1915
    Department of Corrections San Quentin Prison, Inmate Photographs
Gay, Lesbian, Bisexual and Transgender Historical Society of California, San Francisco
    Allan Bérubé Papers
    Louis Graydon Sullivan Papers, 1755–1991
Huntington Library, San Marino, California
    Depositions concerning the charges made before the People's Nominating Committee by Samuel Cowles against Martin J. Burke, Chief of Police, San Francisco, 1864
    Leonard Noyes Scrapbook of Clippings about Crime and Criminals, 1876–80
    Records of the San Francisco Committee of Vigilance, 1856
Library of Congress American Memory National Digital Archive
    "California As I Saw It": First Person Narratives of California's Early Years, 1849–1900
    The Chinese in California, 1850–1925
    Historic American Sheet Music Collection, 1850–1920
San Francisco History Center, San Francisco, California
    Criminal Descriptions File, 1890–1902
    Police Criminal Photos, 1897–98
    San Francisco Board of Supervisors Folder

PUBLISHED PRIMARY SOURCES

American Federation of Labor. *Some Reasons for Chinese Exclusion: Meat vs. Rice, American Manhood against Asiatic Coolieism; Which Shall Survive?* Washington: American Federation of Labor, 1901.

Bancroft, Hubert Howe. *History of California*. Vol. 6: *1848–1859*. 1888. Santa Barbara, CA: Wallace Hebberd, 1970.

Bates, D. B. *Incidents on Land and Water, or Four Years on the Pacific Coast*. Boston: J. French, 1857.

Bennett, W. L. *The Miners' Pioneer Ten Commandments of 1849*. Chromolithograph. Chicago: Kurz and Allison's Art Gallery, 1887.

Boessenecker, John. *Against the Vigilantes: The Recollections of Dutch Charley Duane*. Norman: University of Oklahoma Press, 1999.

Borthwick, J. D. *Three Years in California*. Oakland, CA: Biobooks, 1948.

Buel, John William. *Metropolitan Life Unveiled, or The Mysteries and Miseries of America's Great Cities: Embracing New York, Washington City, San Francisco, Salt Lake City, and New Orleans*. St. Louis: Anchor, 1882.

Carey, Joseph. *By the Golden Gate, or San Francisco, the Queen City of the Pacific Coast*. Albany, NY: Albany Diocesan Press, 1913.

Dame Shirley. *The Shirley Letters from California Mines in 1851–52*. San Francisco: T. C. Russell, 1922.

Derbec, Etienne. *A French Journalist in the California Gold Rush: The Letters of Etienne Derbec*. Georgetown, CA: Talisman, 1964.

de Russailh, Albert Benard. *Last Adventure; San Francisco in 1851*. San Francisco: Westgate, 1931.

DeWitt, Frederick M. *DeWitt's Guide to San Francisco: An Illustrated and Descriptive Handbook for Tourists and Strangers*. 1897. San Francisco: Frederick M. DeWitt, 1900.

Dornin, George D. *Thirty Years Ago: Gold Rush Memories of a Daguerreotype Artist*. 1873. Nevada City, CA: Carl Mautz, 1995.

Doxey, William. *Doxey's Guide to San Francisco and the Pleasure Resorts of California*. San Francisco: William Doxey, 1897.

Evans, Albert S. *A la California: Sketch of Life in the Golden State*. San Francisco: A. L. Bancroft, 1873.

Fairchild, Lucius. *California Letters of Lucius Fairchild*. Madison: State Historical Society of Wisconsin, 1931.

Farnham, Eliza W. *California Indoors and Out, or How We Farm, Mine and Live in the Golden State*. New York: Dix, Edwards, 1856.

Fletcher, Robert Howe. *Ten Drawings in Chinatown by Ernest C. Peixotto with Certain Observations by Robert Howe Fletcher*. San Francisco: A. M. Robertson, 1898.

Heco, Joseph. *The Narrative of a Japanese: What He Has Seen and the People He Has Met in the Course of the Last Forty Years*. Vol. 2. Tokyo: Maruzen, 1895.

Helper, Hinton. *The Land of Gold: Reality versus Fiction*. Baltimore: H. Taylor, 1855.

Higgins, C. A. *To California and Back*. Chicago: Passenger Department, Santa Fe Route [South Pacific], 1893.

Hirschfeld, Magnus. *Transvestites: The Erotic Drive to Cross-Dress*. 1910. Buffalo, NY: Prometheus Books, 1991.

Hirschfeld, Magnus, and Max Tilke. *Der erotische Verkleidungstrieb (Die Transvestiten), illustrierter Teil*. Leipzig: Verlag "Wahrheit" Ferdinand Spohr, 1912.

Johnson, Harry M. *Edith: A Story of Chinatown*. Boston: Arena, 1895.

Jordan, Louis J. *Handbook of the Pacific Museum of Anatomy and Science*. San Francisco: Francis and Valentine, 1868.

Lloyd, Benjamin E. *Lights and Shades in San Francisco*. San Francisco: Bancroft, 1876.

Mayne, Xavier. *The Intersexes: A History of Similisexualism as a Problem in Social Life*. 1908. New York: Arno, 1975.

Mechanics' State Council San Francisco. *Communication from the Mechanics' State Council of California in Relation to Immigration*. Sacramento: D. W. Gelwicks, State Printer, 1868.

Pérez Rosales, Vicente. "Diary of a Journey to California." In *We Were 49ers! Chilean Accounts of the California Gold Rush*, edited by Edwin A. Beilharz and Carlos U. López, 3–99. Pasadena, CA: Ward Ritchie, 1976.

Perkins, William. *William Perkins' Journal of Life at Sonora, 1849–1852*. Berkeley: University of California Press, 1964.

Richardson, Albert D. *Beyond the Mississippi*. 1867. Hartford, CT: American, 1968.

Royce, Sarah. *A Frontier Lady: Recollections of the Gold Rush and Early California*. 1932. Lincoln: University of Nebraska Press, 1977.

Ryan, William Redmond. *Personal Adventures in Upper and Lower California, in 1848–9*. London: W. Shoberl, 1850.

Seacole, Mary. *Wonderful Adventures of Mrs. Seacole in Many Lands*. Oxford: Oxford University Press, 1988.

Soulé, Frank, John H. Gihon, and James Nisbet. *The Annals of San Francisco*. 1855. Palo Alto, CA: Lewis Osborne, 1966.

Stephens, Lorenzo Dow. *Life Sketches of a Jayhawker of '49*. San Jose: Nolta Brothers, 1916.

Stoddard, Charles Warren. *A Bit of Old China*. San Francisco: A. M. Robertson, 1912.

Taylor, Bayard. *Eldorado, or, Adventures in the Path of Empire*. New York: G. P. Putnam, 1850.

Taylor, William. *California Life Illustrated*. New York: Carlton and Porter, 1858.

Vigilance Committee of San Francisco. *Proclamation of the Vigilance Committee of San Francisco*. San Francisco: Agnew and Deffenbach, 1856.

Wilson, Luzena Stanley. "Luzena Stanley Wilson, 49er." In *My Checkered Life: Luzena Stanley Wilson in Early California*, edited by Fern L. Henry. 1937. Nevada City, CA: Carl Mautz, 2003.

Wood, J. G. "Dime Museums." *Atlantic Monthly* 55 (January–June 1885): 759–65.

Workingmen's Party of California. *The Chinese Must Go: The Labor Agitators; or, the Battle for Bread*. San Francisco: Greene, 1879.

Secondary Sources

Adams, Rachel. *Sideshow USA: Freaks and the American Cultural Imagination*. Chicago: University of Chicago Press, 2001.

Adrian, Charles R., and Ernest S. Griffith. *A History of American City Government: The Formation of Traditions, 1775–1870*. New York: Praeger, 1976.

Alexander, M. Jacqui. *Pedagogies of Crossing: Meditations on Feminism, Sexual Politics, Memory and the Sacred*. Durham, NC: Duke University Press, 2005.

Almaguer, Tomás. *Racial Faultlines: The Historical Origins of White Supremacy in California*. Berkeley: University of California Press, 1994.

Altrocchi, Julia Cooley. *The Spectacular San Franciscans*. New York: E. P. Dutton, 1949.

Asbury, Herbert. *The Barbary Coast: An Informal History of the San Francisco Underworld*. New York: Knopf, 1933.

Barnhart, Jacqueline Baker. *The Fair but Frail: Prostitution in San Francisco, 1849–1900*. Reno: University of Nevada Press, 1986.

Baynton, Douglas C. "Defectives in the Land: Disability and American Immigration Policy." *Journal of American Ethnic History* 24, no. 3 (2005): 31–44.

Beebe, Lucius, and Charles Clegg. *San Francisco's Golden Era: A Picture Story of San Francisco before the Fire.* Berkeley, CA: Howell-North, 1960.

Berglund, Barbara. *Making San Francisco American: Cultural Frontiers in the Urban West, 1846–1906.* Lawrence: University Press of Kansas, 2007.

Black Public Sphere Collective. *The Black Public Sphere: A Public Culture Book.* Chicago: University of Chicago Press, 1995.

Boag, Peter. "Go West Young Man, Go East Young Woman: Searching for the *Trans* in Western Gender History." *Western Historical Quarterly* 36, no. 4 (2005): 477–97.

———. *Redressing America's Frontier Past.* Berkeley: University of California Press, 2011.

Bogdan, Robert. *Freak Show: Presenting Human Oddities for Amusement and Profit.* Chicago: University of Chicago Press, 1988.

Boyd, Nan Alamilla. "Bodies in Motion: Lesbian and Transsexual Histories." In *A Queer World: The Center for Lesbian and Gay Studies Reader,* edited by Martin B. Duberman, 134–52. New York: New York University Press, 1997.

———. *Wide-Open Town: A History of Queer San Francisco to 1965.* Berkeley: University of California Press, 2003.

Burton, Antoinette. *Dwelling in the Archive: Women Writing House, Home, and History in Late Colonial India.* New York: Oxford University Press, 2003.

Butler, Judith. *Gender Trouble: Feminism and the Subversion of Identity.* New York: Routledge, 1990.

Cain, Patricia. "Litigating for Lesbian and Gay Rights: A Legal History." *Virginia Law Review* 79 (October 1993): 1551–641.

Califia, Pat. *Sex Changes: The Politics of Transgenderism.* San Francisco: Cleis, 1997.

Canaday, Margot. *The Straight State: Sexuality and Citizenship in Twentieth-Century America.* Princeton: Princeton University Press, 2009.

———. "'Who Is a Homosexual?': The Consolidation of Sexual Identities in Mid-Twentieth-Century American Immigration Law." *Law and Social Inquiry* 28, no. 2 (2003): 351–86.

Casteñada, Antonia. "The Political Economy of Nineteenth Century Stereotypes of Californianas." In *Between Borders: Essays in Mexicana/Chicana History,* edited by Adelaida R. Del Castillo, 213–36. Los Angeles: Floricanto, 1990.

———. "Women of Color and the Rewriting of Western History: The Discourse, Politics and Decolonization of History." *Pacific Historical Review* 61, no. 4 (1992): 501–33.

Chan, Sucheng. "The Exclusion of Chinese Women." In *Entry Denied: Exclusion and the Chinese Community in America, 1882–1943,* edited by Sucheng Chan, 94–146. Philadelphia: Temple University Press, 1991.

Chapman, Kathleen, and Michael Du Plessis. "'Don't Call Me *Girl*': Lesbian Theory, Feminist Theory and Transsexual Identities." In *Cross-Purposes: Lesbians, Femi-*

nists and the Limits of Alliance, edited by Dana Heller, 169–85. Bloomington: Indiana University Press, 1997.

Chauncey, George. "From Sexual Inversion to Homosexuality: Medicalization and the Changing Conceptualization of Female Deviance." *Salmagundi* 58–59 (1982): 114–46.

———. *Gay New York: Gender, Urban Culture and the Making of the Gay Male World, 1890–1940*. New York: Basic Books, 1994.

Cook, James W. "Of Men, Missing Links, and Nondescripts: The Strange Career of P. T. Barnum's 'What Is It?' Exhibition." In *Freakery: Cultural Spectacles of the Extraordinary Body*, edited by Rosemarie Garland Thomson, 139–57. New York: New York University Press, 1996.

Cooks, Catherine. *Doing the Town: The Rise of Urban Tourism in the United States, 1850–1915*. Berkeley: University of California Press, 2001.

Coombe, Rosemary. "Contingent Articulations: A Critical Cultural Studies of Law." In *Law in the Domains of Culture*, edited by Austin Sarat and Thomas R. Kearns, 21–64. Ann Arbor: University of Michigan Press, 1998.

Cowan, Robert Ernest. *Forgotten Characters of Old San Francisco, 1850–1870*. Los Angeles: Ward Ritchie, 1938.

Craddock, Susan. *City of Plagues: Disease, Poverty and Deviance in San Francisco*. Minneapolis: University of Minnesota Press, 2000.

Decker, Peter R. *Fortunes and Failures: White Collar Mobility in Nineteenth Century San Francisco*. Cambridge, MA: Harvard University Press, 1978.

Dennett, Andrea Stulman. *Weird and Wonderful: The Dime Museum in America*. New York: New York University Press, 1997.

Derrida, Jacques. *Archive Fever: A Freudian Impression*. Chicago: University of Chicago Press, 1995.

Dirks, Nicholas B. "Annals of the Archive: Ethnographic Notes on the Sources of History." In *From the Margins: Historical Anthropology and Its Futures*, edited by Brian Keith Axel, 47–65. Durham, NC: Duke University Press, 2002.

Duberman, Martin B. *Stonewall*. New York: Dutton, 1993.

Duggan, Lisa. *Sapphic Slashers: Sex, Violence, and American Modernity*. Durham, NC: Duke University Press, 2000.

Durden, Michelle. "Not Just a Leg Show: Gayness and Male Homoeroticism in Burlesque, 1868 to 1877." *Thirdspace* 3, no. 2 (2004). Online. http://journals.sfu.ca/thirdspace/index.php/journal/article/view/durden/173.

Edwards, Rebekah Lael. "Archives of Uncertainty: U.S. Investigative Narratives of Fraudulent Embodiment, 1900–1920." PhD dissertation, University of California at Berkeley, 2009.

Eng, David. *Racial Castration: Managing Masculinity in Asian America*. Durham, NC: Duke University Press, 2001.

Eskridge, William N. "Challenging the Apartheid of the Closet: Establishing Conditions for Lesbian and Gay Intimacy, Nomos, and Citizenship, 1961–1981." *Hofstra Law Review* 25 (1997): 817–970.

———. *Gaylaw: Challenging the Apartheid of the Closet*. Cambridge, MA: Harvard University Press, 1999.

———. "Law and the Construction of the Closet: American Regulation of Same-Sex Intimacy, 1880–1946." *Iowa Law Review* 82 (1997): 1007–134.

Ethington, Philip J. *The Public City: The Political Construction of Urban Life in San Francisco, 1850–1900*. Berkeley: University of California Press, 1994.

———. "Vigilantes and the Police: The Creation of a Professional Police Bureaucracy in San Francisco, 1847–1900." *Journal of Social History* 21, no. 2 (1987): 197–227.

Faderman, Lillian. *Surpassing the Love of Men: Romantic Friendship and Love between Women from the Renaissance to the Present*. New York: Morrow, 1981.

Fausto-Sterling, Anne. "Gender, Race, and Nation: The Comparative Anatomy of 'Hottentot' Women in Europe, 1815–1817." In *Deviant Bodies: Critical Perspectives on Difference in Science and Popular Culture*, edited by Jennifer Terry and Jacqueline Urla, 19–48. Bloomington: Indiana University Press, 1995.

Feinberg, Leslie. *Stone Butch Blues*. Ithaca, NY: Firebrand Books, 1993.

———. *Transgender Warriors: Making History from Joan of Arc to RuPaul*. Boston: Beacon, 1996.

Finnane, Antonia. *Changing Clothes in China: Fashion, Modernity, Nation*. New York: Columbia University Press, 2008.

Foucault, Michel. *Discipline and Punish: The Birth of the Prison*. New York: Vintage, 1995.

———. *The History of Sexuality: An Introduction*. Vol. 1. New York: Vintage, 1990.

———. *The Order of Things: An Archaeology of Human Sciences*. New York: Vintage, 1994.

Fox, Richard W. *So Far Disordered in Mind: Insanity in California, 1870–1930*. Berkeley: University of California Press, 1978.

Fraser, Nancy. "Rethinking the Public Sphere: A Contribution to the Critique of Actually Existing Democracy." *Social Text* 25/26 (1990): 56–80.

Fretz, Eric. "P. T. Barnum's Theatrical Selfhood and the Nineteenth-Century Culture of Exhibition." In *Freakery: Cultural Spectacles of the Extraordinary Body*, edited by Rosemarie Garland Thomson, 97–107. New York: New York University Press, 1996.

Friedman, Lawrence Meir. *A History of American Law*. 2nd ed. New York: Simon and Schuster, 1985.

Friedman, Mack. *Strapped for Cash: A History of American Hustler Culture*. Los Angeles: Alyson, 2003.

Frost, Linda. "The Circassian Beauty and the Circassian Slave: Gender, Imperialism and American Popular Entertainment." In *Freakery: Cultural Spectacles of the Extraordinary Body*, edited by Rosemarie Garland Thomson, 248–62. New York: New York University Press, 1996.

Garber, Marjorie. *Vested Interests: Cross-Dressing and Cultural Anxiety*. New York: Routledge, 1993.

Gardner, Martha. *The Qualities of a Citizen: Women, Immigration, and Citizenship, 1870–1965*. Princeton: Princeton University Press, 2005.

Gentry, Curt. *The Madams of San Francisco: A Highly Irreverent History of the City by the Golden Gate*. New York: Doubleday, 1964.

Gilfoyle, Timothy J. *City of Eros: New York City, Prostitution, and the Commercialization of Sex*. New York: Norton, 1992.

Gluck, Peter R., and Richard J. Meister. *Cities in Transition*. New York: New Viewpoints, 1979.

Goldberg, David Theo. *Racist Culture: Philosophy and the Politics of Meaning*. Oxford: Blackwell, 1993.

Gross, Ariela J. *What Blood Won't Tell: A History of Race on Trial in America*. Cambridge, MA: Harvard University Press, 2008.

Gusfield, Joseph R. *Symbolic Crusade: Status Politics and the American Temperance Movement*. Urbana: University of Illinois Press, 1966.

Habermas, Jürgen. *The Structural Transformation of the Public Sphere: An Inquiry into a Category of Bourgeois Society*. 1962. Cambridge: MIT Press, 1991.

Halberstam, Judith. *Female Masculinity*. Durham, NC: Duke University Press, 1998.

Halperin, David M. *One Hundred Years of Homosexuality and Other Essays on Greek Love*. New York: Routledge, 1990.

Hamilton, Marybeth. "'I'm the Queen of Bitches': Female Impersonation and Mae West's *Pleasure Man*." In *Crossing the Stage: Controversies on Cross-Dressing*, edited by Lesley Ferris, 107–19. London: Routledge, 1993.

Hanhardt, Christina B. *Safe Space: Gay Neighborhood History and the Politics of Violence*. Durham, NC: Duke University Press, 2013.

Harris, Neil. *Humbug: The Art of P. T. Barnum*. Boston: Little, Brown, 1973.

Heap, Chad. *Slumming: Sexual and Racial Encounters in American Nightlife, 1885–1940*. Chicago: University of Chicago Press, 2009.

Hevey, David. *The Creatures Time Forgot: Photography and Disability Imagery*. London: Routledge, 1992.

Hirata, Lucie Cheng. "Free, Indentured, Enslaved: Chinese Prostitutes in Nineteenth Century America." *Signs* 5, no. 1 (1979): 3–29.

Hsu, Hsuan L. "Personality, Race, and Geopolitics in Joseph Heco's Narrative of a Japanese." *Biography* 29, no. 2 (2006): 273–306.

Hudson, Lynn M. "Entertaining Citizenship: Masculinity and Minstrelsy in Post-Emancipation San Francisco." *Journal of African-American History* 93, no. 2 (2008): 174–97.

Hurtado, Albert L. *Intimate Frontiers: Sex, Gender, and Culture in Old California.* Albuquerque: University of New Mexico Press, 1999.

Issel, William, and Robert W. Cherney. *San Francisco 1865–1932: Politics, Power and Urban Development.* Berkeley: University of California Press, 1986.

Johnson, Susan Lee. *Roaring Camp: The Social World of the California Gold Rush.* New York: Norton, 2000.

Jolly, Michelle. "The Price of Vigilance: Gender, Politics, and the Press in Early San Francisco." *Pacific Historical Review* 73, no. 4 (2004): 541–80.

———. "Sex, Vigilantism and San Francisco in 1856." *Common-Place: The Interactive Journal of Early American Life* 3, no. 4 (2003). Online.

Kanstroom, Daniel. *Deportation Nation: Outsiders in American History.* Cambridge, MA: Harvard University Press, 2007.

Katz, Jonathan Ned. "Coming to Terms: Conceptualizing Men's Erotic and Affectional Relations with Men in the United States, 1820–1892." In *A Queer World: The Center for Lesbian and Gay Studies Reader,* edited by Martin B. Duberman, 216–35. New York: New York University Press, 1997.

———. *Gay American History: Lesbians and Gay Men in the USA.* New York: Thomas Y. Crowell, 1976.

———. *Gay/Lesbian Almanac.* New York: Harper and Row, 1983.

———. *The Invention of Heterosexuality.* New York: Plume, 1995.

Kennedy, Elizabeth, and Madeline Davis. *Boots of Leather, Slippers of Gold: The History of a Lesbian Community.* New York: Routledge, 1993.

Lai, Him Mark, Genny Lim, and Judy Yung. *Island: Poetry and History of Chinese Immigrants on Angel Island.* San Francisco: HOC-DOI, 1980.

Lee, Erika. *At America's Gates: Chinese Immigration during the Exclusion Era, 1882–1943.* Chapel Hill: University of North Carolina Press, 2003.

Lee, Erika, and Judy Yung. *Angel Island: Immigrant Gateway to America.* Oxford: Oxford University Press, 2010.

Lei, Daphne. "Can You Hear Me? Female Voice and Cantonese Opera in the San Francisco Bay Area." *Scholar and Feminist Online* 2, no. 1 (2003).

———. "The Production and Consumption of Chinese Theater in Nineteenth-Century California." *Theatre Research International* 28, no. 3 (2003): 289–302.

Leong, Karen J. *The China Mystique: Pearl S. Buck, Anna May Wong, Mayling Soong, and the Transformation of American Orientalism.* Berkeley: University of California Press, 2005.

———. "'A Distinct and Antagonistic Race': Constructions of Chinese Manhood in the Exclusionist Debates, 1869–1878." In *Across the Great Divide: Cultures of Manhood in the American West,* edited by Matthew Basso, Laura McCall, and Dee Garceau, 131–48. New York: Routledge, 2001.

Li, Siu Leung. *Cross-Dressing in Chinese Opera.* Hong Kong: Hong Kong University Press, 2003.

Lindfors, Bernth. "Ethnological Show Business: Footlighting the Dark Continent." In *Freakery: Cultural Spectacles of the Extraordinary Body*, edited by Rosemarie Garland Thomson, 207–18. New York: New York University Press, 1996.

Longstreet, Stephen. *The Wilder Shore: A Gala Social History of San Francisco's Sinners and Spenders, 1849–1906*. Garden City, NY: Doubleday, 1968.

López, Ian Haney. *White by Law: The Legal Construction of Race*. New York: New York University Press, 1996.

Lotchin, Roger W. *San Francisco, 1846–1856: From Hamlet to City*. New York: Oxford University Press, 1974.

Lott, Eric. *Love and Theft: Black Minstrelsy and the American Working Class*. New York: Oxford University Press, 1993.

Lowe, Lisa. *Immigrant Acts: On Asian American Cultural Politics*. Durham, NC: Duke University Press, 1996.

Luibhéid, Eithne. *Entry Denied: Controlling Sexuality at the Border*. Minneapolis: University of Minnesota Press, 2002.

Margo, Elisabeth. *Taming the Forty-Niner*. New York: Rinehart, 1955.

McClain, Charles J. *In Search of Equality: The Chinese Struggle against Discrimination in Nineteenth-Century America*. Berkeley: University of California Press, 1994.

McClintock, Anne. *Imperial Leather: Race, Gender and Sexuality in the Colonial Contest*. New York: Routledge, 1995.

McDonald, Terrence J. *The Parameters of Urban Fiscal Policy: Socioeconomic Change and Political Culture in San Francisco, 1860–1906*. Berkeley: University of California Press, 1986.

McGarry, Molly. "Spectral Sexualities: Nineteenth Century Spiritualism, Moral Panics, and the Making of U.S. Obscenity Law." *Journal of Women's History* 12, no. 2 (2000): 8–29.

McNamara, Brooks. "'A Congress of Wonders': The Rise and Fall of the Dime Museum." *ESQ* 20, no. 3 (1974): 216–31.

Mercer, Lorraine. "I Shall Make No Excuse: The Narrative Odyssey of Mary Seacole." *Journal of Narrative Theory* 35, no. 1 (2005): 1–24.

Merry, Sally Engle. "Spatial Governmentality and the New Urban Social Order: Controlling Gender Violence through Law." *American Anthropologist* 103, no. 1 (2001): 16–29.

Meyerowitz, Joanne. *How Sex Changed: A History of Transsexuality in the United States*. Cambridge, MA: Harvard University Press, 2002.

———. "A New History of Gender." Paper presented at Trans/forming Knowledges: The Implications of Transgender Studies for Women's Studies, Gender Studies and Sexuality Studies. Center for Gender Studies, University of Chicago, February 17, 2006.

Mitchell, Michael, and Charles Eisenmann. *Monsters: Human Freaks in America's Gilded Age. The Photographs of Charles Eisenmann*. Toronto: ECW Press, 2002.

Mogul, Joey L., Andrea J. Ritchie, and Kay Whitlock. *Queer (In)justice: The Criminalization of LGBT People in the United States*. Boston: Beacon, 2011.

Mohl, Raymond A. *The New City: Urban America in the Industrial Age, 1860–1920*. Arlington Heights, IL: Harlan Davidson, 1985.

Monkkonen, Eric H. *America Becomes Urban: The Development of U.S. Cities and Towns, 1780–1980*. Berkeley: University of California Press, 1988.

Moran, Leslie, Daniel Monk, and Sarah Beresford. *Legal Queeries: Lesbian, Gay and Transgender Legal Studies*. London: Cassell, 1998.

Morphy, Edward A. *San Francisco's Thoroughfares*. San Francisco: N.p., 1920.

Namaste, Viviane K. *Invisible Lives: The Erasure of Transsexual and Transgendered People*. Chicago: University of Chicago Press, 2000.

Negt, Oskar, and Alexander Kuge. *Public Sphere and Experience: Toward an Analysis of the Bourgeois and Proletarian Public Sphere*. Minneapolis: University of Minnesota Press, 1993.

Nestle, Joan. *A Restricted Country*. 1987. San Francisco: Cleis, 2003.

Oaks, Robert F. "Golden Gate Castaway: Joseph Heco and San Francisco, 1851–1859." *California History* 82, no. 2 (2004): 38–58.

Omi, Michael, and Howard Winant. *Racial Formation in the United States: From the 1960s to the 1990s*. New York: Routledge, 1986.

Pascoe, Peggy. *Relations of Rescue: The Search for Moral Authority in the American West, 1874–1939*. New York: Oxford University Press, 1990.

———. *What Comes Naturally: Miscegenation Law and the Making of Race in America*. Oxford: Oxford University Press, 2009.

Peiss, Kathy Lee. *Cheap Amusements: Working Women and Leisure in Turn-of-the-Century New York*. Philadelphia: Temple University Press, 1986.

Pérez, Emma. *The Decolonial Imaginary: Writing Chicanas into History*. Bloomington: Indiana University Press, 1999.

Prosser, Jay. *Second Skins: The Body Narratives of Transsexuality*. New York: Columbia University Press, 1998.

———. "Transgender." In *Lesbian and Gay Studies: A Critical Introduction*, edited by Andy Medhurst and Sally R. Munt, 309–26. London: Cassell, 1997.

Rand, Erica. *The Ellis Island Snow Globe*. Durham, NC: Duke University Press, 2005.

Reiss, Benjamin. *The Showman and the Slave: Race, Death, and Memory in Barnum's America*. Cambridge, MA: Harvard University Press, 2001.

Romesburg, Don. "Don't Fence Me In: Transgendering Western History." Unpublished manuscript, 2000.

Ryan, Mary P. *Civic Wars: Democracy and Public Life in the American City during the Nineteenth Century*. Berkeley: University of California Press, 1997.

———. *Women in Public: Between Banners and Ballots, 1825–1880*. Baltimore: Johns Hopkins University Press, 1992.

Sánchez, Rosaura. *Telling Identities: The Californio Testimonios.* Minneapolis: University of Minnesota Press, 1995.

San Francisco Lesbian and Gay History Project. "'She Even Chewed Tobacco': A Pictorial Narrative of Passing Women in America." In *Hidden from History: Reclaiming the Gay and Lesbian Past,* edited by Martin B. Duberman, Martha Vicinus, and George Chauncey, 183–94. New York: New American Library, 1989.

Sarat, Austin, and Thomas R. Kearns. "The Cultural Lives of Law." In *Law in the Domains of Culture,* edited by Austin Sarat and Thomas R. Kearns, 1–20. Ann Arbor: University of Michigan Press, 1998.

Saxton, Alexander. *The Indispensable Enemy: Labor and the Anti-Chinese Movement.* 1971. Berkeley: University of California Press, 1995.

Schweik, Susan. *The Ugly Laws: Disability in Public.* New York: New York University Press, 2009.

Scott, Joan Wallach. "The Evidence of Experience." In *The Lesbian and Gay Studies Reader,* edited by Henry Abelove, Michèle Aina Barale, and David M. Halperin, 397–415. New York: Routledge, 1993.

Senelick, Laurence. "Boys and Girls Together: Subcultural Origins of Glamour Drag and Male Impersonation on the Nineteenth-Century Stage." In *Crossing the Stage: Controversies on Cross-Dressing,* edited by Lesley Ferris, 80–94. London: Routledge, 1993.

———. "Lady and the Tramp: Drag Differentials in the Progressive Era." In *Gender in Performance: The Presentation of Difference in the Performing Arts,* edited by Laurence Senelick, 26–45. Hanover, NH: University Press of New England, 1992.

Senkewicz, Robert M. *Vigilantes in Gold Rush San Francisco.* Stanford: Stanford University Press, 1985.

Shah, Nayan. *Contagious Divides: Epidemics and Race in San Francisco's Chinatown.* Berkeley: University of California Press, 2001.

Shin, Ji-Hye. "Insanity on the Move: Deportation of the 'Alien Insane' in New York and California, 1882–1930." Paper presented at the annual meeting of the Western Political Science Association, Portland, Oregon, March 22–24, 2012.

Shumsky, Neil L. *The Evolution of Political Protest and the Workingmen's Party of California.* Columbus: Ohio State University Press, 1991.

Shumsky, Neil L., and Larry M. Springer. "San Francisco's Zone of Prostitution, 1880–1934." *Journal of Historical Geography* 7, no. 1 (1981): 71–89.

Silber, Nina. "Intemperate Men, Spiteful Women, and Jefferson Davis: Northern Views of the Defeated South." *American Quarterly* 41, no. 4 (1989): 614–35.

Silverman, Victor, and Susan Stryker, directors. *Screaming Queens: The Riot at Compton's Cafeteria.* Frameline Distribution, 2005.

Somerville, Siobhan. *Queering the Color Line: Race and the Invention of Homosexuality in American Culture.* Durham, NC: Duke University Press, 2000.

Spade, Dean. *Normal Life: Administrative Violence, Critical Trans Politics and the Limits of Law*. New York: South End, 2011.

Steedman, Carolyn. *Dust: The Archive and Cultural History*. New Brunswick, NJ: Rutgers University Press, 2002.

Stern, Alexandra Minna. *Eugenic Nation: Faults and Frontiers of Better Breeding in Modern America*. Berkeley: University of California Press, 2005.

Stoddard, Thomas B., et al., eds. *The Rights of Gay People*. 1975. New York: Bantam Books, 1983.

Stryker, Susan. "(De)Subjugated Knowledges: An Introduction to Transgender Studies." In *The Transgender Studies Reader*, edited by Susan Stryker and Stephen Whittle, 1–17. New York: Routledge, 2006.

———. *Transgender History*. Berkeley: Seal Press, 2008.

———. "Transgender Studies: Queer Theory's Evil Twin." GLQ: *A Journal of Lesbian and Gay Studies* 10, no. 2 (2004): 212–15.

Stryker, Susan, and Jim Van Buskirk. *Gay by the Bay: A History of Queer Culture in the San Francisco Bay Area*. San Francisco: Chronicle Books, 1996.

Stryker, Susan, and Stephen Whittle, eds. *The Transgender Studies Reader*. New York: Routledge, 2006.

Sullivan, Louis. *From Female to Male: The Life of Jack Bee Garland*. Boston: Alyson, 1990.

Sullivan, Nikki. *A Critical Introduction to Queer Theory*. New York: New York University Press, 2003.

Takaki, Ronald. *Strangers from a Different Shore: A History of Asian Americans*. 1989. Boston: Little, Brown, 1998.

Taper, Bernard, ed. *Mark Twain's San Francisco*. 1865. New York: McGraw Hill, 1963.

Terry, Jennifer. "Theorizing Deviant Historiography." *differences: A Journal of Feminist Cultural Studies* 3, no. 2 (1991): 55–74.

Terry, Jennifer, and Jacqueline Urla. *Deviant Bodies*. Bloomington: Indiana University Press, 1995.

Thomson, Rosemarie Garland. *Extraordinary Bodies: Figuring Physical Disability in American Culture and Literature*. New York: Columbia University Press, 1997.

———, ed. *Freakery: Cultural Spectacles of the Extraordinary Body*. New York: New York University Press, 1996.

Toll, Robert. *On with the Show! The First Century of Show Business in America*. New York: Oxford University Press, 1976.

Tongson, Karen. *Relocations: Queer Suburban Imaginaries*. New York: New York University Press, 2011.

Ullman, Sharon. *Sex Seen: The Emergence of Modern Sexuality in America*. Berkeley: University of California Press, 1997.

Vicinus, Martha. "'They Wonder to Which Sex I Belong': The Historical Roots of the Modern Lesbian Identity." In *The Lesbian and Gay Studies Reader*, edited by Henry Abelove, Michèle Aina Barale, and David M. Halperin, 432–52. New York: Routledge, 1993.

Watts, Jennifer. "From the Photo Archive: 'That's No Woman . . .'" *Huntington Library, Arts Collection, and Botanical Gardens Calendar* (July–August 1998).

Weeks, Jeffrey. *Sex, Politics, and Society: The Regulation of Sexuality since 1800.* London: Longman, 1981.

Welke, Barbara Young. *Law and the Borders of Belonging in the Long Nineteenth Century United States.* Cambridge: Cambridge University Press, 2010.

Whisner, Mary. "Gender Specific Clothing Regulation: A Study in Patriarchy." *Harvard Women's Law Journal* 5 (1982): 73–119.

Wright, Les. "San Francisco." In *Queer Sites: Gay Urban Histories since 1600*, edited by David Higgs, 164–89. London: Routledge, 1999.

Yung, Judy. *Unbound Feet: A Social History of Chinese Women in San Francisco.* Berkeley: University of California Press, 1995.

Page numbers in italics refer to illustrations.

African Americans: in arrest statistics, 151n32; discrimination against, 13; freak shows and, 103, 108; slumming tours and, 168n35

Ah Choi, 131

Ah-Choo, 46

Ah Yow, 46

Alien Contract Acts, 125, *127*

Almaguer, Tómas, 21, 45, 155n11

American Federation of Labor, 128

American Museum, 102–3, 110

American Theater, 43

Angel Island immigration station: detention at, 121–22, 130–31, 170n24; history of, 171n29; medical examinations at, 134

Anonymity: city life and, 67–68; gender legibility and, 11, 68; at masquerade balls, 30; racialization and, 94

Anti-Chinese movements: during gold rush, 34–35; immigration law and, 122–28, 131–32; nuisance law and, 68–69, 71–72. *See also* Chinese

Anti-miscegenation law, 13

Anti-prostitution law. *See* Prostitution: criminalization of

Anti-vice movements: emergence of, 43, 46, 50, 67–68; racial bias of,

50–51; spatial regulation and, 50–51; Vigilantes and, 53–54

Archives: imaginative reconstruction of, 120, 132–33; limits of, 15–16, 119, 132, 151n29, 168n1, 170n28; sources from, 15–16, 151n26

Arrest statistics, 16, 151nn31–32, 164n22

Arthur, Chester, 128

Asbury, Herbert, 61, 75, 118

Baldwin, Mamie: cross-dressing arrest of, 92; police court appearance of, 92, *93*; police suspicion of, 82, 161n2

Bancroft, Hubert Howe, 29, 43

Barbary Coast: female impersonators and, 84–85, 96, 101, 114–15; male impersonators and, 99; slumming tours and, 111, 114–16, 118; as vice district, 61, 65, 70, 73, 101

Barnum, P. T., 102–3, 110

Bars: cross-dressing law in, 114; dive laws and, 44, 63–64; female impersonators in, 2, 84–85, 96, 101, 114; during gold rush, 26, 49; as slumming tour sites, 111–14, 116–17

Baskets on poles, criminalization of, 69–70

Bates, Mrs. D. B., 38

Bathing in bay, criminalization of, 44
Baynton, Douglas, 134
Bella Union, 99
Belonging. *See* Citizenship
Bennett, W. P., 32
Berglund, Barbara, 117
Berwick, Carl, 84–85
Blane, Mary, 46
Bloomers, 38–39. *See also* Dress
　reformers
Board of Supervisors. *See* San Francisco
　Board of Supervisors
Bogus Man. *See* Freak-show characters;
　Matson, Milton
Bonnet, Jeanne: courtroom defiance
　of, 142; cross-dressing arrest of, 64;
　gender identity of, 158n9; murder
　of, 65; prostitution and, 64, 144;
　sentencing of, 74
Borthwick, J. D., 29–30
Bottle Meyer's, 17, 84–85, 96, 114
Boyd, Nan Alamilla, 4, 115
Brothels: cross-dressing practices and,
　61–62, 64, 131; during gold rush, 26;
　legal control of, 45–46, *47*, 49–51,
　70–71; as slumming tour site, 111, 113,
　116–17. *See also* Prostitution
Brown, Lizzie, cross-dressing arrest of,
　63–64
Brown, Nellie, cross-dressing arrest of,
　63–64
Budd, James, 32, 40
Buneau, Blanche, 64–65
Burke, Martin, 71
Butler, Judith, 8

California state government: Board
　of Health and, 117; deportation
　procedures and, 136; foreign miners
　tax and, 34, 68; immigration law
　and, 136; inaugural ball and, 32,
33, 40; indecency law and, 144–45;
　masquerade law and, 4; nuisance law
　and, 67; racial discrimination and,
　34–35, 68–69, 123; Vigilantes and, 55
Californios, 24–25, 34
Canaday, Margot, 134, 137–38, 171n40
Cartoons. *See* Political cartoons
Casey, James, 53–55
Castle, Helena, cross-dressing arrest
　of, 83
Chan, Sucheng, 71
Chileans, 34, 45
Chinatown: nuisance law and, 71–73;
　racialization of, 117; as slumming
　tour site, 65, 111–13, 115–18; theaters
　in, 113–14, 119–20
Chinese: cross-dressing arrests of, 63,
　83–84, 94–95; cross-gender repre-
　sentations of, 12, 34–35, 39, 122–28,
　140–41; domestic work and, 34–35,
　68, 124–25, 128; female imperson-
　ation and, 113–14, 119; foreign miners
　tax and, 34, 68; immigration law
　and, 121–28, 130–31; newspaper bias
　and, 16, 63, 80–81, 93–96; nuisance
　law and, 68, 71–72; prostitution and,
　45–46, 50–51, 71, 131–32; racialization
　of, 21, 68, 117–18, 124–28, 140–41;
　slumming tours and, 111–14, *112*, 117–
　18; as stowaways, 121–23, *122*, 130–32
Chinese Exclusion Act: campaign for,
　124–28, *126*, *127*, *129*; effects of, 133;
　immigration practices and, 121–23,
　130–33
Citizenship: cross-dressing law and,
　3, 76–77, 136–38; disability and, 13,
　133–36; gender normativity and, 3,
　12–13, 122–28, 133–38; performances
　of, 83–84; race and, 12–13, 122–28,
　130–33; sexuality and, 123–24, 131–33,
　136–38; as urban belonging, 76–77

City space. *See* Public space

Clarke, Alfred, 57

Clifton, Frank, 104

Coit, Lily Hitchcock, 158n7

Colonialism, 27–29

Colton, John, 36–37

Committee of Vigilance (1851), 52

Committee on Dives and Schools of Vice, 116

Common law, 41–42

Compton's Cafeteria riots, 4

Constitutional psychopathic inferiority, 133, 137

Cook, Jesse Brown, 99–100

Coon, Henry, 41, 59–60, 71

Cora, Belle, 53, 56

Cora, Charles, 53–55

Cowles, Samuel, 145

Criminality, as containment strategy, 13, 66, 77

Criminalization: of bathing in bay, 44; of carrying baskets on poles, 70; of gambling, 44; of indecent exhibitions, 62, 157n2; of injuring public morals, 44; of opium dens, 44; of prostitution, 44–47, 70–71; of public intoxication, 43; of selling obscene material, 44; of sodomy, 62, 157n2; of unsightly beggars, 69–70; of vagrancy, 71; of vulgar language, 44, 62, 157n2; of women in bars, 44, 158n6. *See also* Cross-dressing law

Cross-dressing, as concept, 21–22

Cross-dressing arrestees: Baldwin, Mamie, 82, 92, 93, 161n2; Bonnet, Jeanne, 64–65, 74, 142, 144; Brown, Lizzie, 63–64; Brown, Nellie, 63–64; Castle, Helena, 83; Dessar, Mrs., 65, 115; DeWolf, Eliza, 1, 63, 96, 143–45; Dubia, Mrs., 65, 115; Haisch, Ferdinand, 2, 64, 73, 142; Harrington,

Charles, 114; Johnson, Oscar, 66, 74; Jones, Mary, 161n2; Livernash, Edward, 74, 92; Long, Ernest, 163n15, 165n8; Matson, Milton, 74, 103–5, 146; McCarthy, Mabel, 142; McCarthy, Margaret, 66; Merrel, Charles, 142; Nelson, May, 142; Portica, Geraldine, 87, *89*, 136–37; Roberts, John, 1–2, 81, 86, 90; Ruble, Dick/Mamie, 74–75, 82–83, 142, 146; Salas, Lottie, 66; Sherwood, Sophia, 41; Smith, May, 83, 145–46; So Git, 83–84, 94–95, 142; Stallcup, Elsie, 86, 90; Sullivan, May, 66; Thomas, William, 161n2; unnamed Chinese woman, 63, 94; Wallace, Jennie, 161n2; Wilson, John, 74, 91

Cross-dressing arrests: consequences of, 74–75, 86–93, 136–38; deportation following, 136–38; frequency of, 62, 99, 157n2, 164n22; as mistakes, 82–84; in Oakland, 83–84; racial characteristics of, 93–95; threat of, 73–74; in twentieth century, 4, 146–47, 149n7; in U.S. cities, 4, 165n8. *See also* Cross-dressing arrestees

Cross-dressing law: citizenship and, 3, 76–77, 83–84, 138; as containment, 13, 18, 62, 75–77, 114; enactment of, 2, 17, 41–42, 59–60; end of, 147; exclusionary effects of, 3, 69–70, 75–77, 147; gender normativity and, 5–6, 13–14, 62–66, 77, 139–40; immigration law and, 122–23, 136–38; indecency law and, 18, 42–43, 144–45; legal sex and, 6, 82–83, 139, 152n35; logic of, 21–22, 143; nuisance law and, 10–11, 67–70, 72–73, 77; prevalence in U.S., 3–4, 149n8; public space and, 62, 67–69, 73–77, 139, 161n36; resistance to, 17, 104, 142–46; selective enforcement

Cross-dressing law (*continued*)
of, 62, 65–66, 158n11; as strategy of
government, 3, 5–6, 10–11, 66–70,
72–73; in twentieth century, 4,
146–47, 149n7. *See also* Cross-dressing
arrestees; Cross-dressing arrests;
Policing

Cross-dressing practices: in brothels,
9, 61, 64, 116, 131; in China, 132;
contradictory meanings of, 23–24,
30–32, 65–66, 101; cultural anxieties and, 8, 24, 39, 73, 94; as freakish, 80–81, 86, 91–92, 97, 100–105,
108–10; gender legibility and, 11, 65,
68; during gold rush, 23–25, 29–32,
35–39; as harmless, 9, 13, 65–66, 97;
immigration law and, 121–23, 130–
38; as indecency, 11, 41–43, 144–45;
as individual pathology, 91, 94; as
insanity, 74–75, 83, 91, 96, 134–37,
160n35; as nuisance, 11, 77, 81, 86, 90,
91; persistence of, 77; prostitution
and, 38, 41–43, 131–32, 140, 154n50s;
same-sex intimacy and, 17, 36, 84–85,
104–5, 114, 119–20; as social problem,
41–43, 65–66

Cross-gender representations: of
Chinese immigrants, 12, 34–35, 39,
122–28, 140–41; of Jewish men, 35; of
Native Americans, 169n10; of police
chief, 100; and trans-ing analysis,
9–10; in Vigilante discourse, 57–58,
59; of white politicians, 32, *33*, 58, *59*,
128, *129*

Dame Partington in California, 58, *59*
Dance halls. *See* Masquerade balls
Dash, The, 114–15
Davis, Jefferson, freak-show exhibit
of, 103
Davis, Madeline, 4

Democratic Party, Vigilantes and, 52,
55, 58

Deportation: by California state
government, 136; cross-dressing
practices and, 75, 135–38, 171n40;
detention sites and, 121–22, 130–31;
federal policies and, 135–36; insanity
and, 75, 123, 135–36

Derbec, Etienne, 30

Dessar, Mrs., cross-dressing arrest of,
65, 115

DeWolf, Eliza Hurd: court case of, 96,
143–45; cross-dressing arrest of, 1, 63;
gender identity of, 20

Dime museum freak shows. *See* Freak
shows

Disability: citizenship and, 13; freak
shows and, 103, 107; immigration
law and, 123, 133–36; problem bodies
and, 10–11, 19, 67–69

Dive laws: enactment of, 44, 158n6;
enforcement of, 63–64

Domestic labor: Chinese men and,
34–35, 68, 124–25, 128; white men
and, 32–35

Dornin, George, 23, 30, 40

Dress reformers: cross-dressing law
and, 1, 62–65, 143–46; freak-show
discourse and, 108, 110; during gold
rush, 24, 63

Drunkenness. *See* Public intoxication
Duberman, Martin, 4
Dubia, Mrs., cross-dressing arrest of,
65, 115
Dwinelle, Samuel, 145

Economy: racial stratification of, 34–35,
68; Vigilantes and, 55
Eltinge, Julian, 100
Eskridge, William, 137, 149n8
Ethington, Philip, 54, 57

European Americans: cross-gender representations of, 32, *33*, 58, *59*, 128, *129*; gender normativity and, 16, 93–96, 128, 140; during gold rush, 24, 27–35, 39, 43–46; newspaper reports on, 93–94, 96; prostitution and, 43–46, *47*, 50–51; racialization and, 12, 21, 31, 45, 117, 140; respectability and, 48–50; as slumming tourists, 114–17; white supremacy and, 13, 68–69, 124–28

Fairchild, Lucius, 33
Fairweather, Ellen, 103–4
Family: social order and, 48, 55, 57, 65; in Vigilante discourse, 57–58
Farnham, Eliza, 33, 43
Fast young women, cross-dressing arrests of, 18, 62–64
Federal immigration law. *See* Immigration law
Female impersonators: in Barbary Coast bars, 2, 84–85, 96, 101, 114–15; in Chinatown theaters, 113–14; cross-dressing law and, 114; desire for, 119–20; during gold rush, 98; slumming tours and, 113–15; on vaudeville stage, 97–101, 114
Feminization. *See* Cross-gender representations
Florida Enchantment, A, 107–8, *109*
Foreign miners tax, 34, 68
Fraser, Nancy, 76
Fraud: as criminal offense, 118; cross-dressing depicted as, 91, 94–95, 104; as freak-show entertainment, 104, 110–11; slumming tour displays and, 118
Freak-show characters: Bearded Lady, 103, 107, 110; Big Bertha the Queen of Confidence Women, 105; The Bogus Man, 104; Half Man / Half Woman,

103, 108, 110; Living Skeleton, 108; Missing Link, 103, 108; What-Is-It?, 103, 111
Freak shows: audiences at, 105, 107, 110–11; cross-dressing law and, 97, 102–5, 111, 118–19; cross-dressing performers and, 97, 102–5, *106*, 110–11, 119–20; disability and, 103; in *A Florida Enchantment*, 107–8, *109*; format of, 102, 107, 119; history of, 102, 164n1; jailhouse recruitment and, 105; normalizing effects of, 105–10, *109*; popularity of, 102, 108, 110; racialization and, 102–3, 107, 108; suspicion and, 110–11; venues for, 102. *See also* Freak-show characters
Fretz, Eric, 166n17
Friedman, Lawrence, 73

Gambling dens: criminalization of, 44; during gold rush, 26; as slumming tour sites, 111–12, 116; Vigilantes and, 53–54
Garber, Marjorie, 8
Gardner, Martha, 135
Geary, John, 51–52
Gender identity: cross-dressing law and, 21–22, 64–66, 74–75, 136–37; during gold rush, 35–36; insanity and, 74–75, 135–36; politicization of, 143, 146; sexology and, 78, *79*
Gender illusionists. *See* Female impersonators
Gender legibility: as cultural imperative, 11, 65, 68; policing and, 82, 86, 90
Gender normativity: city space and, 75–77, 139–40; cross-dressing law and, 13–14, 62–66, 77, 139–40; definition of, 5–6; freak shows and, 102–3, 105, 107–11, 118–19; immigration law and, 122–29, 133–38, 140–41, 171n40;

Gender normativity (*continued*)
racialization and, 12, 34–35, 72, 94–95, 124–28; slumming tours and, 113–16, 118–19; vaudeville and, 100–101, 118–19; Vigilantes and, 53–60; whiteness and, 16, 94, 96, 140
Girl miner daguerreotype, 36–37, *37*
Golden Rule House, 46
Gold rush: colonial ideologies and, 27–29; cross-dressing practices and, 23–24, 29–32, 35–39, 98; cultural diversity of, 24–25; dances during, 23, 29–32, *33*, 40; domestic labor during, 32–35; end of, 46, 48–49; gender demographics of, 24–25, 27–29, 40, 48–49; girl miner daguerreotype and, 36–37, *37*; mass migrations of, 24–25; policing and, 52; prostitution and, 26, 42–46, *47*, 154n6; San Francisco and, 5, 25–29
Gross, Ariela, 13
Guangdong Province, 34, 113, 131
Gunter, Archibald, 107

Habermas, Jürgen, 76
Haisch, Ferdinand: cross-dressing arrest of, 2, 64; gender identity of, 20, 144; police surveillance of, 64, 82; private space and, 73, 142; resistance of, 142, 172n5; sentencing of, 73
Hamada Hikozō, 32, 153n27
Harper's Weekly, 125
Harrington, Charles: cross-dressing arrest of, 114; same-sex intimacy and, 119
Helper, Hinton, 35, 126
Hirata, Lucie Cheng, 131
Hirschfeld, Magnus, 74, 78, *79*, 80, 82
Houses of ill-fame. *See* Brothels
Hurtado, Albert, 28
Hutchings, James, 32

Immigration law: California state government and, 123, 136; Chinese exclusion and, 122–28; cross-dressing practices and, 121–23, *122*, 130–38; cross-gender representations and, 12, 122–28, *126*, *127*, *129*; 138; deportation and, 123, 135–36; development of, 123–24, 133, 135–36; disability exclusions and, 123, 133–36; enforcement apparatus, 121–23, 130–37; evasion of, 121, 130–33; gender normativity and, 122–28, 133–38, 140–41; insanity exclusions and, 133–37; nation-state and, 3, 122–23, 128, 138; resistance to, 123, 130–33; sexuality exclusions and, 123–24, 131–34, 136–38
Immorality. *See* Indecency
Indecency: cross-dressing as, 11, 41–43, 144–45; during gold rush, 27, 42–51
Indecency laws: cross-dressing law and, 2, 42–44, 144–45; enforcement of, 62, 116, 157n2; during gold rush, 44–46
Insane asylum: in California, 136, 160n33; cross-dressing cases and, 74–75, 83, 135–36, 160n35
Insanity: cross-dressing practices and, 74–75, 83, 134–37, 160n35; immigration laws and, 133–37; newspaper representations of, 91, 94, 96
Insanity Commission, 75, 135. *See also* Insane asylum

Jail: during gold rush, 26, 52; legal sex and, 74; medical examinations and, 82–83, 121, 152n35, 162n7; as slumming tour site, 111; stripping inmates and, 74, 86
Jenny O., 73, 76, 78, *79*, 80
Jim Crow laws, 13
Johnson, Oscar, cross-dressing arrest of, 66, 74

Johnson, Susan, 33–34
Jolly, Michelle, 58
Jones, Mary, cross-dressing arrest of, 161n2

Kalloch, Isaac, 72
Kammerer, George, 135
Kee, Sam, 83–84
Kennedy, Elizabeth, 4
King, James, 53–55
Kingsley, Omar, 99

Lake, Mrs., 131
Larose, Bert: arrest of, 84–85; as female impersonator, 84–85, 96, 114; prison photograph of, 87, 88
Law and Order Party, 58
Law enforcement. See Policing
Lederer, Sophie, 75
Lee Hoo, 114, 119
Lees, Isaiah, 86, 163n13
Legal sex: certification of, 83; challenges to, 142–44, 146; cross-dressing law and, 6, 21, 82–83, 139, 152n35; definition of, 152n35; jail segregation by, 74; medical examinations and, 82–83, 121, 134, 152n35, 162n7
Lei, Daphne, 94, 113
Leong, Karen, 12
Likely to become a public charge, 133–37
Lingard, William Horace, 98, 100
Livernash, Edward: cross-dressing arrest of, 92; newspaper descriptions of, 92, 95; sentencing of, 74
Local government. See San Francisco Board of Supervisors
Logan, Thomas, 117
Long, Ernest, cross-dressing arrest of, 163n15, 165n8
Looking. See Visibility

Lossen, C., 46
Lott, Eric, 31

Magee, Thomas, 125
Male impersonators: desire for, 119–20; in dive bars, 113; on vaudeville stage, 97–101
Manifest destiny, 25, 45
Masquerade balls, 30–32
Masquerade law, 4
Massett, Stephen, 98
Matson, Milton: courtroom protest of, 17, 146; cross-dressing arrest of, 146; desire and, 104–5, 119; Ellen Fairweather and, 103–4; as freak-show performer, 103–5, 106, 110–11; gender identity of, 17, 103–4; newspaper interviews with, 104–5; sentencing of, 74
McCann, John, 57
McCarthy, Mabel, cross-dressing arrest of, 142
McCarthy, Margaret, cross-dressing arrest of, 66
McCready, Irene, 154n6
Medical examination: at immigration detention, 130, 134; at jail, 82–83, 121, 152n35, 162n7; legal sex and, 82–83, 121, 134, 152n35, 162n7
Menken, Adah Isaacs, 100
Merrel, Charles, cross-dressing arrest of, 142
Merry, Sally Engle, 69
Mexican-American war, 5, 24–25, 28, 34; freak-show dramatizations of, 103; political authority and, 51
Mexicans: cross-dressing law and, 87, 89, 93–94, 96, 136; deportation of, 136–38, 171n40; during gold rush, 27–28, 34, 38, 45–46; prostitution and, 45–46, 50–51; racial construction of, 21, 45; resistance of, 103

Miners' Ten Commandments, The, 32
Minstrel shows, 31, 98
Mittig, Marpha, 133–35, 143
Moral turpitude, crime of, 133, 137–38
Municipal government. *See* San Francisco Board of Supervisors
Municipal Reports, arrest statistics and, 16
Murietta, Joaquin, freak-show display of, 103
Museum of Living Wonders, 102

National belonging. *See* Citizenship
Native Americans: arrest statistics and, 151n32; cross-gender representations of, 169n10; during gold rush, 24, 27–28, 31, 51, 169n10; racialization of, 12, 21
Nelson, May, cross-dressing arrest of, 142
Newspapers: as archival source, 16, 164n22; cross-dressing arrests and, 91–96, 93; cross-dressing law and, 144, 146, 172n12; Milton Matson interview and, 104–5; police court columns and, 91, 163n16; racial bias in, 63, 80–81, 93–95; same-sex intimacy and, 91, 94; slumming tours as source for, 117; surveillance and, 84–85, 162n11; vaudeville reviews in, 99
Nuisance laws: cross-dressing and, 11, 67, 69, 77; problem bodies and, 10–11, 67–73, 91; as spatial regulation, 10, 49, 67–73

Obscene material, criminalizing sale of, 44
Offenses against Good Morals and Decency. *See* Indecency laws
Offensive Trades and Nuisances. *See* Nuisance laws

Opium den: criminalization of, 44; as slumming tour site, 111, 112, 116–18
Oriental and Occidental Steamship Company, 131
Orientalism, 12, 95

Pacific House, 46
Pacific Museum of Anatomy and Science, 102–3
Page law, 124
Parisian Mansion, 61, 75
Parkhurst, Charley, 35–36
People's Party: demise of, 157n36; formation of, 55, 58; local politics and, 55, 58–59. *See also* Vigilance Committee of 1856
Pepper, George, 133–35, 143
Peruvians, 45
Photography: police and, 80, 86–90, 88, 89, 100, 163n15; sexology and, 78–80, 79, 82
Pixley, Frank, 71
Pohlmann, Henry, 75, 135–36
Police court: cross-dressing cases in, 65–66, 74–75, 90–93, 93, 142–46; description of, 90–91, 163n17; newspaper reports from, 91; records of, 16, 151n29. *See also* Police court judges
Police court judges: Coon, Henry, 41, 59–60, 71; Deasy, Daniel, 66, 90; as elected officials, 90; Low, Charles, 146; Rix, Hale, 66; Shortall, Edward, 66
Police department: cross-dressing performances of, 100; during gold rush, 52; as slumming tour guides, 111–12, 116–17, 167n32. *See also* Policing
Police photography: of Bert Larose, 87, 88; of cross-dressing arrestees, 87, 89, 90, 100, 136–37, 163n15, 165n8; description of, 86–87, 163n13

Policing: cross-dressing law and, 62–66, 74, 80–83, 86–87; legal sex and, 152n35

Political cartoons: anti-Chinese movement and, *126, 127, 129*; governor's inaugural ball and, *33*; Vigilance Committee and, *59*

Portel, Bettie, cross-dressing arrest of, 66, 74

Portica, Geraldine: cross-dressing arrest of, 87, 136, 165n8; deportation of, 136–38; gender identity of, 87, 90, 136; newspaper neglect of, 94; police photograph of, 87, *89*, 136–37, 165n8

Prison photography, 87, *88*

Private space: cross-dressing and, 13–14, 67, 73–75, 77, 139–40; public life and, 57. *See also* Spatial regulation

Private sphere. *See* Private space

Problem bodies, 6, 10–12; Chinese immigrants and, 67–72; cross-dressing and, 67–69, 72, 77, 91; disability and, 67–69; immigration law and, 123–24, 133, 138; in police court, 90–91; prostitution and, 67, 70–71; public visibility of, 67–68, 71–72; slumming tours and, 111–12, 116, 118

Profane language. *See* Vulgar language

Prostitution: Chinese women and, 45–46, 50–51, 71, 131–32; criminalization of, 44–46, *47*, 70–71; cross-dressing practices and, 38, 41–43, 131–32, 140, 154n50; during gold rush, 26, 30, 38, 42–46, *47*, 154n6; immigration law and, 123–24, 131–32, 136; at masquerade balls, 30; nuisance law and, 67, 70–71; racial stratification of, 45–46, *47*, 50–51; respectable "ladies" and, 38, 48–50; spatial containment of, 70–71, 161n36; Vigilance Committee and, 53–60; visibility of, 42, 49–51, 56, 70–71. *See also* Brothels

Psychiatric institutionalization. *See* Insane asylum

Public intoxication, criminalization of, 43, 90–91

Public morals, criminalization of acts that injure, 44

Public space: bars, as semi-public, 114; cross-dressing law and, 13–14, 67–70, 73–77, 114, 139–40, 161n36; as gender normative, 14, 75–77, 139–40; nuisance law and, 10, 49, 67, 69–73; public sphere and, 76–77. *See also* Spatial regulation

Public sphere, 76–77, 140. *See also* Public space

Race: construction of, 12–13, 21, 155n11; federal law and, 12–13, 123–24; in freak shows, 102–3, 107–8; gender normativity and, 12, 34–35, 39, 94–95, 124–28; labor market and, 34–35; local law and, 10–12, 68–69; at masquerade balls, 31–32; newspaper bias and, 16, 80–81, 93–96; police photography and, 87; sexuality and, 45–46, 50–51, 71–72; slumming tours and, 113–14, 117–18; state law and, 13, 34, 68, 123; terminology of, 21

Rand, Erica, 134

Redmond, Fergus, 107

Resistance: cross-dressing law and, 74–75, 104, 142–46; immigration law and, 123, 130–33, 143; obstacles to, 76–77; possibilities for, 96

Respectability: European American women and, 27, 48–50, 56–57; prostitution versus, 38, 49–50, 56–57, 154n6; of residential areas, 49, 70–71; urban planning and, 76; in Vigilante discourse, 56–57

Richardson, Albert, 34–36

Richardson, William, 53–54

Roberts, John: court case of, 90; cross-dressing arrest of, 1–2; gender identity of, 20; jailhouse stripping of, 86; police suspicion of, 81–82; sentencing of, 81

Rogers, Maria, 75

Royce, Sarah, 154n6

Ruble, Dick/Mamie: courtroom defiance of, 74–75, 142, 146; cross-dressing arrest of, 74; gender identity of, 17, 74–75, 82–83, 146; insane asylum and, 74–75, 83; medical examination of, 82–83

Ryan, Arabella, 53, 56

Ryan, Mary, 57, 67, 161n36

Sacramento, prostitution in, 116

Salas, Lottie, cross-dressing arrest of, 66

Saloons. See Bars; Gambling dens

San Francisco Board of Health, 72, 128

San Francisco Board of Supervisors: Common Council as precursor to, 52, 72; cross-dressing law and, 2, 41–42, 59–60; indecency laws and, 42–45, 144–45; nuisance laws and, 10, 67–72; proactive government and, 13–14, 42–44, 51–52; problem bodies and, 10–11, 67–72

San Francisco newspapers. See Newspapers

San Francisco police department. See Police department

San Francisco Real Estate Circular, 125

San Francisco streets and neighborhoods: Berry Street, 70; Commercial Street, 61, 75; Dupont Street, 49, 64, 116; Hayes Valley, 64; Kearney Street, 32, 66, 102; Market Street, 83, 102, 105; Mason Street, 70; Mission District, 63, 102; Montgomery Street, 63; Pacific Heights, 70; Pacific Street, 17, 101, 114; Sacramento Street, 63; Stockton Street, 49; Washington Street, 113. See also Barbary Coast; Chinatown

Schweik, Susan, 67–68

Seacole, Mary, 38

Senkewicz, Richard, 55

Sex: at Barbary Coast bars, 84–85, 114; colonial ideologies and, 27–29; cross-dressing practices and, 36, 84–85, 91, 104–5, 114; on slumming tours, 113–14

Sexology, 78, 80

Sexual morality: immigration law and, 123–24, 131–34, 136–38; racialization and, 45–46, 50–51; Vigilantes and, 53–60, 156n34

Shah, Nayan, 12, 72, 117, 134

Sherwood, Sophia, cross-dressing arrest of, 41

Shumsky, Neil, 70–71

Slumming tours: of Barbary Coast, 111, 114–16, 118; of Chinatown, 111–18, 112; cross-dressing law and, 65, 114–16, 118–19, 158n11; description of, 111, 164n1; desire and, 119–20; female impersonators and, 113–15; government investigations and, 116–17; male impersonators and, 115; police guides for, 111–12, 116–17, 167n32; police raids and, 116, 167n32; problem bodies and, 111–12, 116, 118; racialization and, 113–14, 117–18; sex and, 113, 114, 117; as staged events, 118; voyeurism and, 111–13, 112

Smith, May: courtroom defiance of, 145–46; cross-dressing arrest of, 83

Sodomy, arrests for, 62, 157n2, 171n40

So Git: cross-dressing arrest of, 83–84, 95; gender identity of, 142; newspaper reports on, 94–95

Soulé, Frank, 30, 42, 45

Space. See Private space; Public space; Spatial regulation

Spatial regulation: in bars, 114; cross-dressing law as, 13–14, 69–70, 73–77, 114, 139–40, 161n36; at freak shows, 105, 107; immigration law and, 133, 137; nuisance law and, 10, 67–73; of problem bodies, 67–73; of prostitution, 50–51, 70–71, 161n36

Springer, Larry, 70–71

Stallcup, Elsie, cross-dressing arrest of, 86, 90

Stanley, Bertha, 105

Stockton insane asylum. See Insane asylum

Stowaways, cross-dressing practices of, 121–22, 130–33

Stripping: at immigration stations, 130, 134; in jail, 74, 86, 121; by police, 82

Sullivan, May, cross-dressing arrest of, 66

Sully, Lew, 99

Surveillance: by newspapers, 84–85; by police, 19, 64, 80–83; by the public, 83–84

Suspicion: freak shows and, 110–11; police and, 81–83, 152n35; the public and, 83–85

Terry, Jennifer, 10

Thomas, William, cross-dressing arrest of, 161n2

Tilly, Vesta, 101

Transgender. See Gender identity

Transgender studies, 8, 150nn15–16

Trans-ing analysis, 6, 8–10, 139–40, 150n17

Transvestites: The Erotic Drive to Cross-Dress, 78, 79

Twain, Mark, 90, 163n16

Twentieth century: cross-dressing law during, 4, 146–47, 149n7

Unnamed Chinese woman, cross-dressing arrest of, 63, 94

Urban belonging. See Citizenship

Urban development: anonymity and, 67–68; local government and, 13–14; prostitution and, 49–51, 70–71; in San Francisco, 5, 24–27, 49–50

Urban space. See Public space

Urla, Jacqueline, 10

Vagrancy laws, 71, 90–91

Vaudeville: audiences of, 98–99, 101, 119–20; Barbary Coast and, 101; conservative nature of, 100–101; cross-dressing law and, 97, 99–101, 118–19; decline of, 101; description of, 98–99, 164n1; desire and, 119–20; female impersonation and, 97–101, 114; gender normativity and, 100–101, 118–19; male impersonation and, 97–101

Vice district: development of, 49–50, 70–71, 73; as slumming tour site, 111–15. See also Barbary Coast; Prostitution

Vigilance Committee of 1851, 52

Vigilance Committee of 1856: actions of, 52, 54–55, 57–58; formation of, 53–54; "the ladies" and, 56–57; masculinity and, 54, 57–58; membership of, 52, 54–55; sexual propriety and, 53–60, 156n34

Visibility: desire and, 119–20; freak shows and, 102–11, 106, 109, 119–20; gender legibility and, 82, 86, 90; jail

Visibility (*continued*)
and, 86; newspapers and, 80–81,
91–96, *93*, 104–5; police court and,
90–92, *93*; police photography and,
86–87, *88*, *89*, 100, 136–37, 163n15,
165n8; of problem bodies, 67–68,
71–72; of prostitution, 42, 49–51, 56,
70–71; as punishment, 92–93; sexology and, 78–80, *79*; slumming tours
and, 111–18, 119–20; vaudeville and,
98–101, 119–20. *See also* Surveillance
Vulgar language: arrest for, 62, 157n2;
criminalization of, 44

Walden, Charles, 46
Wallace, Jennie, cross-dressing arrest
of, 161n2
Wasp, 125, *127*, 128, *129*
Watts, Jennifer, 36, 154n44
Welke, Barbara Young, 13

Wesner, Ella, 99, 119
Whiteness. *See* European Americans
Wide Open Town, 4
Wilson, John, cross-dressing arrest of,
74, 91
Wilson, Luzena Stanley, 30
Wong Ah Choy: detention of, 121–23,
122; resistance of, 132, 143; as stowaway,
130, 132–33
Woodward Gardens, 102
Working Men's Party of California,
68–69, 72, 124–25
World's fairs, 164n1

Yow On, 121, 143
Yung, Judy, 71

Zoning laws, 13–14, 67, 73, 150n23,
151n24
Zoyara, Ella, 99